UNSILENCED

A Teacher's Year of Battles,
Breakthroughs, and Life-Changing
Lessons at Belchertown State School

by

Howard C. Shane, Ph.D.

Harvard Medical School
Boston, Massachusetts

Boston Children's Hospital
Massachusetts

·P A U L·H·
BROOKES
PUBLISHING CO ®

Baltimore • London • Sydney

Paul H. Brookes Publishing Co.
Post Office Box 10624
Baltimore, Maryland 21285-0624
USA

www.brookespublishing.com

Typeset by Lumina Datamatics, Inc., Norwell, Massachusetts.
Manufactured in the United States of America by
Versa Press, Inc., East Peoria, Illinois.

The events that inspired this book took place decades ago in the late 1960s. The author relied on memory, supplemented by journals, audio recordings, photographs, and newspaper accounts when writing this book. While the information in this book is based on actual events in the author's life, names and identifying details of certain individuals have been changed to protect their privacy. When needed, actual names and identifying details were used with permission. Events, places, and conversations in this memoir have been recreated from and inspired by the author's memories. Selected historical accountings that document conditions at Belchertown State School were also referenced. The chronology of some events has been compressed and altered.

The author and publisher have referred to numerous historical accounts, newspaper stories, and other published books, in addition to the author's own records, in preparing this accounting of life at Belchertown in 1969–1970. The story of *Unsilenced* is not told to disparage any one individual or institution, but to inform today's readers and future generations so that a better life and more opportunity can be ensured for all people, with and without disabilities. If a reader feels there may be an error in a statement made in this book, please contact Brookes Publishing Co. at rights@brookespublishing.com to share that information.

Purchasers of *Unsilenced: A Teacher's Year of Battles, Breakthroughs, and Life-Changing Lessons at Belchertown State School* are granted permission to download, print, and photocopy the Additional Resources document and Discussion Questions for educational, professional, and/or personal purposes. These questions may not be reproduced to generate revenue for any program or individual.

Library of Congress Cataloging-in-Publication Data

Names: Shane, Howard C., author.
Title: Unsilenced : a teacher's year of battles, breakthroughs, and life-changing lessons at
    Belchertown State School / Howard C. Shane, Ph.D.
Description: Baltimore, Maryland : Paul H. Brookes Publishing Co., [2021]
Identifiers: LCCN 2021023551 (print) | LCCN 2021023552 (ebook) | ISBN 9781681255156
    (paperback) | ISBN 9781681255163 (epub) | ISBN 9781681255170 (pdf)
Subjects: LCSH: Belchertown State School—History. | Belchertown State School—Faculty—
    History. | Children with mental disabilities—Education—Massachusetts—Belchertown—
    History. | BISAC: BIOGRAPHY & AUTOBIOGRAPHY / Educators | EDUCATION / Special
    Education / General
Classification: LCC HV897.M4 B47 2022 (print) | LCC HV897.M4 (ebook) | DDC
    371.9209744/23—dc23
LC record available at https://lccn.loc.gov/2021023551
LC ebook record available at https://lccn.loc.gov/2021023552

British Library Cataloguing in Publication data are available from the British Library.

2025   2024   2023   2022   2021

10   9   8   7   6   5   4   3   2   1

CONTENTS

CONTENTS

ABOUT THE ONLINE MATERIALS

Purchasers of this book may download, print, and/or photocopy the Additional Resources document and Discussion Questions for personal, professional, and/or educational use.

To access the materials that come with this book:

1. Go to the Brookes Publishing Download Hub: http://downloads.brookespublishing.com
2. Register to create an account (or log in with an existing account).
3. Filter or search for the book title *Unsilenced.*

ABOUT THE AUTHOR

Howard C. Shane, Ph.D., is Associate Professor of Otology & Otolaryngology at the Harvard Medical School and Director of the Autism Language Program at Boston Children's Hospital. He has designed more than a dozen computer applications used widely by persons with disabilities and holds two U.S. patents. Dr. Shane has received Honors of the Association Distinction and is a Fellow of the American Speech-Language-Hearing Association. He is the 2019 recipient of the  Frank R. Kleffner Lifetime Clinical Career Award. Dr. Shane received the Goldenson Award for Innovations in Technology from the United Cerebral Palsy Association and has authored numerous papers and chapters on severe speech impairment, lectured throughout the world on the topic, and produced numerous computer-based innovations enjoyed by persons with complex communication disorders.

FOREWORD

When our son, Doug Jr., was diagnosed with autism in the 1990s, my wife, Laurie, and I were determined to find the best therapies and interventions to support his development. Despite the advantages our family had due to my public profile and successful professional football career, finding those services was a real challenge—so Laurie and I decided to do something about that. We started the Doug Flutie, Jr. Foundation for Autism with the goal of helping other families who struggle to find and finance services for their children. Twenty-two years later, our Foundation has raised and invested close to $20 million to help these families live their lives to the fullest.

Through our own personal journey with Dougie and two decades of work with the Foundation, we have met so many wonderful professionals who teach, care for, inspire, and provide direct support for people with disabilities. Dr. Howard Shane is one of these people. While his clinical work is groundbreaking, it all stems from his caring, compassionate heart, and his earnest desire to make the world a better place, one person at a time.

As you'll read in this memoir, before Howard was a highly respected doctor and leader in this field, he was a kind-hearted, optimistic young teacher who joined the staff of Belchertown State School in 1969, witnessed the horrific living conditions its residents endured, and knew things had to change. He saw potential in his students where others saw none. He knew their challenges were complicated by their inhumane environment and recognized that they could learn and make progress with the right kind of teaching and intervention. He saw his students as individuals with their own interests, opinions, strengths, and needs, and he found ways to connect with them, even if they couldn't communicate in traditional ways.

I've talked with Howard about his early experiences at Belchertown. Talking to him about his first teaching job is fascinating, sobering, and inspiring. I think of what parents of the children of Belchertown lived through when they learned of their child's diagnosis, back when placement in a state institution was the only real option. I imagine how my son Dougie's life would have been different if he'd been born sixty years ago, without access to the services and supports available today.

I am overcome with gratitude for people like Howard Shane, who dedicated his life to increasing communication opportunities for nonverbal learners and giving them a voice. His contributions have improved the quality of life for countless children, and it all started back in that stark, unassuming classroom at Belchertown.

As you read this book and immerse yourself in a dark era of disability history, you may experience shock, sadness, outrage, and horror. But I hope that you, like me, will come away with a sense of real hope. Thanks to the passion, determination, and pioneering work of Howard Shane and many of his and our peers, my son and other people with disabilities are now able to live more authentically inclusive lives. They have access to life-changing interventions and social and recreational opportunities that families in the Belchertown era couldn't imagine in their wildest dreams. While there is still so much work to be done to improve disability rights and services, progress has increased exponentially over the last 40 years. My wife, my colleagues, and I are honored to work alongside Howard—and thousands of other professionals and families who share our convictions—to help make sure this march of progress never ends.

Doug Flutie
President & Co-Founder, Doug Flutie, Jr. Foundation for Autism
Former NFL, CFL, and Heisman Trophy-winning Quarterback
www.flutiefoundation.org

AUTHOR'S NOTE

The events that inspired this memoir took place decades ago, beginning with my first day at Belchertown State School in the late 1960s. As I wrote the book, I relied on my memory, supplemented by journals, audio recordings, photographs, and newspaper accounts. While the information in this book is based on actual events in my life, the names and identifying details of certain individuals have been changed to protect their privacy. (When needed, actual names and identifying details were used with permission.) The events, places, and conversations in this memoir have been recreated from and inspired by my memories, and the chronology of some events has been compressed and altered, while still accurately capturing the essence of my time at Belchertown.

Because this memoir tells the story of true events that took place in 1969 and 1970, there are instances where outdated and inappropriate terminology is used to describe or refer to people with disabilities. This terminology is used sparingly, only in direct dialogue, and only when needed to convey the mindset of the time. In my four decades working in the field of augmentative and alternative communication, I have been glad to see that terminology evolve along with our attitudes toward people with disabilities. As language continues to evolve, I urge professionals—who set an example for others—to keep both seismic shifts and the individual preferences of people with disabilities in mind when it comes to terminology. Today, person-first language is preferred by some individuals, while other people embrace terms such as "disabled" and "autistic." If you aren't sure which words to use, ask your communication partner to clarify the terms they prefer.

The ADA National Network website says it best: "Words are powerful. The words you use and the way you portray individuals with disabilities matters." As a communication professional, I couldn't agree more. This book will give you a window into the words and actions our society once used to limit and dismiss people with disabilities—but it's my hope that you'll come away with a fresh appreciation for how far we've come, and a renewed determination to keep pushing forward.

ACKNOWLEDGMENTS

This book has been five decades in the making.

For the first thirty years, I pondered whether I should even write it, and then took another few decades to actually start putting words to paper. Over that stretch of time, I received suggestions, encouragement, critiques, and helpful insights from many generous people. If you are not directly mentioned, I still want to thank all of those friends, colleagues, and students over the years with whom I have discussed my time at Belchertown State School and the book that it inspired.

Several professors from my graduate program at the University of Massachusetts offered me invaluable guidance, and I am forever grateful. Most importantly I am indebted to the late Dr. Henry Peirce, who became the mentor and friend that I hope every young adult—with no clear life path—finds. My gratitude also goes out to the late Dr. Jay Melrose for teaching me how to write, and to Dr. Harris Nober for pressing me to pursue one more academic degree. Dr. Ian Thomas, you were one crazy driver and a true innovator.

I also want to thank Ed Hebert, who became the first head of the newly formed Communication Disorders Program at Belchertown State School. Ed gave me extraordinary latitude to pursue my abiding interest in creating an effective communication device.

Many thanks to Katherine Anderson, who provided several photos contained in this book. Her extraordinary historical knowledge of Belchertown State School, including its extensive archival materials, was extremely helpful.

I also want to extend my appreciation to the late, great Burt Blatt, another of my mentors from Syracuse University, who spent Christmas in Purgatory and demonstrated what it means to put everything on the line for the right cause.

I will be forever grateful to the entire team at Brookes Publishing: Melissa Behm for believing the story needed to be told; Rachel Word for making early comments and improvements; Jen Lillis for providing her remarkable talent that greatly enhanced the writing and indirectly schooled me on how to be a better storyteller. And most importantly, I owe so much to my incredible editor Sharon Larkin, who put up with me, guided me, and helped smooth out and better tell this story.

A very special thanks goes to Lisa Miori Dinneen, the most insightful special education administrator on the planet, who offered comments and suggestions that contributed to this book.

Thanks to Dr. William Kiernan, friend and confidant, who offered insightful thoughts and suggestions, and Dr. Warren Gleckel, who made it clear that this book could offer aspiring special educators insight about the horrors of the past and their role in not repeating them.

Thanks also to Heidi Campbell, parent, teacher, and advocate, who convinced me as to the relevance of this book for parents of a child with a disability; to Ellie Belknap, who read an early draft and insisted I complete the writing; to Marilyn Buzolitch, a speech-pathologist-extraordinaire whose careful reading gave insight to a better book; to Bronwyn Hemsley, the finest speech pathologist in all of Australia, who provided helpful edits, comments, and suggestions; and John Costello, who's been my closest colleague for nearly four decades and was continuously supportive of my getting this book finished and out into the world.

Thanks go out as well to Missy and Doug Fyffe, who reignited the fire and convinced me to do a major revision of *Unsilenced*; Kevin and Lynn Brennan—a layman and professional who separately offered encouraging words that kept me on track; and Charlie Zatzkin, a pal with a creative brain who willingly shared his insights.

I wish my parents were here to celebrate this with me. From them I learned early on I wasn't required to be silent.

Lastly, I extend my greatest appreciation to Kathryn Dawson Shane, my wife, best friend, greatest critic, fiercest fan, and behind-the-scenes advocate. Her suggestions and edits made *Unsilenced* a far better book.

This book is dedicated to my students
in the infirmary building classroom at
Belchertown State School, who taught me
so much more than I ever taught them.

PROLOGUE

I stare at the screen of my laptop, biting my inner cheek as I often do when I am anxious, all the while questioning the wisdom of sending this email. When faced with such inertia, I rely on a tried-and-true strategy to force myself to act. I imagine a familiar digital screen showing the number seven, immediately followed by a steady countdown. I don't recall its origin, but this is the same strategy that propels me like a starter's pistol to instantly leave the warmth of bedcovers for a bathroom visit, the same strategy that caused me as a teenager to launch myself from a high ledge into a cold-water pond at an abandoned rock quarry. On this occasion, not unlike the others, when the countdown hits one, I click send.

"Done," I whisper at the very moment I dispatch this decisive email. I've just announced my intention to step down as the director of a clinical center for children with special needs at Boston Children's Hospital—a department I've spent decades building. On this day, like most, I have a hectic schedule that includes several family consultations, where we'll explore ways to enhance their children's communication—often with technologies my center has developed that provide a substitute for a biological voice. In fact, most of my patients over the past forty years have been unable to communicate through the typical means of speech that many of us take for granted.

I take a moment and scan my office, the memorabilia and the photos, both of my family and of those who have significantly influenced my career and, by association, my life over the years. My eyes fix on two photographs prominently placed on a shelf behind my desk—one of Henry Peirce, a former professor at the University of Massachusetts, who thankfully tossed me a lifeline, and another of Ron Benoit, a former student with a profound disability who, although unable to speak, taught me much about strength, survival, dignity, and friendship. Both men jumpstarted a career for me fifty years ago, and I will always be eternally grateful.

It began in 1969, at a school with a name that's repellent to modern ears: Belchertown State School for the Feeble-Minded. Located in the sleepy town of Belchertown, Massachusetts, it was a grim institution where children with a wide range of disabilities were warehoused for nearly a century. At that time, parents of children with disabilities had few alternatives when it came to raising and educating their children. Support services in the form of medical, educational, and/or therapeutic interventions didn't exist. As a result, children with disabilities ended up in places like Belchertown, forced to suffer the indecency of horrific institutional placement.

In the years before Belchertown, I was a typical college student, consumed by my own life, my friends, nights out drinking, and meeting girls. The Vietnam War was a looming concern for me and all my friends. While I hoped my minor in education would allow me to avoid Vietnam, I learned shortly before graduating that the government had done away with deferments and instead had instituted the draft. My number was thirty-seven.

A previous football neck injury freed me from the horrors of war, but I would come to learn that the simple act of birth had condemned Ron—the young man who would become my student when I went to teach at Belchertown—to his own personal nightmare: a brutal life of isolation, neglect, and indignity. Ron and others like him had not left their homes willingly. They had been forcefully drafted into the unnatural and hellish setting of the institution.

When Ron's mother, Mrs. Benoit, arrived at Belchertown State School in the spring of 1964 alongside her then-eight-year-old son with cerebral palsy and no verbal speech, she was resigned to the fact that as a single mother with an irreparably damaged back, she could no longer care for her son at home. At eighty-five pounds and growing, Ron was just too heavy for her alone to bathe and maneuver onto the toilet or into his wheelchair.

Holding back tears and with hollow eyes, she was met at the red brick administration building by the institution's sanctimonious superintendent, Dr. Lawrence Bowser. Dr. Bowser was famous for saying he preferred to meet new families in person to inform them firsthand about his "progressive policies."

"Good morning, Mrs. Benoit," he said. After the niceties were out of the way, he went on to inform her of the forward-thinking therapies her son would receive, as well as the institution's enlightened education program. As he spoke, the bewildered mother felt herself becoming more relieved as she bought into his disingenuous sales pitch. In fact, the superintendent's entire lecture could be summarized by his closing sentence: "Don't you worry one bit. We'll take wonderful care of your son."

Following that final remark, the frightened and confused boy, who had never spent a single night away from home, was wheeled away by a silent and unsmiling attendant.

For Mrs. Benoit, her ride home was a mixture of sadness and relief. She wanted to believe what Dr. Bowser had relayed and hoped that in little time, her Ron would be back to his usual cheerful self. How could she have known that Ron would spend his days alone and isolated, with little human contact except that of the stranger who changed his soiled clothes, or the aide who dressed him in a scratchy, unfamiliar nightgown? How could she know that his carefully packed suitcase and much-loved stuffed monkey were tossed onto a heap of other residents' baggage in a damp room in the basement?

I stumbled into Belchertown, fresh from college, without an inkling of what lay behind its walls. Once there, I was determined to make life better for Ron and all of my students. I soon became known by the administration as an obstinate, rule-breaking troublemaker whose disruptive ideas about educating and supporting people to become more independent were in direct opposition to Belchertown's status quo.

Looking back, I believe my defiant behavior was a reflexive reaction to the horrifying conditions and multiple indignities I witnessed at every turn. No doubt, complacency could have become acceptance and, over time, I would have lost the capacity to differentiate normal from deviant.

But that wasn't the case here.

My resistance, both passive and overt, to the school's customs and norms seemed to give me strength and helped shape an enduring philosophy about that which is unjust, inhumane, or simply unfair. If there is a message here for the next generation of teachers and clinicians serving people with significant disabilities—or anyone for that matter who is charged with the welfare, education, or safety of another human—it is this: "It may be easy to recognize right from wrong, but it's harder to stand up for it."

I am reminded of a remark Winston Churchill made at the Harrow School commencement in 1941. He stated, "Never give in. Never give in. Never, never, never, never—in nothing, great or small, large or petty—never give in, except to convictions of honour and good sense." Remember, when you are doing all in your power to support a person in need with your expertise, or fighting for whatever it is that you know in your soul must be defended or you deem as necessary, never, never, *never* give in. Never give up. Let good sense, common sense, and a conviction of honor be your guide.

And so the story begins. The perfect storm? Perfect timing? Lost souls coming together? Who knows? What I do know is that we all became friends, and we all found a way to move our lives forward, and it all began in the earthly purgatory known as Belchertown State School.

This is the yet-untold true story.

CHAPTER 1

I glanced quickly in my rearview mirror. My vintage car was beginning to fall apart, and I needed to extend the life of the turn signal required by the state to pass inspection. Spotting no cars behind me, I made a sharp right turn without signaling off Route 21 and onto the grounds of Belchertown State School.

It was an early September afternoon in 1969. I had graduated from the University of Massachusetts, Amherst, that spring with a major in sociology and a minor in education. I was a typical college kid, moving from one step to the next without much forethought. After a congenital neck condition—exacerbated by an old football injury—delivered me from the Vietnam draft, I decided to find a teaching job. One of my fraternity brothers heard about a teaching position in this institution for people with physical and cognitive disabilities just ten miles outside Amherst, and after a mail-in application and a telephone interview, I'd landed the job. I would later learn that teachers actually seeking work at Belchertown were in short supply.

Belchertown State School was one of several facilities for people with intellectual disability. Historically, it had been called the State School for the Feeble-Minded, and it was operated by the Commonwealth of Massachusetts. I learned that these facilities, dotted around the state, were generally named for the small rural communities in which they were located, so in Massachusetts we had Belchertown, Monson, and Wrentham State Schools. I knew almost nothing about teaching or about people with disabilities, but I was glad to have a job and eager to get started.

This institution, and ones like it throughout North America, existed because separation and segregation were the norm at the time for people with disabilities. The birth of a child with a disability was often greeted with social stigma, and confused parents were typically advised to put their children away in the care of a state or private institution and forget about them. I came to learn that the parents who made this decision were mostly not uncaring people, but were themselves victims with little information and few options. The challenges of raising a child with a disability seemed insurmountable, with no resources from the state and no doctors or religious institutions to help them find their way. State institutions like Belchertown were intended to be humane solutions to the painful and awkward problem of accommodating people who would seemingly never fit into normal society.

I drove slowly along a paved roadway surrounded by well-kept lawns and a scattering of large maple and oak trees. The gently rolling terrain was typical of rural, Western Massachusetts. There wasn't much difference between these grounds and those of any beautiful college campus or country club, but I felt an unusual awareness of the space, a prickling in my neck, despite the lovely setting.

I'd given myself plenty of time to make mistakes in the unfamiliar drive, and now I was early for my appointment with the institution's academic director. I turned off my radio and stopped near a groundskeeper who was down on one knee trimming grass, his blue work shirt thrown on the lawn in the late summer heat.

"How ya doin'?" I yelled out. "Can you tell me where to find the school building?"

The fellow stood up slowly and exchanged the clippers in his hands for his long-sleeved shirt. With the radio off, I thought I heard distant calliope music as he approached my car, but I dismissed it because it seemed so out of place.

"Drive straight ahead, and don't take either of the right or left side roads you come to. When the road begins to curve to your left, you look to your right, and the big brick building with the stone steps will be the one you're looking for. There's a parking lot just past the building. Can't miss it."

"Thanks," I said. As I started to pull away, I heard the music again. I turned back to ask where it was coming from.

He pointed toward a pretty meadow off to the right, on the other side of which stood a one-story steel building at the top of a knoll. "Up there at the merry-go-round. See that building at the top of the little clearing?"

"Must be fun for the kids," I said. As I drove forward, I could see one wooden horse after another through the large opening at the front of the building facing the meadow. Children sat on the brightly painted mares and stallions, some bobbing up and down and others sitting stationary.

Still half an hour early, I parked my car alongside the road and started walking across the mowed field to get a better look. Off to my left, a platoon of over a dozen women were advancing up the knoll on their way to the carousel, dressed in mismatched and ill-fitting clothes. Most sported an identical hairstyle, a bowl cut just below the ears with Dutch-boy bangs sliced straight across the forehead. Rather than walking along with swinging arms, they each marched with one arm extended forward and the other back, touching or nearly touching the person in front and behind. From my vantage point, they looked like a string of paper dolls being propelled through the field by a gentle breeze.

I realized I had misjudged who was riding the merry-go-round. The people who appeared to be children when viewed from a distance were actually adult men. They looked a bit disheveled because their clothes were wrinkled and mismatched, but their faces revealed a definite look of contentment. There was something unnerving about the sight of adults—regardless of their intellectual abilities—being entertained with a ride intended for children, but I knew as a neophyte and outsider I had a great deal to learn.

I walked back to my car and drove on according to the groundskeeper's instructions, but my mind lingered on the peculiar image of adults gleefully riding a merry-go-round with no actual children in sight. Finding the gravel lot next to the two-story brick school building, I parked and then climbed the wide granite steps that led up to a landing at the front entrance. From there I turned and looked back across the grounds. It really was a beautiful day, with a nearly cloudless sky. The bright afternoon sun was warm but not uncomfortable. And yet... something was wrong. People... where were the people? The only living creatures I had seen were the groundskeeper and the handful of adults at the carousel. I knew that nearly two thousand people lived at Belchertown, but the place looked mostly deserted. The setting was orderly but empty. I was beginning to feel like I was in an episode of *The Twilight Zone*.

At the top of the stone steps sat a handsome young man of about twenty years of age, not much younger than me.

"Hey—can you tell me where I can find Mrs. Sharp's office?" I asked him.

He looked up and cupped his hand over his eyebrows to shield his blue eyes from the sunlight. "You Mrs. Sharp! You Mrs. Sharp!" he loudly blurted out.

I looked at him more closely. He wore an ordinary white t-shirt and loose jeans that partially covered a pair of black patent leather shoes. His hairstyle alone should have been a dead giveaway that he was not a worker taking a break but rather a resident just killing time. His dirty-blond hair was cut at one length just above his ears, the rest cropped closely to his scalp—similar to the hairstyles of the women I'd seen parading toward the carousel.

"Leo, what are you doing here?" snapped a sharp female voice. "You know you're supposed to be in your building!"

A matronly woman strode out onto the landing. She wore a brown flowered dress and heavy black leather shoes, and her face was pinched into a scowl. At her words, Leo jumped up, scurried down the steps, and darted off around the building. "I'll be with you in a moment," she said to me smoothly, and then turned and hurried back into the school building, yelling, "Alert security! Leo's on the loose again!" I heard the striking of her leather soles on hardwood and the echoing of her shouts as she disappeared down the long hallway. When she was out of sight, I decided to try to track down Leo myself. As I came around the corner, I caught a glimpse of his white shirt as he slid behind a huge oak tree. He was mostly hidden at the angle from which I approached, but as I circled around, I saw he was splayed frozen against the tree.

A security officer emerged from the school building and marched right to Leo's hiding spot. "Okay, Leo, I see you. It's time to go back to B Building." The guard reached out and grabbed the young man by his arm, then marched him back toward the school. "Son, this needs to stop," the panting guard said. "I'm getting tired of chasing after you."

I was curious how the security guard knew with such precision where Leo tried to hide. I had only to turn and look up at the school building for an explanation. There I spied the matronly woman from the steps staring down from a large first-floor window. The moment our eyes met, she drew back and vanished. I started back toward the school building for my appointment with Mrs. Sharp, feeling pretty confident that we had actually just met.

As she opened the main door to the building, she introduced herself as Mrs. Dorothy Sharp, Academic Director for Belchertown State School. "Now, that made for a rather inauspicious beginning to your tenure with us, Mr. Shane," she offered.

"What's the story with him?" I asked, recalling Leo being led away. "He looked pretty scared. He won't be punished or anything, will he?"

"Leo?" she said, then paused. "He's not in your class, so he's not your student, and if he's not your student, then he's not your concern," she responded with finality as we entered her office. Slipping behind her desk and sitting down, she continued: "Belchertown State School operates efficiently because everyone follows rules, without which there'd be chaos. We need to operate as a rule-based, fine-tuned machine for the safety of all the residents." She looked at me for a moment. "Now, on to why you're here. You have to keep in mind that while we run a school, this institution is also a lifelong residence for everyone who lives here. That is why you'll see adults as well as children who live and are educated here. I'm proud to say that our educational program is a model for the entire state school system. You will be working with both 'trainables' and 'educables.' Many of them are crippled, as well." She gazed at me with such intensity I squirmed in my seat. "What has been your experience working with crippled children?"

"Very little, actually, but I'm looking forward to learning," I said. At this point, I was just relieved that I didn't have to admit I had no experience with "trainables" and "educables," whatever they might be. I'd had a semester of student teaching in history at Amherst High School during college, but that was the extent of my teaching experience. I'd learned nothing in school about working with children with disabilities, and other than a few visits to a family friend with Down syndrome, I'd never spent any time around people with disabilities. I knew what Mrs. Sharp meant by "crippled," but I hadn't thought the word was used anymore. I could guess, of course, what the other labels meant. I cringed at how dehumanizing they sounded. The word "demeaning" came to mind. I had to school my expression as she continued.

As Mrs. Sharp spoke, she leaned slightly forward and never took her eyes off me. The intensity of her posture and unwavering facial expression made me uneasy. If she was attempting to use body language to prove who was boss, she was succeeding.

"School officially starts next Monday, so you will have a few days to get oriented. Most of our classrooms are in the school building, but you have been assigned to teach in the infirmary. We'll take a tour of that building shortly, but I just want to say a few words about your assignment. The

infirmary houses young and adult residents who require medical attention, many of whom are confined to wheelchairs or spend their days in bed.
Most of your students will not be able to walk, and many don't talk. Your
classroom is in the basement, but the students live on the two floors above."
Without missing a beat, she asked, "Do you have an educational philosophy
as it applies to the retarded?"

The word "retarded" also made me cringe, but I moved on. "Well, this
is my first job, so I'm not very experienced, but I'm certainly eager to learn.
As far as philosophy, I guess I would have to say that everyone learns and
excels when doing something of strong personal interest."

She stopped me before I could continue and asked if I thought that
idea applied to "retarded children" as well. I was lucky she'd interrupted
me because I didn't have much philosophical fuel in my tank. However, I
did suspect that personal motivation was indeed important for children—
with or without disabilities—and I was comfortable reiterating that fundamental principle to her.

Without another word, she pushed a thin spiral notebook across her
desk in my direction. "We have only a few days before school begins, but I
thought you should look at this curriculum guide."

I picked it up, nodded silently, thumbed through it quickly, and moved
to tuck it into my briefcase. As I fumbled with the latches, it might have
become obvious to Mrs. Sharp that I was a briefcase neophyte. Truth be
told, this was my first day lugging around a briefcase. Even that morning I
wondered whether I was actually trading up when I grabbed it and not my
battered backpack.

At that moment, the phone rang, and Mrs. Sharp picked it up before
the first ring had ended. "That's all right," she said, staring out the window.
"He can stay in his room for a while. He'll be fine."

I assumed the call was about Leo, but I knew Mrs. Sharp wasn't about
to clarify anything for my benefit.

She hung up the phone and turned back to me. The room was silent
except for the strumming of her manicured fingernails on the desktop.
After an awkward moment, she folded her hands together in a manner
which seemed to indicate that she was ready to move onto a new topic. "I
think this is a good time to review some school policies. I'm referring to the
rules I've created so that the education department remains on course. As

I said, rules are intended for the safety of the residents and to allow me to keep track of staff performance. I'm sure you understand that."

"Yes," I responded, wanting to seem agreeable.

"The first rule is," she began, "school begins at eight a.m. sharp and ends promptly at two p.m. Teachers usually arrive by seven thirty. I assume that works for you."

I nodded.

She signaled her approval with a small smile and a raised eyebrow, then leaned toward me and, punctuating each word, said, "Number two, never, never, never, ever transport a student in your car."

"Makes sense to me," I said.

"Rule three: Do not allow more than two students at a time in the elevator that brings students to your classroom—and I mean never."

This one confused me. I wondered if it was a problem because of the weight of more than two students or perhaps some state regulation that I wasn't experienced enough yet to understand. I wanted to ask her to clarify, but Mrs. Sharp barreled on with the next regulation. "Rule four: Residents are rarely allowed to leave the grounds for field trips, shopping, or visits to private residences."

"Quick question about this."

"Of course."

"Mrs. Sharp, are you saying that no one ever leaves?" I asked politely. I was sure that there must be safety and liability issues, but I felt uncomfortable with the suggestion that people who lived there were essentially captives. The finality of a no-leave policy suggested for me a life sentence without ever having committed a crime.

"Well, of course some people occasionally get to leave. They can go with family, and some do—especially for holidays. Long-time volunteers who become attached to some of our residents can request to take a person out. Just to be clear, the residents aren't exactly in lockdown, but we certainly do not have a come-and-go policy, and permission needs to be granted." She paused briefly. "Our door-locking policy comes next. It's pretty simple, actually. The rule is if you open it, lock it. Remember, that applies to every door and every cabinet."

She rolled her chair back, signaling we were through, and as she shifted her focus to the side drawer of her oversized wooden desk, I felt my shoulders relax. I hadn't realized as they crept closer to my ears throughout the conversation. I was simultaneously intimidated by her brusque efficiency and suspicious of her callous discussion of the residents.

She rummaged in the drawer of her desk, retrieved a set of keys, and slid them across her desk to me. The key ring contained three keys and an oval brass plate engraved with *Belchertown State School 836*. She explained that the large skeleton key fit the main doors of the infirmary building. The other keys opened my classroom and got me into cabinets and desk drawers.

"Lastly, we have a mandatory monthly staff meeting. There are eight teachers based here in this building who teach about eighty residents. That staff meeting will include you even though you will be teaching in the infirmary rather than in the actual school building. The non-infirmary students can walk and don't require constant medical attention."

"Mrs. Sharp," I said, "is there a dress code for the staff?"

"Well, you won't be required to wear a tie, if that's what you're asking. Now, of course, you might from time to time see Dr. Bowser, the superintendent, in the building, but he isn't actually part of the school department. You'll know him because he normally wears a coat and tie—a rare fashion statement in this institution." This line could have been interpreted as a joke if she'd cracked a smile, but I was getting the feeling that Mrs. Sharp was the furthest thing from a joker.

Given the events of the day, I was beginning to suspect that these staff meetings would take me to foreign territory. I was a little overwhelmed and frankly uncertain that I had the right training for my position or for any position at the institution. It was sinking in that I had taken a full-time job for which my education hadn't prepared me. Now that I was actually at the school, I knew I hadn't—and likely couldn't—have anticipated the difficulties and conflicts that would arise in a state facility where people were seemingly prisoners. I didn't want to discuss much more about teaching until I at least had the opportunity to meet my new students and see my classroom.

As if reading my mind, Mrs. Sharp stood, retrieved a large black leather pocketbook, and moved toward the door. "Then we're off to visit the infirmary," she said. When we got to the bottom of the steps, she asked, "Do you mind driving? My husband has my car today."

"Not at all."

As we approached my car, I was startled to see a tiny smile tug at her lips. "You drive a... isn't this a taxicab?"

"This isn't just a taxi, Mrs. Sharp. This is an authentic British taxicab." I loved this 1951 black Austin Taxi, with its right-hand drive, jump seats, and glass window separating me from any passengers. I could count on lots of space for friends and lots of people staring when I drove past. I'd never been afraid of being a little different or standing out in a crowd.

I opened the large back door, and Mrs. Sharp shifted her black pocket-book to climb into the spacious back seat. I slammed her door shut, jumped into the front seat cubicle, and slid aside the glass divider.

Before I spoke another word, she said, "Straight ahead."

The infirmary stood about a hundred and fifty yards down the road from the school building, so the trip was brief. The campus itself consisted of ten dormitories for men and women and three nurseries for children under the age of six. To care for the considerable residential population, there was also a laundry building, kitchen, storehouse, hospital, private housing for staff, a power plant, and, of course, the infirmary. The school opened in 1922, built on eight hundred acres of former farmland. It surprisingly still operated a farm, which supplied a fair amount of the institution's food and employed some of the residents. It was a self-contained community that kept the residents safe but separate from the nearby town. The two-story infirmary, like most of the other buildings on the grounds, was constructed of red brick. Wings extended from either side, flanking the main section, each ending with a porch enclosed by screens to keep the insects out and black iron bars to keep the residents in. INFIRMARY was inscribed over the main entrance.

We were greeted by the frantic cries of a lanky redheaded teenager with freckles that covered his entire face. "Can I ride in your car?" he yelled from a clump of bushes in front of the left wing of the building. I knew the boy had Down syndrome because as a child, I had often visited Sam, my aforementioned family friend. Sam, who also had Down syndrome, lived in a noisy, smelly nursing home, and even as a young kid, I had felt sad that he had to endure a life of loneliness in such wretched conditions, spending most of his time staring out the window.

This boy's hair was cut in a shorter version of the bowl style. He wore a long-sleeved shirt with multicolored horizontal stripes tucked into pants that looked clean but were extremely wrinkled. His zipper was down, and the hem of his shirt stuck out through it.

"No rides today," I said as he approached the car.

"Jimmy Kearns, zip up your pants and go wait for us over there." Mrs. Sharp pointed toward the front door of the building. Jimmy's demeanor quickly changed from delight to nervousness as his head went down and his zipper came up. "Do you know what he was doing behind that bush?" Mrs. Sharp inquired.

"I think so," I answered without hesitation.

"There is a lot of that going on here. What do you know about curbing such behavior?"

I indicated that I would look into it. In that moment, an unsettling understanding of the real-world problems I would have to face and solve in my new position began to creep into my mind. Here was a behavior, masturbation, that most young men would consider normal—in private, of course. But here, the residents had no privacy unless they snuck out and hid in a bush or behind a tree. This was my first inkling that very normal sexual behaviors were seen as deviant under pretty much all conditions here, and that controlling, not normalizing, the behavior was the goal at Belchertown. A normal act was abnormal at the institution, whether private or not, and it would be part of my job to determine a way to control it. I was extremely uncomfortable with the knowledge that I would likely have to find a way to influence or control the sexual behavior of other men or women.

She suggested, "Perhaps you might consider dealing with this in your classes this year. How about doing it as part of sex education?"

Jimmy approached us as we moved toward the infirmary, putting an end to the uncomfortable discussion.

"Jimmy, say hello to Mr. Shane, the new teacher," offered Mrs. Sharp pleasantly.

I asked, "Do you live here, Jimmy?"

"Me live in the infirmary. Can I ride in your car?"

"I don't think that's a good idea right now, Jimmy."

Together the three of us climbed the steps to the heavy door of the infirmary, where I entered a world I could never have imagined existed.

CHAPTER 2

As I stepped into the hallway with Mrs. Sharp and Jimmy, I was engulfed by a thick wave of heat and a powerful, completely foreign odor. It came not from a single source but from a convergence of foul smells that weren't difficult to place: urine and feces, sour milk and rotting food, unwashed flesh, dirty sheets, and medical ointments, with a whiff of piney cleaning solutions. All those elements interacted in the swelter to produce a unique and overpowering stench. I was temporarily incapable of speech.

Mrs. Sharp seemed not to notice. She shoved the door shut behind us with a terse reminder: "If you open it, lock it!" Jimmy scurried ahead, where a short, broad woman in a white nursing uniform intercepted him and led him gently down the corridor. The nurse removed keys from her belt and used one to open a door, through which they both disappeared. After the door slammed shut, I heard metal turn on metal again. The hairs on the back of my neck prickled.

"I need to find the head nurse," said Mrs. Sharp with a sigh. "Wait here."

Mrs. Sharp walked away, and I shifted from foot to foot in the hall, trying to acclimate to the environment. The stench was overwhelming. Could I ever get used to it, the way Mrs. Sharp seemed to have? I realized that if I were to take this job at Belchertown State School, I'd be smelling this every day.

And these sounds—this is what I'd be hearing every day, too.

The space seemed to explode with loud, inharmonious, and disturbing noises associated with the supervision of so many human beings. Some of the sounds were common—the thump of laundry bags hitting tiled floor, the slamming of doors, the clanging of metal pails against a baseboard, the clatter of dishes being stacked. More alarming were the steady sounds of humans in distress. Screaming and moaning. Crying, from both men and women. They were wailing and hollering, painfully and unrelentingly. It seemed to me that what I was hearing was an endless anguished protest. I was rooted to the spot and unable to move. I felt shocked and horrified. The sounds reverberated in the empty hall.

Mrs. Sharp made a breezy return from the offices down the hallway. "Mr. Shane," she said. "I would like to introduce you to the head nurse, Mrs. Bernice Dalton."

"Howard," I offered, as I reached out to shake her hand.

"And I prefer Bernie," she said with a smile. I estimated Bernie to be in her mid-forties. She had a triangular face with high cheekbones, light blue eyes, and reddish-brown hair that she neatly tucked into her nurse's cap. She was dressed in a traditional white nurse's uniform and white leather shoes.

She took a few minutes to orient me, explaining that the two residential floors separated the sexes, with women and girls as young as ten on the first and the men and boys on the second. I was shocked to realize that adults and little children shared a living space in this stark, unsavory environment. The infirmary's echoing hallways were a far reach from the raucous playgrounds, cheerful classrooms, and cozy bedrooms I associated with children. I was horrified to think that these children woke alone to the screams of unrelated adults, with no parents or family to comfort them.

Bernie went on to explain that residents of the infirmary had either a physical disability requiring a wheelchair, a pair of crutches, or a walker, or a medical condition that required medication. I was vaguely familiar with epilepsy and cerebral palsy but was unacquainted with hydrocephaly, microcephaly, spina bifida, and autism, among many others. I'd never heard many of the terms Bernie was using, and it struck me that the very act of keeping people with disabilities separate from society in places like this meant that the rest of us had no cause to ever learn about them. I was witnessing firsthand the hidden warehousing of human beings. I wondered how long it took to get used to this. Within two hours of being at Belchertown, I'd learned I was going to have to deal with sex education, overpowering assaults to the senses, adults living with children, children growing up without the hugs and comfort of familial love, disabilities and disorders I'd never heard of, an oblivious society, and a stodgy, rule-driven academic director. Having first been simply grateful to be employed, now I marveled at how I'd stumbled into an entirely foreign world.

I was Alice, and I had tumbled down the rabbit hole.

Bernie turned to me with a smile. "It's been a while since we've had a new teacher, Howard. Welcome," she said. In my overwhelmed state, I didn't respond. After an uncomfortable silence, she offered, "How about a tour of the building? Meet some students, some staff, and see your classroom? To your right is our elevator. It's used for everything around here. Unfortunately, it works only about half the time."

Bernie's comment instantly transformed Mrs. Sharp's facial expression from boredom to annoyance. I reflexively braced myself for a rebuttal.

Mrs. Sharp remained silent as Bernie hit the elevator button. The pockmarked door moved only a few inches before reversing direction. She hit the button again, this time pushing the door open by hand, revealing several bulky gray laundry bags that had blocked it. The other side of the elevator shaft opened to the outside loading dock, and over the bags, I spotted the heads of a couple of men in their mid-thirties. I knew at once from their telltale haircuts that they lived here, and I surmised that they also held jobs on the grounds. While we were trying to get onto the elevator from inside the building, they were pulling bags in from a truck on the other side.

I asked about alternatives for getting to school if the elevator was down.

"This is the only way for students to get to your classroom. Your only choice is to cancel school until it's fixed," Mrs. Sharp replied tersely. "And by the way, this is the only elevator on the grounds, and it's only here because most of the patients in this building are crippled."

Bernie flinched, but then interjected, "And our kids are heartbroken if they have to miss school."

"Can I meet the kids?" I asked.

With that, Bernie continued down the corridor past the elevator and held open the door to the children's ward. Upon entering, I knew that moment would become a defining one in my life. I would never be able to erase my first visit to Ward 1.

The room itself was cavernous, with a high ceiling covered by stained acoustic tiles, walls the color of mustard, and a speckled linoleum floor. Banks of tall, double-hung windows covered much of the upper half of the walls. Torn and faded shades, some with missing drawstrings, were stretched over half the windows. The stench that assaulted me in the hallway followed me to this part of building. Because the smell was a little less pronounced, I figured this was the result of my senses mercifully acclimating.

But more than the smells, sights, and noises, it was the number of humans within the space—mostly children, dozens of them, along with the

furnishings and implements needed to bed, transport, and contain them—
that would become etched in my mind.

Four rows of metal beds and cribs, some large and some small, dom-
inated the room. Each mattress was wrapped in a dull white sheet and
covered by a flimsy tattered blanket and a tiny pillow encased in a gray-
ish pillowcase. The bars on the cribs were dull chrome, with no decorative touches to arouse interest, and there were no mobiles in the space
above the children's beds to capture and hold their attention. Many of the
cribs were occupied even though it was only early afternoon. The beds
were laid out with a thin passageway between them that enabled the
attendants as well as any ambulatory girls to walk or be guided about the
room. Between the cribs was a jumble of personal objects: chests of drawers, small steamer trunks, and a variety of wheelchairs and carts, some
ancient and in disrepair.

Three large sheets of posterboard detailing different types of sched-
ules were taped to one of the walls. The first schedule was titled BOWEL
MOVEMENT and listed each girl's first name. Next was a column labeled
DATE AND TIME, and next to that a column intended to capture a description. Here I read details such as "diarrhea," "little loose," "bloody," or
"normal." The bathing schedule hung next to the bowel movement chart.
The posted dates revealed that most girls received a bath every other day.
The last chart was a monthly calendar that showed work schedules for
the attendants.

I was struck by the lack of privacy in posting such personal information so openly in such a belittling manner. I couldn't fathom how it would
feel to have exceptionally personal information about my hygiene or bathroom habits shared so publicly.

The entrance to a multipurpose bathroom and changing room was
without a door. The room was tiled on six surfaces, with walls matching
the mustard tiles from the main ward. The focal point of the room was a
large stainless-steel washtub and a changing table large enough to hold
residents of all sizes.

Not surprisingly, the closer our contingent got to the washroom,
the more pungent the odor became. The bathroom and toilets were
grimy, and the floor and walls were discolored and stained. Probably
contributing more to the smell, however, were the soiled bed linens and

clothing piled in two corners of the room. The open doorway allowed anyone, visitor or worker, male or female, to peer directly into this ladies' room.

Along one wall of the main room, I spotted two large, padded platforms with wooden sides, onto which some of the girls had been deposited— some on their backs, some on their sides, others with their heads tucked right into the Naugahyde surface. It was obvious that the reason those girls didn't get up and jump off the platforms was because they couldn't. The wooden boxes nearly devoured their small bodies. It was a painful reminder that these were children.

As I scanned the room, I saw girls of all ages everywhere—on the beds and floor, in wheeled chairs and carts. They ranged in age from about five years to their late teens. I didn't observe any interaction among the girls. Many sat quietly, just staring into space. Others watched attentively as the attendants went about their work. Many of the girls were unable to walk or sit up, and were stranded as they sat in wheelchairs or remained in bed. Some of the girls were rocking, twirling, hand flapping, or making sounds that I perceived as chilling and eerie. I was almost paralyzed by what I was observing. In spite of their environment, in spite of the severe physical restrictions they lived with, the faces of these girls were still soft and innocent.

White-uniformed nurses and attendants, all women, moved amongst the clutter of young bodies and beds and wheelchairs and bags of laundry. Beds were stripped, diapers changed, medications administered, food delivered, unresponsive children fed, children loaded into wheelchairs for trips to the toilet, children cleaned and dressed, and on and on. I could see that caring for a roomful of girls with severe disabilities required order and routine. The interactions between staff and children were not uncaring or cruel, but rather efficient and somewhat mechanical. I told myself that their workloads were too demanding, that they were probably far too busy for the types of casual exchanges that stimulate growth and development. But I knew those girls deserved more.

"How many girls live in this room?" I asked.

"Never more than forty." Mrs. Sharp answered as calmly as if she were informing me about the number of girls who tried out for the local soccer team.

"Forty," I repeated. Forty children were housed here in this room alone. I didn't need a degree in special education to understand how this environment would negatively affect human potential.

There was so much that was peculiar, unsettling, and disheartening about what I had seen in this ward, but it wasn't simply that all these children were housed together. After all, the idea of three hundred people living in one building wasn't in and of itself abnormal. College dormitory life, military barrack life, and even life in a penitentiary had a similar arrangement. But even in these settings, they didn't all bunk together in a single room. In the case of these kids, it was clear they had been unwittingly thrown into these circumstances, and they had few, if any, alternatives. What I found most distressing was that they had no privacy. These residents of Belchertown State School had no opportunity to collect their thoughts, to engage in private conversation, to be intimate, to cleanse themselves alone or use a toilet without someone seeing them. Breaking a rule by hiding in a bush or behind a tree was apparently the only way to achieve alone time in this place.

As I consciously tried to block out this entire scene, I knew that despite my efforts, what I'd seen, smelled, and heard today would be engraved in my brain forever. It would be a memory that never fully faded, jolting back to mind throughout my life with no antecedent, and no warning.

But something else happened to me on that first day, in that grim, overcrowded room—something more profound and positive than simple horror.

I had been shocked into having an educational philosophy.

CHAPTER 3

When I had arrived at Belchertown only a few hours earlier, the story in my head had been all about me. What would this new job be like, and how would it affect my life? I had been central to the narrative. But as I left the ward on the heels of Mrs. Sharp and Bernie, dazed at the atrocious conditions I'd just seen, my own plights or misgivings were far from my mind. All I could think about was how I could help change this environment. How I could help these kids.

In the few steps it took to walk down the hall into the next ward, I became a celebrity of sorts. It had been a very long time since there had been a teacher in the infirmary, and the kids—as well as the staff who cared for them—were excited.

As we entered the ward for older students, Bernie announced my arrival with unconcealed enthusiasm.

"Pauline, he's finally here! I want you to meet our new teacher," she said, gesturing toward a shy woman. "Mr. Shane, I want you to meet Pauline, one of our best attendants. She's in charge of most of your students. Pauline's been building you up for the past few weeks."

Pauline beamed and shook my hand. "I'm very glad you're here," she said nervously, staring at the floor. "My girls have been waiting for a teacher for more than a year now. I hope you decide to stay."

They'd been waiting *a year*? I knew the tenure of teachers who had come to work at Belchertown had historically been short-lived, but my plan was to stay. After what I'd just witnessed in the ward, I wasn't going to let those kids down.

"Hi, Mr. Shane," said a small voice behind me, the words perfectly articulated.

I turned around to find a young girl lying on her back in a plywood cart. She was the size of a toddler, with a tiny torso, arms, and legs. From her feet to her eyebrows, she appeared to be a small but typically developing child, but the upper part of her head was extremely large, with her skull stretched out like an overinflated balloon. She wore a wrinkled navy-blue dress with a white border around the short sleeves and neck, white shoes, and blue socks. I noticed at once that the bottoms of her shoes were as clean and shiny as the tops. She wasn't able to sit or stand, I realized, because her slight body couldn't support her head. I had a million questions—but asked none. I turned and crouched down to get nearer to her. "Hi," I said. "Who are you?"

"Wendy," she answered.

Pauline stepped in. "Mr. Shane, Wendy is the sweetest girl in the entire world."

"Good, I'm glad," I said, "because I'll need some sweet girls in school this year."

Wendy smiled.

"How old are you, Wendy?"

"Eight years old," she volunteered.

"Wendy has un-arrested hydrocephalus," Mrs. Sharp interjected. "That means she has water on her brain. The water is really spinal fluid that just kept pouring into her head as an infant, and it kept getting bigger and bigger. Her head weighs more than twenty pounds. It might be the biggest head in the U.S." The callous, clinical way she said this made my stomach clench.

"Imagine that," I offered. "Say, do we have a budget for snacks? I bet Wendy loves snack time."

Mrs. Sharp regarded me shrewdly. "Mr. Shane," she said, "does the description of medical conditions make you uncomfortable?"

"Not really, but I would prefer not to talk about this right here."

"Wendy doesn't mind people talking about her, do you, Wendy? Lots of people come to visit her because of her head. She's kind of famous, you know."

I caught a quick glimpse of Pauline and Bernie. They were likely used to Mrs. Sharp's insensitive opinions; they handled the awkward moment by disconnecting entirely. They looked away. Ironically, Mrs. Sharp's most enthusiastic listener was Wendy, who looked back and forth between us as we sparred nonverbally about the appropriateness of this discussion.

"Are you my new teacher, Mr. Shane?" Wendy inquired.

"Yes, I am, and school starts next week, so you'd better be ready." I gave her a nod and a smile. "I'll see you later, Wendy."

I moved toward a teenager sitting in a wheelchair who had been looking in our direction. Bernie made the introductions this time. "Ruth, this is Mr. Shane. You know already that he's the new teacher now, don't you?"

Ruth immediately looked up in an exaggerated fashion, and she smiled.

"Are you having a good day?" Bernie asked.

Ruth remained silent, but her eyes shot up quickly again.

Bernie explained that though Ruth couldn't speak, they had developed a basic communication system that depended on Ruth responding to a series of yes/no questions. "Ruth, can you please show Mr. Shane how you say yes?"

She looked up.

"And how you say no?"

This time, Ruth's face molded into a pout, and she looked down.

"Now, Mr. Shane, why don't you ask Ruth a question just to be sure you've got her system down?"

Instinctively, I knew this was more an opportunity to affirm Ruth's competence than to prove my skill at interpreting facial expressions. I obliged. "Okay, Ruth. Do you like music?"

She signaled yes immediately.

"Have you heard of the Beatles?"

She raised her eyes.

"The Rolling Stones?"

She shrieked, and her eyes shot up immediately.

"Ah, are they your favorites?"

Her eyes shot up with such swiftness that her body and wheelchair shook.

"Do you know the song 'Honky Tonk Women'?"

Again, she responded with combined eye movements and a loud squeal.

"Really! Is it a Beatles song?"

She pouted no.

"Righteous Brothers?"

Another pout.

"Rolling Stones?"

Her eyes shot up.

"Don't think you can fool Ruth," Bernie whispered loudly. "Trust me, even though she doesn't talk, she understands everything—and I mean everything."

Ruth burst into laughter, which ended in a long coughing spell. Even as she coughed and struggled for air, she refused to let go of her wide grin. I said goodbye, warning her to be ready for some challenging schoolwork beginning Monday morning. Her facial expression all but said, "I was born ready."

Bernie pulled me aside to confide that Ruth had been sent to Belchertown because her mother could no longer manage the physical lifting required to care for her. Ruth's family was very loving, and they visited regularly. They brought care packages, so Ruth was spared the institutional uniform, instead always wearing contemporary clothing that fit. She'd clearly managed to avoid the barber of Belchertown, because she sported a flattering short hairstyle.

Bernie also told me that Ruth was an intelligent teenager who was, in her words, "trapped within her own body by cerebral palsy." Her life at Belchertown was mostly bearable because the direct care staff, and especially Pauline, treated her as normally and with as much dignity as the setting would allow. When she was bathed or used the toilet, they made an effort to afford her some privacy. Respect also meant talking directly to her, not conversing in the same room about her, and making an effort to discuss age-appropriate topics. Bernie's short tutorial ended with an appeal that I pay particular attention to Ruth and try to make school the place where she could learn to become a better communicator.

After agreeing that I'd make every effort to help Ruth develop her communication skills, I introduced myself to a young woman sitting in a wheelchair nearby.

"Carla, meet your new teacher," Bernie said. "Mr. Shane, this beautiful young lady is Carla Dalton, who is Ruth's best friend."

Carla was a pretty, dark-haired fourteen-year-old who, like Ruth, had cerebral palsy. She leaned forward in her seat, straining against a tightly fastened seat belt. Using what seemed to be every muscle in her body, she pushed against the back of her seat, twisted her head up and to the left, and said what sounded like, "Hi."

Bernie told me that some of the girls in the ward had forged close relationships. Even without being able to speak, they had managed to achieve successful communication through facial expressions, directed glances, and movement. While Ruth and Carla shared similar challenges from cerebral palsy—with bodies that were affected by irreparable damage to their brains—the nature of their respective motor difficulties was entirely different. Ruth sat very still and stiff in her chair, and when she did move, it was indeed extremely slow. Carla, on the other hand, had a type of cerebral palsy that caused her body to be in constant motion. As a result, she was thin and muscular, and she sweated profusely. Overall, she looked tense, and her muscles strained in whatever body part she struggled to control. When she attempted to speak, the intricate movements required of her mouth and throat caused her to stiffen to the point that veins in her neck protruded. Her vocal tract constricted, and the resulting speech sounded like air being forced through the tiny opening of a balloon. Sometimes it came out in loud bursts, and at other times it was soft and indiscernible.

As we were speaking with Carla, a girl in the adjacent crib began to make a persistent throaty sound in rhythm with the flapping of her arms. The sudden noise briefly captured everyone's attention. Carla repeatedly looked to me and back to the girl, and even a rookie could have recognized she meant to express something.

The girl in the crib wore a white hospital gown with an unsecured back, the tie strings dangling. She looked to be about twelve or thirteen years old, with dark black hair, ivory skin, and deep brown oval eyes. As she flailed her arms and shook her shoulders, she kept her head steady all the while, her eyes fixed on the wall.

"What about her?" I asked Carla—but realized right away that I needed to ask yes/no questions. I tried again: "Carla, do you have something you want to tell me?"

"Yes."

Bernie stepped in. "Are you wondering if Jennie is going to school?"

Carla let out a strangled "yes."

Through glances and strained yes and no vocalizations, Carla was able to start and expand on a discussion about Jennie. Her strategic glances were filled with meaning, and she knew how to take full advantage of powerful nonverbal tools.

As I moved toward Jennie, Mrs. Sharp stepped in front of me. As quickly as Jennie's arm-flapping and sound-making had started, the girl now became absolutely still. She sat cross-legged on her mattress, staring without emotion through the bars of her crib.

"Will she be one of my students?" I asked.

Mrs. Sharp, who had been silent for the past several minutes, spoke up. "No, of course not. Sending Jennie to school would only be a waste of time. Look at her. She just sits and stares."

"Mrs. Sharp..." Bernie began.

"I know, I know," Mrs. Sharp interrupted. "The staff thinks that having some new experiences, some 'stimulation,' might affect her. Well, I'm not buying it, and I'm not going to budge on this one. She's not even trainable. She has no sense of the world around her. It's like she's in a coma with her eyes open."

I realized that while the teacher in me reared up ready to prove a point, the diplomat had kicked in. I knew not to fight Mrs. Sharp at that point. She was coming off in every situation as a rigid administrator. As she moved away, I murmured to Pauline that maybe moving Jennie closer to the door, where she would get more stimulation, might help pave the way to the school.

"Great idea," Pauline whispered back. "I'm going to move her this afternoon."

Carla pushed back and seconded Pauline's approval with a loud yes.

"Hey, Carla, let's try to give her more interesting things to do and to look at," I suggested. "We can work on that together, okay?"

A smile and another yes followed.

Mrs. Sharp was abruptly ending this part of our rounds, motioning for us to follow her out of the ward. I scanned the room and was gripped by the thought that nearly forty other children hadn't made the cut and would not be starting school on Monday. What disability was so extreme that they wouldn't benefit from a few hours away from this dull, dreary room?

As the three of us retreated from the ward, I noticed that Pauline had already taken the initiative, and Jennie, still motionless in her crib, was being moved to her new bed location. The screeching sound of her crib, caused by wheels that likely had been stuck in one spot for years, became the alpha sound in the cacophony of the room. I wondered if the noise of the wheels or the shift in her surroundings was penetrating her seeming indifference.

We took the stairway to the second floor, where the boys and men lived. Mrs. Sharp effortlessly selected a key and opened the door to a hallway that looked identical to the previous one. I looked down and saw a slender teenage boy kneeling just beyond the threshold as we stepped into the hallway. He had a sharp nose, thin lips, dark eyes, and a short crew cut. He rested firmly on his bent knees, his tattered pant legs extending several inches beyond his feet. As Mrs. Sharp re-locked the door, the boy reached out his hand and perfectly enunciated one word: "Keys."

Mrs. Sharp peered down at his hand as if it were a dinner entrée she didn't order. Then, without acknowledging his request, she returned her attention to locking the door and dropped the big key ring into her purse. Once the keys disappeared, the boy's face fell. He turned away slowly and propelled himself to a wheelchair parked several feet away, using only his arms and dragging his legs behind him. He effortlessly hoisted himself into the seat and wheeled away. The chair was way too big for his small frame, but he maneuvered it easily and rolled out of sight.

"What was that all about?" I asked Bernie.

"That's Danny Brookes," Bernie told me. "Danny has lived in this building since he was an infant. I don't think he's spent a single day off grounds, even out of this building, in the thirteen years he's lived here. As you just witnessed, he loves keys. It's amazing to see how quickly he gets to the entrance from anywhere on the floor the moment he hears keys jingling." She paused briefly. "All he wants to do after he gets your keys is just lock the door for you." Bernie gave Mrs. Sharp a hard look, but Mrs. Sharp inhaled deeply as she shut her eyes, tucked her chin, and shook her head a few times from side to side. There was no mistaking that the boss was unmoved.

"That Danny never seems to give up, but I don't feed into his nonsense," she said. "The only way to stop him from doing this is to stop handing over our keys. He's in your classroom, Mr. Shane, but I'd suggest not giving him your keys."

Bernie rolled her eyes as Mrs. Sharp turned to lead us down the hall. I needed some time to think more about Danny, his keys, and what Mrs. Sharp had said about his behavior. I would need to consider how his fascinations might stem from the boredom of growing up in a place like Belchertown. I recalled Jennie's arm-flapping downstairs, and Jimmy's excursion into the bushes in front of the building. If keys were a strong interest that brought him joy, then I'd find a way to incorporate that interest into my teaching. The fact that he had any passion at all after thirteen years in this institution made him, in my eyes, truly exceptional.

"Ward 5," Mrs. Sharp announced as we turned into another cavernous room. "Some of these boys will be in your class."

Not more than ten feet from the entrance, a man of about forty with a blond crew cut and piercing blue eyes approached. His clothing had been ironed, his face was clean-shaven, and his nails clean and trimmed. "Pencils?" he asked softly. "Do you have any pencils?"

"Scoot along, Ed," said Mrs. Sharp. Her tone was cool, but she addressed him with less antipathy than she did the other residents. "None of us have any pencils." She turned to me and said, "Ed doesn't belong in this institution. He should be in a facility for psychotics, but he's been here for almost thirty years."

After what I'd witnessed in my first hours at Belchertown, I didn't think anyone belonged in this institution, but I held my tongue. "You mean he hasn't left the building in thirty years?" I asked. My question had an edge that I hadn't really intended, and I shot a glance at Mrs. Sharp to see her reaction. She said nothing, just turned away and called to an attendant outside the entrance to Ward 5.

The attendant had thin dark eyebrows and jet-black hair that contrasted with her stark white nurse's uniform. She was talking to a gaunt elderly man whose fingers moved constantly in a rolling motion. His clothing and the stubble on his face marked him as a resident. Mrs. Sharp ignored the man and spoke directly to the nurse. "Nancy, we're looking for Teddy McNeil, Dennis Russell, and Ron Benoit." She glanced at her student roster and added, "And Danny Brookes, but we saw him heading toward the other end of the hall."

"Teddy, Dennis, and Ron are in the ward. Danny probably went to the dining room," Nancy answered irritably.

Bernie took it upon herself to introduce me. "Nancy, meet Howard Shane. He's the new teacher."

"Oh, yeah, the hippie teacher Dennis mentioned. I heard you were coming up. Nice to meet you."

"Ha! A hippie? I guess it's my hair." I touched the shaggy 'do instinctively. "Who's Dennis?"

"You'll meet Dennis Russell in a few minutes," Mrs. Sharp snapped. "Although I thought it was decided he wasn't going to be allowed to go to school this year. He's a real troublemaker."

"He's only thirteen, and he just needs a little guidance," offered Bernie. She rarely looked at Mrs. Sharp directly. "I think deep down, he's eager to learn. He deserves another chance." Turning to me with a smile, she asked, "You can handle a hellion, can't you?"

"I can handle a hellion," I responded. I sensed that, compared to Mrs. Sharp, Bernie had a much better grasp of who these kids actually were and what they needed.

Mrs. Sharp sighed. "He'll just waste your time, and I wouldn't do it, but..."

"I'm willing to give him a chance," I interrupted.

"Fine, give it a chance," Mrs. Sharp snapped as she glared at Bernie. It was becoming increasingly clear that the tension between the two was longstanding. I just prayed we could get through the tour before they tore off the gloves and went at it.

Nancy sliced through it. "These are the greatest kids in the world—so, hippie or not, just be a good teacher. Your predecessor didn't last a year. I don't think she even liked the kids. A real lousy teacher and a real loser!"

I admitted to myself that I certainly thought I could be a good teacher. But the fact that the one before me had left before the year's end—I didn't want to admit it, but that rattled me a little.

"Come on, Nancy, let's not scare him off before he's even begun," warned Bernie. Cheerily, she added, "Teddy, Dennis, and Ron, right?"

I pushed open the right-hand side of the double doors, and we moved into a large room. It was a carbon copy of Ward 1, only this ward was filled with boys—boys in cribs, boys in wheelchairs, boys staring vacantly at walls, or wailing or flapping their hands. The smell and the commotion were nearly identical to the girls' ward. A very slender boy with missing clumps of white-blond hair roamed past, walking barefoot on the balls of his feet. His path took him directly into the tiled toilet and bathing area, and he was gone.

Noticing a pencil on a wooden table next to the entranceway, I picked it up and slid it over my right ear. My companions had moved to a bedside, and I joined them.

A teenage boy sat on one of the thirty or so identical metal beds in the ward, repeating, "I don't have to go to school. My father is coming next week to take me home." A wheelchair sat next to the bed, and a set of wooden crutches leaned against the metal headboard.

"Dennis, you can still go to school until he gets here, can't you?" Bernie interjected, her voice filled with compassion.

"Hi, Dennis," I added. "I'm the new teacher, and I'd like you to be in my class."

"You're a shithead!" he cried. "I don't want a shithead for a teacher."

"I'm a lot of things, but I'm not a shithead," I insisted.

"Okay, then you're an asshole."

"Now you're getting warm."

He cracked a smile.

"Look, Dennis, come to school, and if you don't like it, you and I will talk about it."

"But I might miss my father when he gets here."

"Dennis, I promise I will find you if he comes," offered Bernie.

"She's right, Dennis," I said, but noted her use of the word "if" rather than "when." "We'll let you know the moment he arrives. What do you say? How about giving it a try?"

He sat in silence for a moment, contemplating.

"I'll think about it," he conceded.

I suspected he'd be in school on opening day.

Bernie grabbed my arm and escorted me down the row of beds toward the back of the room. Mrs. Sharp remained with Dennis. She hadn't said a word earlier, but now that Bernie and I had taken our leave, she'd become awfully chatty with him. I hoped she wasn't discouraging him from attending school.

Once we were out of earshot, I asked about Dennis's medical condition. Bernie explained he had spina bifida, a birth defect that had caused his spinal column not to close entirely in the womb. "His legs are paralyzed, but as you can see, he talks normally," she said.

"Yes, indeed... for a sailor," I offered, with a large grin.

Bernie ignored me. "Dennis doesn't have any intellectual problems—other than the ones you'd expect from living here for so long. Did you happen to see the suitcase next to his bed?" she asked. "That suitcase has been sitting there, packed and waiting, for more than three years. The father who's supposed to be taking him home has never visited. Dennis is angry, confused, and alone." The same pragmatic tone remained in her voice. "Initially, I thought—now, there is a boy who only experiences one emotion: anger. I know now that he also feels deeply, deeply sad."

All at once, I was envisioning abandonment, abuse, depression, and despair. I was at a loss for words again.

Bernie placed a hand on my shoulder. "I know how lousy you feel," she said. I looked into her eyes but remained silent. "Many of us have that same reaction day after day. Last week, Dennis convinced a new attendant to dial an outside number for him from the office telephone. Of course, he was trying to call home, but the number had been disconnected. After the call, he just lay on his bed for two days, refusing to speak to anyone." She leaned in, her expression grave. "I wish I could tell you that you've seen and heard the worst of it, but you'll quickly find that the more you learn and the more you see, the worse it gets and the more you hurt."

At this moment, the steady noise of the ward was being drowned out by three voices vying for airtime in my head. One voice was yelling, "I am not prepared for this, so just bolt as fast as you can!" Another was more of a gesture: my hands covering my ears in an attempt to prevent anything I have been hearing and learning to travel to my brain, because I wouldn't know what to do with such sadness, despair, or longing. The third voice sounded more like me. It said it was the voice of reason, and that even though this was all new, confusing, and even frightening, I would handle it—and try my damnedest to do something about it.

Bernie somehow must have realized that I'd settled on the third-voice option. She offered me a little smile and said, "Let's meet Ron; he'll cheer you up."

Ron Benoit was another teenager with cerebral palsy who was living there because he'd grown too big for his family to care for at home. Like Ruth, whom I had just met on Ward 1, Ron had a family that visited frequently—especially his grandmother, who came to see him at least twice a week.

Bernie knew I was overwhelmed, and she fed me each new piece of information slowly and deliberately. For some of the children, I sensed she was willing her aspirations for them to become my objectives as well.

The intensity of her support for Ruth, and now Ron, was obvious. She would ensure that these two children got everything this barren environment could deliver. She repeated that except for an inability to control their arms and legs, and except for an inability to talk, these two were typical teenagers. I sensed she was preparing to hand off some responsibility to me. She would continue to handle the chores surrounding daily living, but the care and nurturing of their minds was now being placed in my hands.

A weighty responsibility for a kid at his first job in the "real world."

An older woman was sitting on the side of the bed next to a handsome boy I assumed to be Ron. She was well dressed in bright casual clothes. Her eyes were the same shape and shade of pool-blue color as the smiling teenager's.

"Mrs. Chapman, Ron, this is Mr. Shane. He's going to be Ron's new teacher," said Bernie.

I touched Ron's arm. "Hello, Ron. Nice to meet you, and how nice to meet your grandmother, too." I smiled at Mrs. Chapman.

She looked at me with a warm smile. "I'm delighted that Ron is going to have a teacher again. Now, I don't mean to be disrespectful, but are you old enough to be a real teacher?" Her remark was sincere and endearing. Ron could hardly contain his laughter.

Bernie laughed along with Ron. "He doesn't miss a thing."

"Mrs. Chapman," I replied, "I'm old enough to be a teacher. Only time will tell if I'm good at it."

Ron glanced up, bringing to mind Ruth's system for affirming a statement. Ron, however, looked up with a rapid eyes-only glance, while Ruth's signal had been an upward gaze that included her eyes, eyebrows, and forehead. Although Ron couldn't say a word, his nonverbal behavior spoke volumes.

"He's very smart, you know," Mrs. Chapman added.

"So everyone has been telling me. But I'll have to find that out when he gets to school," I said, with a wink to Ron.

"One more thing, Mr. Shane," said Mrs. Chapman. "Could we arrange some parent–teacher conferences? My daughter, Ron's mother, isn't able to visit as much as I can, but I know she wants to check up on how he's doing and see how we can help."

"That would be great. I'd be happy to." Given the events of the past hour, I never thought I'd hear a request for an ordinary parent–teacher interaction. "Ron, I need to go now. Do you have any questions for me?"

His eyes flew upward, and he smiled. I interpreted this as a yes.

"Is your question about me?"

Up shot his eyes. Yes again.

"Are you wondering if I'm a hippie?" I hadn't forgotten that word travelled fast at Belchertown.

His head moved slowly from side to side.

"Where I'm going next?"

Another head shake. Ron looked at his grandmother and then quickly glanced back at me. Well, that was easy.

"You want to know how old I am?"

A huge grin appeared on his face, and he looked skyward, indicating a clear and definite yes.

"I'm thirteen, same as you." I replied.

I watched a smile appear on his face, followed by a facial expression that said, "Very funny. You've had your fun. Now how old are you, really?"

"I'm twenty-two," I stated, carefully watching Ron's face and wondering how he would react.

His next subtle facial expression essentially said, "That's more like it."

I was amazed at how effectively he could communicate such complex thoughts through subtle body and facial movements and eye shifts. This brief exchange had made one thing clear: the inability to talk was not the same as the inability to communicate.

Before we could leave, Mrs. Chapman stopped me. "You don't suppose we could have our first conference today, do you?"

"Sure. How about after I meet Teddy and finish my tour?" I looked over at Bernie, who nodded approval. With Mrs. Sharp still engaged some distance away, I agreed to meet Mrs. Chapman at the main office in an hour and said my goodbyes.

Bernie pointed out Teddy McNeil, the last young man I'd meet in the boys' ward that morning. He was alone in the back of the ward, sitting hunched over in a wheelchair and staring into his lap. I walked over, extended my hand, and said, "Hi, Teddy. I'm your new teacher." Bernie watched from a distance.

Teddy raised his head and shook my hand. He had a round face and brown hair with bangs cut straight across his forehead. He wore a wrinkled plaid shirt and khaki pants. "It's not safe to talk in here. It's not safe in here."

I let go of his hand. "What's not safe?"

"To talk here. Don't say another word."

"We're not safe? Are we safe anywhere in the building?"

"Only in the scrub room."

"Why in there?" I asked.

"Because you can't hide the bugs in there. The rest of the ward is bugged."

"Really?" I was intrigued—not about the presence of supposed listening devices, but by the depth of his imagination.

"Nah," he said. "I was just testing whether you were paranoid."

"I was lying back there. I'm not the new teacher," I said, playing along. "Actually, I'm here to find all the bugs in the building. Perhaps you can help. Have you seen any?"

"Only the cockroaches at night. And you thought I was retarded."

"Whoever said I thought that?"

"No one, but everyone thinks you are if you live in this place."

"Well, I don't. You'll never hear me use that word. All I care about is whether or not you're coming to school next week."

"That's not ALL you care about," said Teddy.

"Well—"

"You care about your mom. And food. And air—"

"Okay, good point."

"And the Red Sox, probably."

"All right, you got me. Maybe you should be the teacher." I laughed. I enjoyed this banter, but my growing unease about smart and clever teenagers living in this institution was only heightened.

While Teddy wasn't able to walk due to cerebral palsy, he moved around efficiently in a hand-powered wheelchair. His speech was clear and articulate. Even from this brief encounter, I could see he was intelligent and possessed a clever sense of humor, a considerable amount of sarcasm, and plenty of insight.

"So, are you signing up for school or not?" I inquired.

"I guess so."

"You don't sound very excited about it."

"It's always the same thing," he sighed. "Go down the elevator, go to the classroom, color some pumpkins, cut out some tree decorations, listen to some records, and then go back up the elevator."

"This year we're going to do some reading and some math," I said.

"My mother taught me how to read. I even have some books in the box under my bed."

"What do you like to read about?"

"I like to read *Playboy*."

I noticed Bernie's eyebrows shoot up at that remark.

He was testing me, feeling out the edges of my tolerance. I liked his style.

"Have you ever read a *Playboy*?" I asked.

"No, but I saw some of the pictures once. The girls didn't have any clothes on."

"But that's not reading. That's looking at pictures," I pointed out.

"Can I read *Playboy* in school?"

"If that's what you really want to read, then you can read it in school."

"Then I do want to come to school, all right!"

"Can we wait a few weeks before we read any magazines? I'd like you to practice on some other books first."

"I can't hold a pencil. See these fingers?" he said, holding up his right hand to reveal fingers that did look twisted. "I'm too weak on this side to do things right."

"I can try to teach you to hold a pencil if you want."

Stealthily, Mrs. Sharp appeared behind us. "I see you have met Mr. McNeil."

"Yes, I have, and he's raring to go to school."

"Mr. Shane said we're going to read *Playboy* in school, Mrs. Sharp," Teddy said, with the same innocent delivery of someone referring to a class assignment of *Huckleberry Finn*.

"Teddy, I didn't say *we* were going to read *Playboy*."

"Did too. Didn't he, Bernie?"

Before Bernie got dragged in, I replied, "No, Teddy, what I said was *you* can read *Playboy* in school."

"I doubt that will happen, Teddy," said Mrs. Sharp, "but Mr. Shane will find plenty of other things for you to do. Isn't that right, Mr. Shane?"

Teddy, thankfully, remained silent and allowed the issue to die.

I had already decided that using each kid's interest to engage them—whether that interest be pencils, keys, or *Playboy*—was the best way to help my students learn. I planned to customize the curriculum for each student. If *Playboy* would motivate Teddy to read, to learn a concept, or to grapple with a new idea, then *Playboy* (though probably a redacted version) would be used.

As our group turned to go, Teddy signaled for me to come nearer. I approached, and he cupped his hand to his mouth to indicate that he wanted to tell me something privately. I leaned closer.

"I'll come to school like I said, but it won't do any good."

Since the group had headed toward the door and out of earshot, I straightened up and said in a soft voice just above a whisper, "What won't do any good?"

"Teaching us about school stuff won't do any good. What's the difference what we learn? Don't you know the only way we'll ever get to leave this place is in a hearse?"

I was stunned by his candor and unsure of how to respond. My natural instinct was to try to convince him he was mistaken or that he was being overly dramatic, but from what I had seen and heard so far that day, his conclusions were, sadly, the truth—or close to it, at least. In any event, Teddy wasn't interested in my reaction, so he spun his chair around and headed toward his bed.

"You might be very wrong about that, Teddy," I called after him. Even as I said it, I knew my response was weak and perhaps even self-serving. I really couldn't think of anything else to say.

We left Ward 5 and found Ed, the man obsessed with pencils, stationed at the entrance. I pulled the pencil from behind my ear and handed it to him without saying a word. With pencil in hand, he withdrew swiftly into Ward 2 without looking at me or making a sound. It was a simple, short interaction, but it made me smile—I'd connected Ed with his special interest, and I couldn't wait to do the same for the rest of my students.

"Well, that finishes our tour of the wards," Bernie said. "Howard, do you have any questions?"

"Just one," I said, my mind whirring with plans and ideas. "Can we check out my classroom?"

CHAPTER 4

A s the elevator descended to my new basement classroom, Mrs. Sharp filled the silence in a predictable way: by rattling off more rules and regulations.

"Two standard wheelchairs can fit in this elevator at a time," she said, staring straight ahead at the closed doors before us. "If you transport a student who lies in a cart, that number may shrink depending on the size of the other wheelchair. Don't let the attendants fool you by taking the students one at a time to your classroom. They can find plenty of ways to waste time."

"Mrs. Sharp, I take issue with that," Bernie said quickly, surprising me. "The attendants have the toughest job in the building, and if they do take one student alone at times, it's only because the elevator is already jammed with laundry bags or a food cart."

Mrs. Sharp said nothing, just rolled her eyes as the elevator lurched to a stop. As soon as the doors opened, she marched out ahead of us, her heavy shoes echoing in the corridor. Bernie looked at me and shrugged. "You'll find there are often very... different opinions about the staff and the residents. Let's go see your classroom."

My classroom was located at the end of the narrow, poorly lit basement corridor. I had hoped the walls might be painted light blue or yellow, something more appropriate for a school setting, but they were covered in the same mustard tile from the rest of the building. The basement floor was cement and painted an institutional gray. I felt comfortably cool for the first time since entering the infirmary, and I was relieved that the putrid smell of the upper floors had been replaced by the stale odor of a basement.

I peeped through the windowed door of the classroom to see Mrs. Sharp already standing by a large wooden desk at the front. With her arms crossed and her mouth a tight line, she looked the part of a very stern teacher. No doubt she'd been one before making the transition to administrator, and I wondered if she had been as humorless and cold before she took on the responsibility of running the entire school program. Though she was completely at ease with the residents, in her authoritarian way, I hadn't seen any warmth when she interacted with children in the wards.

Scanning the room, I found it dull and nondescript. Three rows of fluorescent light strips cast a cold glow; the only hint of natural light peeked in through a basement window high in the wall. There were blackboards behind the desk and on the back wall, and a large bulletin board stretched along the longest side wall. I sat down at one of two large rectangular oak tables in the back corners of the room. The words *sturdy, functional,* and *adequate* came to mind.

The tables may have been adequate, but little else was. I saw no materials or supplies at all. No books, paper, or pencils. No remnants of student celebrations, holiday decorations, calendars, or student art. No hint that education had ever been approached in this space. The spirit of past teachers and students was entirely missing.

"What do you think?" Bernie said softly, joining me at the table.

"I... think I can work with it," I told her—but inside I was thinking, *Can I?*

"I think so too." She ventured a smile. I wondered if she believed in me as much as she seemed to, or if she was just glad to have someone else here to share her responsibilities.

"Bernice." Mrs. Sharp's voice intruded. "Let's wrap up the grand tour, shall we? There's work to be done."

"If you don't mind, I'd like to hang back for a few," I told them. "Since my work doesn't start until Monday."

Mrs. Sharp stared at me as if I'd sprouted antlers. "Suit yourself, Mr. Shane. I'll trust you can see yourself out."

After they left, I walked slowly around my new teaching space, contemplating exactly what I'd done when I'd accepted this job at Belchertown. Had I landed a job as a history teacher at a local high school, the subject matter and students would be familiar and comfortable; I would have been in my element. Instead, I felt adrift in an educational netherworld where the entire setting was disturbing and my boss was—overbearing, to say the least.

On the other hand, the students were affable and appealing, and I sensed that every one of them had great potential. It would be my responsibility to help them fulfill it, to make school monumentally important for each student. Given how empty and barren the rest of their lives were, I needed to make education meaningful and joyous. I would have to fight through my uncertainties and insecurities, because my convictions just wouldn't let me treat this like a standard teaching job.

I searched the room, trying to dream up ways to make this nondescript and soulless space come to life.

I really had my work cut out for me.

When I finally left my new classroom, vowing to brainstorm more that night, I found Ron's grandmother waiting outside the nursing office. She looked older standing there than when we had met in the ward.

"Hi, Mrs. Chapman," I said, remembering our meeting. "Why don't we go outside and find a comfortable place to sit?"

We walked toward the parking lot, where we found a battered wooden bench in the shade of a tree. She sat down wearily and rested her hands in her lap, worrying a linen handkerchief with her thin fingers.

"This is a dreadful place," she began. "The attendants are nice people, but they aren't parents, and they don't care for the children the way a parent would. I begged my daughter not to put Ron here, but she felt she had few resources and nowhere to turn."

"How long has Ron been here?" I asked.

"Five and a half years." She shook her head. "Ron's father doesn't live at home anymore. My husband and I were the only help his mother had, and neither of us had the strength to help with lifting and bathing—especially my husband, after his heart attack. We all cried so much after we left Ron here that first day. The only one who didn't cry was Ron, and I think he was just being strong for all of us. He's such a wonderful boy. I'm very afraid that he'll lose his spirit."

"I can understand that." I repeated.

"My grandson has a wonderful spirit, and it shows in the sparkle in his eyes. The longer he lives here, though, the more it's going to fade. I'll tell you, if I was younger, I'd take him home myself." She paused and took a deep, shuddering breath. When she continued, her voice was soft, but unwavering in her conviction. "Nobody should have to live like this. It's like a prison here. Even old people in nursing homes have it better. I want you to help him."

"I'll be a good teacher, and that should help a great deal," I offered.

"No, I mean really *help* him. Be sure he gets a good education so he can get out of here someday. Do you know he hasn't had a teacher since he got here?"

"I'll do the best I can. I promise."

"Mr. Shane," she said, looking me straight in the eye, "I want to trust you and believe what you're telling me. You have to help my Ron."

I paused, searching for words. I had no idea what this school year would bring or what I could actually accomplish. It was depressing to think that I was the best option this heartbroken woman and her grandson had—but I knew I had to try. Despite being clueless and feeling completely inadequate, especially given the magnitude of her request, I told her what she wanted to hear.

"You can count on me, Mrs. Chapman," I said, with an encouraging smile and a look I hoped conveyed a seriousness of purpose. What else could I do? I made a note to myself that I would keep in mind what I had promised, and do everything I could to deliver.

After my appointment with Mrs. Chapman, I headed directly to Mike's Roadside Tavern, a nearby place I had frequented as a student. I checked my watch as I walked through the doors and into the familiar space. Two o'clock. It wasn't my custom to drink that early in the day, but my introduction to Belchertown had me caught in a whirlwind of conflicting emotions. I needed to sit over a beer and sort through my thoughts.

"I thought you graduated," said Jack, the bartender. He was standing at the bar sink, washing glasses, and I dragged a bar stool closer to him so we could talk. With the exception of the couple making out in the corner booth, the place was empty. It looked entirely different in sunlight than it did in the evening, when the students piled in and filled the wood-paneled room with cigarette smoke and laughter. The jukebox was playing, but so softly I couldn't recognize the song.

Jack and I had grown up in the same town in another part of the state, and although we weren't close friends then or now, that history was enough of a bond for us to discuss more than beer nuts and last call.

I groaned and dropped my head to the bar, cupping my hands protectively on top. "You still sell beer in this place, don't you?" I muttered.

Jack poured my draft and set my beer on the bar in front of me.

I took a long, cool sip. "I just had one of the most incredibly—no, the most incredibly strange day of my life," I said.

I watched Jack shift from bartender to therapist, a role he was likely familiar with from engaging with students and their multitude of problems, both big and small. He settled in, leaning forward and resting his elbows on the bar. "I started my new job today," I told him. "I'll be teaching out in Belchertown, at Belchertown State School. You know it?"

"I see the signs for it, but I don't have a clue about what goes on there," he admitted.

"Yeah, you and me and everybody else in America. Jack, going to this place is like visiting a foreign country. When you drive in, you think you're at a country club. The grounds are beautiful, but if you do a deeper dive and actually go into one of the buildings, you find thirty to forty people crammed together in squalor and filth."

"It can't be that bad," he said, stepping away from the bar and pulling another glass from the dishwasher.

"It's worse," I said. "And I signed up to work there."

I poured my heart out to poor Jack about the details of my day. What I'd seen in the wards. The coldness of Mrs. Sharp. The emptiness of my future classroom. The promises I'd made, that I wasn't sure I could keep.

"Wow, Howard." Jack shook his head. "Honestly, I can't imagine working there. And from the sound of it, neither can you. You're not trapped, you know. Maybe you ought to just pass on this job and find something a little easier."

You're not trapped. Jack's words echoed in my head. He was entirely right: Unlike the residents I'd met that day, I had alternatives. I wasn't trapped in a place with no escape route. I could leave anytime I chose.

And that was the very reason I knew I had to stay.

I'd been given the gift of freedom, something these kids had never known. And the least I could do with that freedom was freely choose to stay and help them. I could deal with the smell and the noise and an unpleasant and uptight school administrator. I could deal with all of that, and I could keep the promises I'd made, although I didn't have any idea how. I was young and energetic and creative, and I'd figure it out as I went along.

"Another beer?" Jack said.

"Sure," I said. "Thanks for your help."

Jack shrugged, unaware of the epiphany he'd just helped me have. Though fear and uncertainty gnawed at me, another feeling was growing strong: the belief that I could make a real difference at Belchertown.

CHAPTER 5

School started in three days, so I had seventy-two hours to get ready—at least as ready as I could be.

First, I went to the hardware store, where I purchased a stockpile of number two pencils and a brass key ring, and I had duplicate keys made for all the classroom storage cabinets. In a local antique store, I found several skeleton keys, including one with an accompanying lock set, and asked the proprietor to call me if she came across any more. I also purchased colored folders, a length of rope and some clothespins to hang artwork, and some decorative edging to brighten up the bulletin boards. With my starting teacher's salary of roughly five thousand dollars a year, I didn't have much money to work with—but the items I'd bought were essential to my evolving formula of teaching success, so I'd have to deal with any budget shortfall later.

At the supermarket, I bought a variety of snacks and soft drinks, having come to the easy decision that nothing prepared by a state school kitchen would ever be served or consumed in my classroom. This led to a related decision that the classroom could not and would not resemble the stark environment two floors above it. I wanted an upbeat refuge filled with happiness and authentic learning, which was a tall order with the current color scheme, flooring, and furniture. I hoped once school got under way, my students might enjoy themselves and perhaps, just momentarily, forget they lived at Belchertown.

Now that I had gathered some supplies to outfit and brighten the classroom, my mind turned to the question of what exactly I was going to teach on Monday. I felt an initial sense of relief when I realized the curriculum guide Mrs. Sharp had given me was in my briefcase, but I scanned its contents and realized this was not going to provide the help I was seeking. It was nothing more than an outline of areas of instruction, including generic topics such as hygiene and dressing for "trainable" students and reading and math for those who were considered "educable." For both groups, the instructor was urged to include music, art, and nature. Teaching methods or actual instructional sequences were missing.

I was on my own, so I decided to do what I did best: take a more unconventional approach. As a first step, I knew I had to start reading about children with intellectual and physical disabilities, and I had to start right away.

I went straight to the UMass library and gathered and studied what special education materials I could find. I discovered quickly that the state of special education in the United States was pretty bleak. U.S. schools educated only one in five children with disabilities, and many states had laws to exclude children with severe disabilities from attending public school altogether. The few curriculum guides I managed to track down were rudimentary, recommending that children with intellectual disabilities first learn functional self-help skills and then acquire the knowledge that would enable them to work a menial job. For a child with some academic promise, a person Mrs. Sharp would likely label "educable," a watered-down elementary school curriculum focusing on basic literacy and math was recommended. I emerged bleary-eyed from the library with a handful of practical ideas—but nothing exciting or inspiring. But even if all the teaching resources in the world had been at my disposal, I still wouldn't be sure how to use them effectively with the students at Belchertown. My introduction to the wards had profoundly affected my thinking. I'd been completely unprepared for the conditions under which the students—my students—were forced to live. I thought of Teddy's words: "Don't you know the only way we'll ever get to leave this place is in a hearse?"

This wasn't going to be easy. These children were growing up almost entirely isolated from the outside world. Very few were lucky enough to have parents who visited regularly, and even those who did rarely left the school grounds. I knew instinctively that preparing lessons and activities without acknowledging these conditions would be wrong, in both a practical and ethical sense. I was being forced to construct a new teaching reality—one that had to consider the students' unique living circumstances.

Truth be told, I was excited by this challenge; it was, to me, an invitation to be creative and original. It was the 60s, and it was mostly okay to experiment, to be "out there" with fresh ideas and approaches. My overall teaching strategy was still evolving, but I knew I had a few tricks up my sleeve to shake up the students and get them thinking about school in a whole new way.

Of course, the success of any trick depended on its execution.

Over the weekend before school was to start, I made a second visit to my classroom. I was eager to inspect the supplies I'd been given, arrange the classroom, and review student records—and I also hoped that revisiting the room might spark some fresh thoughts about instructional approaches. While walking from the parking lot to the infirmary, I spotted Ed standing alone near the front entrance. His shirt pocket held several brand-new pencils.

Even from a distance, something about Ed separated him from the other residents. As he got closer, I realized what it was: Ed looked like an average guy on the street. Unlike the other residents I had seen, his clothes were free of wrinkles and were not ripped or tattered. His leather shoes matched and were polished. Not one button on his white shirt was missing or undone. A brass belt buckle was properly positioned on his body, and the zipper on his trousers was up. I knew Ed had a sister who managed his clothing needs, but he also had the physical skills, aptitude, and interest to manage his wardrobe, coordinate, and dress himself without reminders day after day.

I nodded to him. "Ed."

When he recognized me, he began to walk quickly in my direction. As he approached, I noticed that all the pencils in his pocket had the eraser side down and unsharpened writing ends facing up. Clutched tightly in his right hand was a collection of new sharpened pencils. I started to hand him a new pencil I had stored behind my ear, and he turned his body away from me and rotated his wrist back, as if I were passing him a baton in a relay race. With the pencil now firmly grasped in his fist, he shuffled away quickly. Under his breath, I heard him mutter, "Thank you."

"You're welcome," I shouted after him as he walked beyond the entrance, heading toward the opposite side of the building. I watched him go, a smile tugging at my lips. Here was the first hint of evidence that I could connect with a resident at Belchertown. That I could do some good here. I headed for my classroom, feeling optimistic about what awaited me there.

At the entrance to the infirmary, a handwritten sign just above a rusty button read PUSH TO RING DOORBELL. An attendant I had not yet encountered opened the door and offered me a friendly, comforting smile. She had blonde hair with some brown roots showing and round wire-rimmed glasses. After explaining that I was the new teacher and had forgotten my keys, I asked her to open the door into the stairway so I could get to the basement classroom. I took a deep breath of the last fresh air I'd have for a while, followed her inside, and disappeared down the deserted stairway. On the landing halfway to the basement level, a door led outside; through its window, I spotted a pleasant grassy area with several empty picnic tables. I could easily imagine holding class there from time to time.

I stepped into my classroom and surveyed my surroundings. With the exception of the wooden cabinet in the corner, now stuffed with the supplies Mrs. Sharp mentioned would be brought over, the room was unchanged since my first visit. I quickly inspected the materials and found nothing inspiring, just a jumble of shabby art and writing supplies and a cardboard clock. Not surprisingly, there were no workbooks or reading books, fictional or otherwise. Although it had been one of my motivations for coming back to the classroom, I didn't even bother looking in the storage closet to crosscheck its contents with the order sheet that lay on my desk. I knew that inventory control was one area where Mrs. Sharp would excel. I realized I'd been left entirely to my own devices. Other than that order sheet, the sparse curriculum notebook, and the set of impenetrable rules I'd been given during my interview, I'd received almost no guidance from Mrs. Sharp. I knew nothing about the school's expectations of me, much less for my students. I had hoped she might leave me some paperwork detailing how the infirmary classroom had been run in the past or how other teachers on the campus organized their classes, but there was nothing. The student records I had requested were piled on the desk, but when I paged through them, I found that backgrounds on half the students were missing, three folders were empty, and two records were for people I had never heard of. I stuffed the records in my bag so I could examine them later.

Doubt was beginning to set in again. There were no inspirational words chalked on the blackboard, no folders filled with sensible ideas hidden in a desk drawer. I hadn't even settled on a seating arrangement because I wasn't sure how many students would come in wheelchairs. Come Monday morning, I would have to figure this out on my own, with no support.

I trailed my fingers along the mustard tiles lining the wall, a layer of dust gathering on my fingertips. These cold, unwelcoming walls still held no pictures or student work to provide warmth and cheerfulness. I hoped that would change soon—if I could figure out what I was doing. I had one more weekend to think about it, and then I'd be thrown in the deep end.

I hurried out of the empty classroom and ducked out the back door, avoiding the upstairs entirely.

CHAPTER 6

When we anticipate major events, we usually do so with either enthusiasm or dread.

I felt both that Monday morning on my first day teaching at Belchertown.

While I couldn't wait to greet the students and begin my teaching life, I was terrified to confront my own shortcomings and the outcomes of the decisions I was about to make. What if I just wasn't cut out to be a teacher? I didn't want to let the kids down.

Anyone who watched me confidently unlatch the front door and march to my classroom surely wouldn't have known I was experiencing profound self-doubt. All I had going that morning were a few initial lessons I had prepared so I wouldn't be standing flat footed in front of my students with nothing prepared and nothing to say. I'd tried to further bolster my confidence that morning by donning a button-down shirt and necktie. If I weren't up to the intellectual challenge of the position, at least I'd look the part during my collapse. I speculated that only two men would be sporting neckties on this first day of school at the institution—Superintendent Dr. Bowser and me. I figured I might just make it a habit, if I survived my first day.

On my way to the infirmary, I stopped at the school building to touch base with Mrs. Sharp. It was seven a.m., and I suspected she might already be in her office. In fact, she was out, but she had left an envelope with my name taped to the door. It contained the final class roster, another key for my ring with no explanation of what it unlocked, and a bulleted note with three reminders:

1. Staff meeting every Tuesday at eight a.m. sharp.
2. Stop by the business office in the administration building to complete health and tax forms.
3. Contact me with any questions.

I pocketed the key, crumpled the note, and headed toward the infirmary. I noticed in the distance several attendant-led lines of residents marching from the dormitories toward the main school building. There was a precision to the residents' cadence and the timing of the lines, which arrived at the front door at exactly the same time, like clockwork.

I entered the infirmary, unlocking and locking the door as I'd been instructed, and headed for my classroom, arriving right on time. Beside the blackboard, I tacked up the colorful signs I'd made the night before. I also had a plan up my sleeve for the back-right corner of the room, and I hoped it would work.

But fifteen minutes after the official starting time, none of my students had arrived yet. My heart pounded in my chest. Needing a distraction, I turned again to the notes I had taken over the weekend while reviewing the school records which were sparse and incomplete but did reveal some background information on several of the students. I read the following:

Dennis Russell was literate and could read, "... at least at a third-grade level." The term "uncooperative" appeared in every report I reviewed.

Teddy McNeil recognized a few sight words and had limited math skills.

Ron Benoit and Ruth Sienkiewicz's communication had always been a central concern. One former instructor wrote that Ron "understands pictures and objects," while a note written two years later revealed that he "... understands better than anyone else in the class."

Carla Dalton was considered "lazy." The note didn't illuminate any reasoning behind this label.

Danny Brookes wouldn't pay attention or stay still.

Wendy Short had "cocktail party" speech. (I had to look this one up in my medical dictionary; it meant she had a tendency to talk a great deal without producing any real content.)

I sighed at the pile of records before me. Nearly every student's characteristics and abilities were framed in a negative way. Nothing at all about their individual learning styles, personal interests, or passions. I thought of the progressive educational culture I'd been so inspired by at the University of Massachusetts School of Education, where I'd learned that recognizing individual differences was vital to successful teaching. Why had no one viewed these children as individuals yet? Why dismiss the speech of an eight-year-old child as superficial, or label a lively young girl as "lazy"?

There was no sense dwelling on these records, I told
have to gather those insights myself. Besides, input from
or administrators might even lead me astray or infect m᾽
unconscious bias.

I glanced up at the clock that hung over my desk. My first class was
now twenty-five minutes late. Then, it hit me that I didn't want a clock to
have such prominence in my classroom, so I took it down. I retrieved the
instructional cardboard clock from the storage cabinet and placed it on the
chalk tray, setting the time to eight-thirty. I had resolved that school would
become an oasis for the kids, as dissimilar as I could make it from the carefully controlled existence just one and two floors above, where every ward
displayed a clock and the attendants were bound to follow a schedule for
eating, dressing, bathing, and even toileting. Pleased that I had done something small but meaningful to set my classroom apart, I sat on the edge of
my desk and awaited the invasion.

Laughter finally resonated through the basement as the first wave of
students came down the hall. Ron entered first, his chair pushed by a man
in his early twenties whom I estimated to be at least six and a half feet tall.

"You must be Howard Shane," he said. "I'm Bob Bergquist, a physical
therapy grad student. I've been assigned here three days a week for the next
year."

When we shook hands, my hand disappeared into his. He was so tall
I had to look up when we spoke. Bob had a light complexion, blond hair, and
a wide, friendly smile that made his cheeks flush and his eyes crinkle.

"Ron, is this guy okay?" I asked.

Ron pouted and looked down, signifying no. He broke into a big grin,
and Bob crouched down beside him and said in a slightly raised voice, "You
big nincompoop—and after I gave you a free push, too. Now tell him what a
great guy I am."

Same pout, same smile.

"Sorry, Bob, looks like you struck out," I said. The interaction between
Bob and Ron was friendly and genuine, and I liked how naturally Bob
responded to this teenager's clowning around.

"I had something I wanted to tell you," Bob said to me, straightening up,
"so I hopped a ride on that elevator from hell. I wanted to meet you anyway,
and I figured this would be as good a time as any."

"What's on your mind?"

Bob pulled me to the side, out of Ron's hearing range, and offered me a heads-up about a little surprise Dennis Russell apparently had in store for me. When I asked how he knew, he just smiled and told me there were no secrets in the building.

Before I could respond to Bob or think too much about my impending "surprise," Danny Brookes entered, propelling himself in his wheelchair. As he rolled in, he discovered my state-issued key ring dangling in the classroom door, where I had left it for him. He deftly retrieved the key from the keyhole, barely slowing his forward progress. He rolled directly to me and handed over the keys.

"Thanks, Danny!" I said. "And here's a set I put together for you to keep. This key here is for the storage cabinet." I pointed to the cabinet in the corner. "I want you to be in charge of that key. Whenever we need to get into the cabinet, I will be calling on you. Is that okay?"

He didn't respond to my question. Instead, he grabbed each of the keys in succession with an inquisitive look on his face. Without actually speaking, he asked, "And what are these keys for?"

"Over time, you'll find out what those are for," I told him. "Right now, keep your keys safe, and I'll try to get you even more."

Bob had been watching Danny too, and he extended an offer. "Danny, I have a key to the physical therapy storage locker upstairs that you can put on your ring. Just find me after school, and I'll get that key for you."

Danny extended his hand to me and said something I couldn't understand. I grabbed his shaking hand in mine, and we smiled broadly at one another. Still smiling, Danny shook Bob's hand, then wheeled over to examine the items I had placed on the table at the side of the room. It was a hodgepodge of toys, tools, and implements that would eventually be part of the curriculum that was germinating in my head. Danny completely ignored the small pile of outdated *Life* magazines, but I was gratified to see him bounce the ball; look though the magnifying glass; pull on the Slinky; brush aside the yardstick, a measuring cup, an assortment of sponges and a few glass jars; and fumble with the switch on the flashlight.

I exchanged glances of triumph with Bob. I had read once that the word "therapist" is derived from the Greek word "therapon," meaning comrades in a common struggle. It would help to have a comrade around here, and I suspected that Bob could be that person.

"Bob, can you wait here for just a second with the class? I'll be back in just a moment."

"Sure thing," he said.

I grabbed my coffee cup off my desk and dashed out on a quick, secret mission—one related to the Dennis surprise Bob had warned me about. When I returned, Bob greeted me with a grin. "I'll see you guys later," he told the class. "I'd better get back upstairs before someone misses out on the magic of my therapeutic touch."

"Thanks for stopping by," I said. Then, I murmured to him, "and thanks for the tip. I'll let you know how it turns out."

He nodded and headed for the door. "Hey, Teddy," he said on his way out, mimicking the steering of a car with two hands. "Nice driving."

Teddy McNeil was making his way through the doorway. His movement was hampered by an apparent right-sided weakness that resulted in a hard push by his left hand followed by several smaller forward thrusts by his right one. The result was slow but steady progress of the chair in a straight line. "I'm coming, I'm coming," he announced. "I told the old ladies upstairs that I didn't need anyone to push me around. Hey, where are the girls?"

"They haven't made it down yet," I said. "Maybe they found something better to do."

"Yeah, like escaping!" he offered.

"Teddy, no one would dare escape on a day when school is in session. If you're planning on escaping, save it for the weekend or when I'm on vacation."

"Ron," Teddy said, "do you think we can put off our breakout for a few months?"

Ron blinked to signal yes.

"Thank God," I said. "I think I'd have to close school down and declare a national holiday."

They laughed together. Both boys understood sarcasm and clearly a great deal more.

I followed Ron's gaze, and it took me to Dennis Russell. Just outside the door, Dennis was leaning back in the canvas seat of a wheelchair and balancing on the two large wheels, with the two smaller ones suspended in the air. Last week, during my initial tour of Belchertown, I had noticed that he used a set of crutches to get around, but today he had chosen to move about in a wheelchair. In the background, the sound of the female students making their way from the elevator to the classroom echoed down the long corridor.

This was the moment Dennis chose to make his move. With a burst of speed, he headed straight for me, and now I understood why he'd chosen to travel by wheelchair. As he advanced, I calmly watched him get closer. His cheeks were extended like a chipmunk, but I knew he wasn't hoarding nuts. All eyes followed his course.

I sat at the edge of my desk, slowly sipping from my coffee mug. He reached me and stopped abruptly, drew his head back, and then thrust it forward, spewing a mouthful of spit. Just as he released, I raised my hand and deflected the saliva off to both sides. A little fell on my pants, but most of it just ended up on the floor. Then, I let him have the entire mouthful of water I'd been conserving from the mug I'd filled in the hallway fountain minutes before. My aim was perfect. The water splashed on his face, soaked his bangs, and then spilled down his shirt.

He looked shocked by my retaliation. For a moment, he just froze. Then his body seemed to go limp, and he slumped in his chair like a released marionette. His face flushed red with anger. It was painful to observe. Water dripped off his chin, and the wet spot on the front of his shirt was growing. I was distressed but steadfast in my determination not to show any kindness at that time.

The room remained quiet. All eyes stared in disbelief. Dennis slowly turned, wheeled himself out of the room, and headed back toward the elevator. I stepped out the door after him and yelled, "Dennis, when you come back tomorrow, either don't spit or bring a raincoat."
He kept wheeling away from me.

I followed him up the corridor, where I ran into Pauline, who was pushing Wendy's cart toward the classroom. "Would you be sure that Dennis gets back to the second floor safely? I'll take Wendy the rest of the way."

Pauline took one look at Dennis and asked, "What happened?"

"Just a difference of opinion. He spit at me; I spit at him. My aim was better." I lowered my voice so Dennis, who was now about fifteen yards up the corridor, couldn't overhear. "Please ask Nancy if she could keep an eye on him. Tell her that he's pretty upset."

"I will, Mr. Shane. You mean you really spit at him?"

"Sure, I'd spit at anyone who spit at me. Wouldn't you?"

She stared as Dennis made his way up the corridor. Then, with her fingers cupped over her nose and mouth, she said, "I'll tell Nancy."

I pushed Wendy into the classroom and set her up in a spot that would let her see as much of the room as she could from her cart. Ron looked confused.

"Do you have a question?" I asked him.

He looked up quickly to signal yes.

"We both want to know how you knew Dennis was going to do that," Teddy replied.

"Is that your question, Ron?" I inquired.

He blinked immediately.

Not wanting to betray Bob, I said, "It was easy. I picked up a strong signal as he came down the corridor and then read his mind as he entered the room."

Teddy stared at me as I proffered my explanation. He turned to Ron and then back to me and asked, "Okay, then what am I thinking right now?"

Without hesitation, I responded: "You're wondering why I'm a teacher when I could have been on television, reading minds." Before he could answer, I continued, "You're also thinking that wasn't a very nice thing to do—and you know what? It wasn't. But if Dennis comes to school every day and decides to spit on me, I'm going to have to ask him to stay upstairs in the ward. I think he's better off down here. Don't you agree?"

Ron blinked, and Teddy nodded.

"So, I thought, if my spitting will stop him from doing that again, he'd be a lot better off." I took a step toward Ron with a broad smile. "Ron, right now I know you're hoping I don't spit at you. Well, don't worry—I have no more plans to spit in this room. Come on, let's greet the girls, and we can talk about this another time."

Looking back on this water incident many years later, I had to admit I acted impulsively. My knee-jerk reaction was the result of my inexperience as a teacher, and perhaps my immaturity. Nowadays, of course, this kind of retaliatory gesture wouldn't fly in a school setting, though I do believe my knee-jerk reaction ultimately cemented my relationship with Dennis, and that might not have happened had I just avoided his attack.

I strolled over to greet Ruth and Carla as they were pushed into the classroom. "Welcome, ladies," I said, and to the attendants I added, "Thank you for bringing Ruth and Carla to school."

"Our pleasure," replied the young woman standing behind Ruth's chair. "I've known Ruthie for a long time—right, Ruthie? I live right near her house in Springfield."

Ruth's eyes shot up, and she kept looking at me.

"Ah-ha, I already knew you grew up in Springfield, Ruth," I revealed, with a big grin on my face, "because I read all about you last night!" I paused briefly. "I learned something else about you."

Her expression grew serious, her gaze unwavering.

"I found out you have a brother whose name is the same as mine. Howard."

She let out an audible laugh, and her entire body contracted in delight.

The attendants disappeared down the corridor as two more women came through the classroom door. They were Belchertown residents, whom I guessed to be in their early to mid-thirties. One was in a wheelchair and was pushed along by the other, who had an unusual gait herself and seemed to gain stability from leaning against the wheelchair. The pair stopped, and the woman in the wheelchair handed me two manila folders with the names Paula Rivers and Barbara Cohn on the tabs.

"I assume one of you is Paula?" I said.

The one sitting laughed and replied, "Yes."

"And are you Barbara?"

The woman standing just looked at me, not speaking.

There was a handwritten note from Mrs. Sharp attached to the folders. I retreated to my desk to review the materials. I asked Teddy to tell the class about all the listening bugs in this place while I concentrated on the note. Teddy took to the task enthusiastically.

Mr. Shane,

I know you won't mind that I have added two more students to your class roster. They haven't attended school in some time, and I received a call from their state representatives just yesterday, who asked that we

extend the courtesy of continuing their education. You will find their
school records attached. I started one for Barbara because she actually has
never been to school.

   Sincerely yours,

   Dorothy Sharp

   I dropped the note on my desk and took a deep breath to shake off the annoyance of receiving this unexpected, last-minute curveball. With the exception of Danny's keys jingling as he examined them, the room was now silent. This moment marked the transition from anticipating a classroom filled with students to the reality of actual people arranged in a rough approximation of a semicircle. I slowly scanned the group, stopping for a brief moment to focus on each individual.

   "Well," I said, eyeing their expectant faces. "Welcome, Barbara and Paula. Good morning, everyone. Welcome to the first day of what's going to be a fabulous school year. There is one other student, Dennis, who will be joining us at some point soon. Now that everyone is here, school is officially started. First, I'm going to review the roll. Who knows what the roll is?"

   "We have rolls at breakfast," Wendy replied in her unmistakable high, sweet voice.

   "That's wonderful, Wendy." I couldn't help beaming at her. "This one is called the roll call. It means that we need to see who is on the class list and if they are present. When I call your name, give me a signal that you're here. Let's see now. Is Danny Brookes here?"

   Danny nodded, but his eyes remained fixed on the set of keys I'd given him.

   I repeated, "Danny, are you here?"

   The sound he emitted was a close approximation to "yuh," which was clear enough to identify as a yes.

   "Wendy Short?"

   "I'm here," she said. At eight years old, she would be my youngest student. I took note of the fact that she couldn't lift her head to look around, and I wondered how I might be able to open up more of the world to her.

   "Carla Dalton?"

   A strangled, "Me," emerged from the girl sitting next to Ruth.

   Very seriously: "Teddy Benoit?"

Ron Benoit and Teddy McNeil exchanged glances. Without missing a beat, Ron squealed and blinked yes at the same time that Teddy said, "Here." We went on for several exchanges: "Benoit McNeil?" "Ron McNeil?" These boys, one unable to speak and neither able to walk, were clearly going to be my class clowns. Ruth Sienkiewicz, who had been sitting in silence, now moved frantically in her chair with a huge smile on her face.

"Oh, *you!*" I said to her. "Are you Teddy Benoit?"

She beamed and shot her eyes up, indicating "Yes!"

I watched Barbara, who didn't seem to be following this exchange. In fact, she had a blank look and seemed generally perplexed by the unfamiliar world of my classroom. I wanted her to feel included, so I walked over to her, extended my hand, and said, "And I know this is Barbara Cohn, and she has a sister named Karen who wanted her to come to school!" I had just quickly read about Karen in her chart, which had also told me that Barbara had Down syndrome and had never attended school in her nearly three decades at Belchertown.

Barbara looked up at me, smiled, and took my hand. While holding her hand firmly, I patted it several times, hoping to convey through my gaze that she was welcome. However, if she was the mind-reader I had feigned being moments before, she would have known that my brain was awash with sadness and dismay that someone nearly two decades older than all but one classmate was just now attending school for the first time. She was a teenager when I was born. While it is not uncommon for a college professor to be younger than students who matriculate at an older age, I felt awful that this student was having her first educational experience this late in life.

I turned to Paula beside her and asked, "Are you sure you're Paula Rivers?"

She shyly raised her hand and said, with rising intonation, "Yu-uup."

I suspected that her speech difficulty was related to cerebral palsy, which would also explain her need for a wheelchair. This exercise went on for a few more minutes as I tried to understand the strengths and needs of the group, to loosen them up, and to familiarize myself with the methods my students would use to communicate. This lesson reinforced for me that kids are kids, and most of them like to be gently teased and have fun as long as they felt safe. I also resolved to learn more about their interests, families, and friends, since they responded so positively to the few details I already knew.

The trick would be learning how to accommodate everyone and keep all my students engaged. I had two adults to teach as well as the children. My students had a wide range of learning and support needs that had to be addressed. I would have to figure things out, and fast.

We'd just finished our roll call game when the door to the classroom opened and a teenage boy was wheeled into the room. He was lying on his side on a stretcher. He wore a colorful pajama top, and his lower half was covered with a white flannel sheet. Nancy pushed him into the room and said, "This here's Jack Pappas. He's all yours for the next few hours. One other thing: Mrs. Sharp told me to tell you that you shouldn't worry about having more students than you expected." After delivering Jack and that unexpected message from Mrs. Sharp, she left.

"Nancy!" I yelled out the door.

I chased after her as she continued to walk away. She shook her head, eyes cast down.

"It's not my fault," she insisted. "Don't take it out on me."

"I have no issue with this boy being in my class." I caught up to her and stopped us in the hall. "He's welcome here, early or late. But I do have an issue with him coming to my class dressed in his pajamas. I'd like the kids to dress as they would if they were going to Belchertown Junior High. I want them to know that coming to school is special and means dressing appropriately. I want them to feel safe, smart, and dignified in this space, and wearing clothes instead of pajamas will help set that mood."

"Look, Miss Manners," she said, scolding me with her index finger and staring me down. "I have been here since six thirty a.m., getting these boys ready for your precious little school. My shift doesn't start until seven. Everyone was bathed, put into clean clothes, and had their hair combed—so don't start throwing your schoolhouse teacher crap at me."

I tried to apologize for being so critical, but she kept talking.

"You know I was thrilled that Jack was allowed to go to school—he should have been here in the first place. It's unfortunate that he came in his PJs, but it was either that or he stays upstairs, waiting his turn for the bathtub."

"All right, all right. I'm sorry," I said sincerely, knowing I was taking out my frustration on a professional who was doing her best in a tough situation. "I got a little carried away, but I want to set the right mood for the class, and I don't want to do it by making you angry. I really need your help."

"Fair enough," Nancy said, but I could tell she still had her guard up. "We work our asses off up there in that pit, and we don't need to hear any of your complaints when things don't go perfectly. Nothing in this place goes the way it's supposed to go. Too much to do, too little time, too small a staff."

"I understand completely. I apologize. I was a jerk."

"Sure, we're cool," she said, gently squeezing my forearm.

I headed back to the room with a heaviness in my chest. I'd only been on the job for an hour, and I'd already spit at a student and insulted a colleague. I didn't know what the rest of the day—let alone the year—would bring, but I hoped I could turn things around.

CHAPTER 7

Barring any further additions, I would have ten students to teach this year—swollen from a roster of eight students just six minutes before. That final number, of course, would depend on whether I could convince Dennis to return.

I returned to class, officially welcomed Jack, and announced that there would be no further distractions.

It was time to begin.

I walked to the yellow posterboard sign with bright blue letters that spelled out, RULES THAT RULE. Under my catchy title, I had written four lines in the same bright blue letters, each sentence covered by a sheet of newspaper. I informed the class that we all have to live by rules and that they would have to follow these four. I didn't bother to mention that I didn't particularly like rules myself and often broke them.

"Okay, gang," I started. "Let's see what you will have to do to be good citizens in this classroom." With that, I tore off the first sheet of newspaper, revealing the first rule. With a long wooden pointer, I touched and read each word in succession, affecting the deep, resonant voice of a radio announcer: "Never. Make. Fun. Of. Anyone. In. The. Room." Then I repeated in my regular voice. "Never make fun of anyone in the room. Teddy, can you read that?"

"Sure, don't make fun of anybody."

"Close enough," I said. "And now for the second rule. Barbara, please pull this down."

I knew Barbara was having trouble following what I was saying, but she was attentive. When she didn't respond to my request, I extended a corner of the newspaper toward her and asked her again to take down the paper. This nonverbal cue was enough for her to make her way over to me and pull off the newspaper. I immediately said, "Awesome job!"

"Can anyone read this second rule out loud?" I asked, hoping to further assess who else could read.

Jack, who was lying flat on his stomach with his head supported by his right hand, pushed both elbows into the bottom of the cart and arched his back. He read evenly and without hesitation, "Laugh at all the teacher's jokes."

"Great job, Jack," I said, pleased to see that he was both literate and engaged. I was also impressed that he could remain attentive despite having to look at the room while lying down. "And that, by the way, is a great rule you should never, ever forget."

"What if the joke isn't funny?" Jack asked.

"Impossible. All my jokes are funny."

Ruth's face changed immediately to a distinct pout that signaled no.

I walked to her side and asked indignantly, "Do you mean to say that not all my jokes are funny?"

With that, her body extended, and her eyes shot up. "Yes!" she signaled.

"Ha!" I said. "Believe what you want, but before long, you will all be begging me to stop telling so many funny jokes and stories because your sides are hurting from laughing so much. Danny, please tear off the paper so we see Rule Three."

He complied, wheeling to the blackboard to remove the newspaper.

I read, "Always compliment your classmates for trying." I turned back to them enthusiastically. "Now this is a really important rule. If someone tries, I expect to hear someone show or say, 'Good job,' 'Nice work,' or 'That was great.'" I looked at Ruth. "Hey, Ruth, how would you say, 'Good job'?"

She immediately raised her head and squealed. I then went around the class, asking each one to explain how they would compliment the others. When it was Barbara's turn, she giggled and clapped her hands.

I pointed to each rule in succession. "One, two, three, and, and..." I repeated as I tapped the next card several times. "Paula, one, two, three, and..."

"Four," she said, speaking her second word since entering the room.

"Exactly right, Paula. Rule number four is, and I quote, 'No peeking at anyone behind the screen in Independence Hall.'" Everyone looked confused. "Let me explain what I mean. Everyone, look in the back of the room." After I said this, I turned Ruth and Ron's chairs and Jack's cart to improve their line of vision. Without being asked, Barbara spontaneously spun Paula around. "Barbara, can you turn Carla and Wendy around too?" I said, pointing to both girls. I was pleased that she followed my instruction and was eager to help her fellow classmates.

With everyone situated, I took a large eraser off the chalk tray and tossed it at the wooden screen blocking their view of the back-right corner of the room. It hit the target with a dull thud, leaving a chalk mark on the wooden screen and a cloud of chalk dust in the air. "Behind that screen," I said, "is what I'm calling Independence Hall. This is a place where you can go and work or just think and know that no one will bother you. This is a private area. The rule is that no one is allowed to peek around the screen when someone is in there."

I gave the students a brief and simplified history of the real Independence Hall in Philadelphia. I wasn't preaching rebellion as much as I was encouraging self-determination and respect of self and others in an environment of freedom, privacy, and fun. While I was not an experienced teacher or therapist, I took care to adapt my speech and gestures as much as possible to try to reach every student.

Whether I was preparing the kids for unlikely emancipation from Belchertown or an entire life within those walls, I believed their education had to emphasize the skills that would allow them to be more self-reliant. The three Rs of traditional education were certainly important, but surely *reading, 'riting, and 'rithmetic* were insufficient for the schooling of children who had been stripped of liberty and had not yet experienced freedom and privacy.

My classroom's Independence Hall would be the place to acquire skills that most people simply took for granted. I envisioned this as a place where the students could learn to operate a can opener, use a pair of scissors, fasten and unbutton, zip and tie. Hygiene would be given some priority. Teeth would be brushed properly, hair fixed, or deodorant applied. While some of the students had disabilities that prevented them from independently performing some personal activities, others simply needed the opportunity, experience, or instruction to achieve such things on their own.

Finally, Independence Hall would be a place where the students could just be alone and feel safe. The reality that they had little understanding of privacy or an awareness of freedom saddened me. I knew my goals for this corner of my dingy classroom were lofty, but I hoped the students would get into the spirit of the project.

"Any questions?" I asked. I got blank looks, but I still felt hopeful. "And now, finally, for a fifth rule." For this, I went to my desk drawer and retrieved another sheet of the oak tag board I had used to make the first four rules, wrote on it with a black marker, and then taped it on the board under the other four.

"Teddy?" I tapped the new sign with the wooden rod to signal for him to read.

"Don't spite. I mean don't s—don't spit. Don't spit!" he repeated triumphantly.

"You spitted, Mr. Shane," Wendy pointed out.

"I did, and so I broke the rule. But I'll try not to do it again."

"Do you promise?" she asked.

"I promise. I won't spit in school ever again. Guys, I know that together we'll make some more rules, so I've left room for them under here. Does anyone have any more rules to add today, right now?" I waited and studied the silence while scanning the students' faces, knowing that a response could come from either spoken words or from facial or body expressions. *Expectation* would be my new mantra. I expected things from these students, and what would come to make the real difference in their performance was their coming to understand this. For many of them, no one in their lives had ever expected anything from them.

Things were about to change.

I'd selected the Apollo 11 moon landing as my first topic to teach. The moon landing was, of course, a huge event that had occurred only a few months before I landed at Belchertown—another remote and barren part of the galaxy. Not only was the moon landing recent, but it also offered essential ingredients to make a lesson appealing to this diverse group: an exciting story about real people and an observable yet faraway object that had captured the fascination of so many that summer.

Only four of the students—Ron, Ruth, Jack, and Teddy—were aware that the landing had occurred. My students all seemed to listen as I read the first lines of a brief news story about the event and then asked Jack to continue the reading out loud. After this introduction, I began to engage the students in some activities that would capitalize on their curiosity and help reveal their knowledge, understanding, and abilities.

Barbara, I learned, could pick out the color of the moon from a color chart I had brought from a paint store. She was able to trace a circle, and Danny could color it in with a yellow crayon. Ron could indicate with his eyes where I should add a crude rocket drawing. From the photos I brought in, Paula could point to a ladder on the picture of Neil Armstrong descending from Apollo 11, and Wendy could count to three when shown a photo of the three who had made this historic landing. Teddy could pick out associated words I wrote on the board, including "Apollo," "Armstrong," and "11," as well as the phrase, "That's one small step for a man, one giant leap for mankind."

As the day progressed, I found myself mentally correcting the school records I had inspected. Carla was most definitely not lazy. Wendy's speech wasn't empty or superficial. I did find it hard to understand some of my students—when Paula or Carla asked a question, Teddy or Jack often served as an interpreter—but I quickly adapted and knew my ear for understanding would improve as I became more familiar with the students and their speech patterns. For now, I was just trying my best to engage each student in a way that helped me get to know them better and made them feel included.

Near the end of the day, I assigned what was probably their first homework assignment ever: to look out a window and gaze at the moon.

As three p.m. arrived and the attendants began to appear outside the classroom door, I was filled with a sense of both optimism and dread. I was excited about how much had been done, but I hadn't completed nearly as much as I had hoped. In my inexperience, I hadn't anticipated that everything would take twice as long as planned. I was exhausted.

On the other hand, there were small victories. I'd learned many things about my students. I'd opened a new corner of the galaxy to them, in some small way. And Teddy, thank goodness, had not yet inquired about *Playboy* magazine.

I eyed Pauline and the other attendants loitering outside the classroom door. I took the cardboard clock from the chalk tray, then stood on my desk chair to hang it where the real clock had once hung. In this elevated position, I had the attention of the entire student body while I cranked the hands to show three o'clock. In response, Danny held up three fingers.

"Put your hands up higher, Danny, and let everyone know that it's three o'clock," I said. "Guess what that means? 'That's all, folks.' But before you go for today, I want to know what character says that on television."

Ruth suddenly stretched her body, and a grin spread across her face, signaling that she had a response. The speed with which she reacted suggested she undoubtedly knew the answer.

After only one full day of knowing Ruth, it was clear to me that the method by which she communicated, by responding to questions, was workable but not very efficient. It required that I take on more responsibility in the conversation and be good at posing questions. If I didn't ask the right question, she wouldn't get her ideas out to the world. There had to be a better way.

"So, Ruth, do you know who says, 'That's all, folks'?"

Eyes up again.

"Okay, Ruth, you react when I get to the correct answer. Red Skelton?"

Her face remained flat.

I waited three seconds. "The Road Runner?" Two seconds later: "Porky Pig?"

With that, her eyes shot up to signal, "That's the one."

"Did you all hear that?" I addressed the class. "Ruth is absolutely correct. Danny, would you tell the attendants to come in?"

One of the attendants from Ward 5 came over to push Ron out, but I stopped her and said, "Oh, Ron, before you leave, I have a question for you."

As the attendant went to look at the students' artwork of the day to give us a minute together, Ron looked at me attentively.

"Do you like Ed?" I whispered. For some reason Ed and his many pencils had stayed in my mind since our contact a few days ago. I figured that if he could be as fastidious with some classroom tasks as he was with his personal grooming, he might be a positive addition to the management of the schoolroom.

Ron signaled yes with little hesitation.

Next I asked, "Do you trust him?"

This time, he slowly blinked, but at the same time, he leaned his head against the headrest of his chair, which meant no.

"Is that a maybe?" I asked, doing a little interpreting.

His eyes blinked immediately, and I added "maybe" to my nonverbal glossary.

"Do you trust him enough to let him push you to school?"

Quick blink.

"Because I was just thinking about asking him for some help, but I wanted to be sure it was all right with you."

Again, he blinked.

"All right, then. I'm going to work on this idea some more. See you tomorrow!"

I grinned at Ron as the attendant came to roll him away. I couldn't wait, in fact, to see all my students tomorrow.

But there was one student who still needed a visit from his teacher today.

CHAPTER 8

Ireally wasn't looking forward to reliving the morning's spitting contest. Despite my rather aggressive stand that morning, I wasn't a person who took any pleasure from confrontation. I wasn't afraid of it, but I'd never seek it out and certainly didn't reap gratification from disagreements or conflicts of any kind.

I found Dennis sitting on his bed, pulling at some loose threads on the sleeve of his jersey. His metal crutches were propped up next to him, his wheelchair nowhere in sight. He turned away when I approached.

"You know," I said, "I'm the one who should be mad. Nobody likes to be spit on. Did you like it when I spit on you?"

Dennis didn't react, other than to tuck his chin further into his shoulder. My main objective was for Dennis to return to my classroom, but I also believed he needed to see my point of view, even if he didn't completely agree with it. Otherwise, if he did return, there would be ongoing tension that would be disruptive to the entire class.

"Well, did you?" I asked again.

His "no" was barely audible.

"Are you coming back to school?" I asked, figuring it best to get right to the heart of the matter.

"Why should I?" he said, loud enough to get the attention of an attendant mopping the floor three beds away.

"Because you can learn some new things. Maybe help you get ready to get out of this place. Besides, I need your help in the classroom."

Dennis looked straight at me now. "That's a bunch of shit! You don't need any help, and I'm never getting out of this crap hole. You're just saying that to get me back."

"That's not true. There are too many students for me to do a good job teaching. I need some help, some extra help. You already know how to read, so you could help some of the other kids when you're not learning some things yourself."

Now he was looking at me. "How do you know I can read?"

"I have a folder about when you went to school, and it told me you could read," I said. "It also says you can add and subtract. I need someone like you to help me."

62

His lips moved, but I couldn't make it out.

"Can you say that again? I couldn't make out what you said."

Softly, staring at the floor, he said, "Okay."

I realized I'd been holding my breath and exhaled with relief. I was thrilled he had agreed to come back. "But Dennis, if you spit again, then you will be banned from school for a week, and every time after that, it will be for another week, and so on. Are we clear about that?"

"Uh-huh."

I placed a paper cup filled with water on the dresser next to his bed. I pointed to it and said, "There it is." I really wasn't sure if this was a good idea, but I assumed that whether I was sprayed or not, it would put an end to our little skirmish.

"What's that for?" he asked.

"I call it revenge. I'm giving you one chance to get back at me for what I did—but just this one chance. Then, we're even."

Dennis sat immobile and stared at the cup, his head no doubt filled with a hundred mischievous thoughts—like the long-term consequences of actually letting me have it or the story he could tell around the ward about the sweetness of revenge.

To remove any doubt of my sincerity and to legitimately put this event in the past, I picked up the cup and handed it to him. "Here. I want you to get this spitting out of your system."

He emptied the contents of the cup into his mouth, then leaned back and pursed his lips into the unmistakable, universal spitting posture. I moved closer to him and stared. He leaned back further. I closed my eyes, ready for the stream of water. Then, with two noisy gulps, he swallowed it.

I smiled. "You had me there. You're a good actor. I really thought you were going to do it, but I am glad you didn't."

With that, I got up and headed out of the ward. As I walked, I turned back to him and yelled, "See you in the morning!"

Outside the door, I found Nancy in a heated discussion with another attendant about her date from the night before. She glanced up at me with a hint of irritation.

"No, no, finish your conversation. I'm sure your love life is much more interesting than what I want to talk about," I declared dramatically.

Nancy laughed and cut off her discussion to deal with me. I was learning quickly that in this building, which was so horrific in so many ways, I was surrounded by a crew of good-natured and extremely caring people.

"You're not going to spit on me, are you?" she asked.

I smiled and shook my head. "I have a question about Ed that I thought you might be able to answer."

"I've known him for a long time," she confirmed.

"That's what Bernie told me. I need some extra hands in the classroom, and I was thinking about trying to get him to help out. Things like pushing kids in their chairs, running errands, I don't know—just stuff that comes up."

"Ed is a sweet guy. He's not aggressive, but he is very solitary. He might not want to get that close to people, especially teachers who might spit at him." She gave me a little grin. "But seriously, I think he's your guy if he'll do it."

"Actually, I have one other Ed question, if you don't mind."

"Shoot."

"His clothes," I said. "Does he have a butler or something? He just always looks so neat. It's like he has a staff to press and prepare his clothes and a valet to help him get dressed in the morning."

Nancy smiled, leaned toward my ear, and whispered, "I think it's related to his pencil collecting." She smiled. "Did you ever see the way he keeps his pencils stored?"

I shook my head.

"Well, he stores them according to color, length, if they're sharpened or new, and so on. It's the way he keeps all his other things, too. He's a neat freak and likes everything just so. As far as where he gets his clothes and why he's always so polished—well, he has a family that visits a lot. His brother, who I think might even be his twin, is always bringing him things. Every week someone in his family stops by, picks up dirty laundry, and brings back clean clothes for the week. So he always looks fresh." She paused, "Any more questions? They need me in the ward."

"That about does it. Thanks for your advice," I said, as she hurried off.

I had one more stop to make. As I entered Bernie's office, she looked up from the papers stacked on her desk.

"How did it go? I hear you had a little water fight with Dennis." She raised an eyebrow.

"Well, yes," I admitted. "Besides that, I think the day went just fine. Word sure travels fast in this place." I collapsed into her guest chair.

"Make that your second lesson about the infirmary. Keep things to yourself unless you want everyone in the building—staff and residents alike—to know your business."

"Okay, but what's the first lesson?"

Now she looked at me with a solemnity she likely reserved for handling serious personal matters. "Lesson one is to be careful to avoid letting the lives of the residents weigh you down. You need to learn that you will never be able to control certain things around here, and often it's those very things that hit you the hardest."

I nodded, acknowledging her warning, but I didn't feel ready to put into words what I was thinking. Instead I moved on to a practical question, which was easier to talk about. "I would like your permission to ask Ed to give me a little assistance in the classroom. I checked with Ron Benoit to see if he would mind Ed being his transporter and asked Nancy if she had any reservations. They had no objections."

She lifted her eyebrows but stayed silent.

"Mainly to help with transporting the residents, especially Ron," I added. "But I can imagine if things work out, he can just be an overall assistant. My class has a few extra bodies. I could use some more manpower."

"I have no problem with that," she said, nodding. "He's manageable and cooperative, and God knows he could use the diversion."

I hesitated for a moment, trying to compose a question that had been troubling me since I first met Ed. "I have to ask: why is he in this building and not one of the dormitories with the men who don't have a physical disability?"

"Mainly because he has a seizure disorder. Most of the time, they're under control, but he needs someone, a nurse, to give him the meds to prevent the seizures."

"But you don't see any risk or problems if he helps me out?"

"Unofficially, no, I don't. Officially, you may get some pushback from someone from the School Department," she said with a slight grin.

"Well, that's great," I said, ignoring her warning about Mrs. Sharp. "I'm going to ask Ed if he's willing to help the class. Thanks for your help." On my way out the door, I stopped and turned back to her for a moment. "Oh, and Bernie, you don't need to worry about me. I won't let this place get to me. Besides, my heart is made of asbestos—I'm fireproof and bombproof."

"Yeah, right," she retorted, sarcasm dripping from every word. "I can already tell from your behavior that you won't get involved." She smiled and returned to her paperwork.

Bernie had my number, more than she even knew. Although I had been associated with Belchertown for only a short time, I realized already that this place and my students could consume me. My mind was full—racing with ideas for how to help the students, while also struggling to accept the terrible circumstances of their lives within these walls. Not long ago, my life had been removed from such personal anguish, but the details of that period already seemed distant.

During my conversation with Jack at the tavern, he had indicated that I could quit this job anytime I wanted, try to find something easier. The notion hadn't felt quite right to me then, and it definitely didn't feel right now.

After my first day, I was all in.

I found Ed hanging out in the dining room, watching some resident workers stack dishes into a large industrial dishwasher. I was discovering that this was his style: he observed from just far enough away to not be part of any actual group.

"Hey, Ed, got a minute to talk?" I said, approaching him.

"Pencils?"

"How many pencils do you have, anyway?"

"Can I have a pencil?" he said. Was he simply ignoring me, or did he not understand my question?

"Ed, I want you to be a helper in the schoolroom. Will you come at eight-thirty and stay through the day? I'll give you pencils for helping. From now on, no more free pencils. You have to work for them." I paused to gauge his response. He might have been mulling it over, but it was hard to read his face. "So, Ed, how many pencils do you have?"

"Hundreds of pencils—and I want more."

That answered that. "So... will you work with me for pencils?"

"Okay. Can I have a pencil now?"

"Sure. Let's just call today's pencil a signing bonus." I pulled an unsharpened pencil out of my pocket and offered it to him. "You're now in charge of pushing Ron to school every morning. Can you remember that? Tomorrow, I also want you to sharpen pencils in the classroom."

Ed took the pencil and started to move away, but I called him back. "Ed, can you read what it says on that new pencil?"

Ed held the pencil between the thumb and forefinger of both hands and rolled it around several times, stopping occasionally.

"Dixon Universal 2," he said. Then, he walked off repeating the phrase, the pencil now stored in the front pocket of his unwrinkled white shirt.

Our exchange had confirmed what my gut had told me: Ed could read.

When I finally tracked down Bob Bergquist, it was just after four p.m., and he was conducting therapy in Ward 4 on the first floor. The room was identical to all the others, but it was crowded with elderly women. This particular ward had been skipped during my first tour, most likely because its residents were far removed from school age. Their lives had undergone a double tragedy: They had spent years here, cast away as children to live a woefully dull and uneventful life in decrepit conditions, but they had also aged out of the small scraps of normalcy some of their younger counterparts now received— like fragments of an education, or the occasional trip home. Their entire lives had played out here, in what would likely be their first and final home.

Most of the women apparently spent their days in bed, because the majority of the iron cribs were occupied when I entered. I suspected that almost all of these women were potential candidates for physical therapy, since a high percentage of them had cerebral palsy. Bob was a physical therapy student in training, brought to Belchertown along with others to work under the direction of a consultant from Springfield College. But it was obvious from the sheer number of residents with significant physical therapy needs that the help of a few students would not be sufficient.

I spotted Bob in the middle of the room, stretching the leg of a white-haired woman whose facial expression wavered between discomfort and relief. I watched as a huge smile enveloped his face, and I overheard him telling her in a soft voice, "Now when I put your leg down, don't you go and kick me." I suspected she tolerated this necessary stretching because of Bob's steady stream of encouragement and funny quips he kept up as he moved her through the exercises. I could tell that Bob was committed and empathetic with his patients. His height allowed him to conduct the exercises while hovering over the resident, offering face-to-face encouragement.

I clutched the bars of the iron bed, listening to Bob's banter, and then asked, "How are we doing today?"

"We're great," he said. "Lucy here is doing a fantastic job with her exercises."

I couldn't tell whether Lucy fully understood the meaning of Bob's comment, but I was struck by the way she came alive in response to his voice and personal attention, her smile bright and her blue eyes sparkling.

"I'm glad," I said. "Hi, Lucy—I'm Howard."

"I'd venture a guess that our day is going a bit better than yours," said Bob. His eyes darted quickly to mine, eyebrows raised in question.

"So, you heard?"

"It traveled the infirmary pipeline faster than it took you to wipe the dribble off your chin. I will add there hasn't been much sympathy for poor old Dennis around here today. He's been a terror lately."

"He'll come around," I replied. After my exchange with Dennis, I sincerely believed he was on board for giving school a try. "In any event, I did want to thank you for your heads-up about his little plan this morning. In the long run, it may help improve this situation with Dennis, so thanks."

"Actually, I felt like a snitch."

"Well, that's true, but it did help me out," I said. "Do you drink beer?"

"Depends on who's buying."

"I thought we might catch the happy hour at the saloon in town—and I'll buy. Let's call it a reward for the tip that kept me relatively dry today."

It's said that friendships often form faster and are more enduring when initiated under stressful circumstances. Sitting in a slightly sleazy local bar down the road from the school, Bob and I spent the evening becoming fast friends.

Bob was an easy guy to talk to, and we shared a love for sports—especially the Red Sox. I think that connection allowed us to easily talk about our families and ourselves. He grew up in Connecticut and was completing his degree at Springfield College. A cartoon illustration over the bar—in which two drunks decided that it didn't matter if a glass was half empty or half full, because there was still room for beer—sparked the revelation that he was an amateur cartoonist himself. As one beer turned into several, I realized Bob's sense of humor clearly clicked with mine.

"To Mrs. Sharp!" Bob said, hoisting his pint of draft beer.

"To Mrs. Sharp," I concurred. "May her influence on the lives of my students last no longer than the foam in this glass of cheap domestic beer."

Our discussion eventually led to the question of what exactly had brought us to Belchertown State School in rural Western Massachusetts. Bob had attended Springfield College in nearby Springfield, Massachusetts, because of its renowned physical education department. Although he enrolled there to become a high school physical education teacher, one course with Sherrod Shaw—a distinguished physical therapy instructor—instantly convinced him to become a physical therapist. His internship at Belchertown State School was an intensive "hands-on" experience as part of his graduate school curriculum.

As for myself, I'd spent the last four years at college drinking beer with my buddies and putting just enough energy into my coursework to ensure I passed, so my social life could continue uninterrupted. I'd been on track for an easy teaching job, an easy life—until Belchertown had come along and set me on a whole new path.

Undoubtedly, some of this conversation was fueled by alcohol, but drunk or sober, Bob and I were convinced there was a reason why we ended up in this specific town, and in this specific place. Neither of us put much stock in fate, but a small part of me knew that the universe was playing a role here. The reality was that both our lives had taken a radical turn, and now we were both somewhere we never expected to be—a place where we had the opportunity to change lives, and have our own lives changed in the process.

As the evening wore on, our voices got louder, as did our opinions about Belchertown and how it was run.

"Oh, let me guess how much support Mrs. Sharp is giving you!" Bob's voice rose above the roar of the crowd. "Would zilch be accurate?"

"You should see the school records she left me with!" I waved my beer around. "Incomplete! Missing! Nothing but insults and negativity. Those kids never got an education, ever."

"Such is life at Belchertown State School." He shook his head.

"I mean, until now? The term 'school' has had zero relationship to whatever took place there."

"Yeah, well, it hasn't been a school," said Bob. "It's been a warehouse."

"Yes! Exactly! They should be ashamed, calling Belchertown a state school."

"Soothes the parents, I guess."

"God knows they can't just call it Belchertown State Human Warehouse." I took a long swig of beer and set my mug on the bar with a loud thump. The room seemed to have quieted around us. I glanced at the other patrons, who returned my gaze with cool stares. A man seated at a corner table slowly exhaled his cigarette, staring at me the whole time.

It abruptly dawned on me that the tavern was probably filled with men and women who either worked at the facility themselves or who were related to or lived next door to someone who did. I realized for the first time that there was another human side to the equation. The institution I was so effortlessly berating fed their children, paid their mortgages, and probably even kept this bar operating. It was easy to criticize the state and the institution because those were more or less abstract concepts. If this state school were to shut down, where would the townspeople work? The existence of Belchertown State School and its connection to the fabric of the community suggested to me I had a lot more thinking to do before I could reconcile the horrors of the institution with the human element that surrounded me.

Chastened, I suggested to Bob that we ought to keep our voices down.

"Good call," he agreed, peeking at his watch. "Whoa—actually, we should probably head home. It's getting late."

I left the bar that night believing I had found a spiritual brother. Another human who saw the world, or at least a small part of it, as I did. Another person who was shocked by the circumstances under which the human beings at Belchertown lived. Bob and I had spent the evening being impudent and irreverent—and, in many respects, free. By contrast, that same evening of the first day of school, all residents of the infirmary were compelled to be in bed by seven-thirty p.m.

As I stepped out into the cool evening air, I reminded myself that seven-thirty was late enough for the moon to be visible. I could only hope that the attendants had fulfilled my request: to wheel or walk every student to a window that night so they, too, could observe the bright half-moon hanging in the cloudless evening sky.

CHAPTER 9

"No," was the first word Mrs. Sharp uttered when she looked up and saw me in the doorway of her office.

It was the end of September, and I'd been feeling more relaxed as my enthusiasm for teaching grew. Mrs. Sharp had continued to ignore me—until today, when I'd sent a written request to bring the students out to the meadow just behind the infirmary for a nature walk.

In as calm a voice as I could manage, I said, "But, Mrs. Sharp, I only want to take my students as far as the tree line behind the building."

"I said no."

"But why? I can't think of one good—"

"It will cause chaos in the wards! It's impossible to get the residents dressed and down the back ramp," she shouted as she stood up behind her desk.

I was taken aback. In all her unpleasantness, I'd never heard Mrs. Sharp yell before.

Leaning over her desk, she glared at me. It took an effort not to glare back. For the past month, she'd offered me no support at all. No teacher training had been planned, no in-service days were ever set aside for me and the other teachers in the building, and very little in the way of curriculum development was discussed. I'd felt completely on my own.

By now, I realized my meadow request was a lost cause with her, and I didn't care if I inflamed her even more. "Imagine how much they might learn from hearing the sound of footsteps or wheels crushing leaves, the sensation of snow on their hands or cold on their cheeks. Wouldn't this be a great way to explain weather and experience nature? As of now, they're always trapped in the infirmary."

She sat down very slowly and smoothed her skirt. "Mr. Shane, thank you for your ideas," she said in a calm, clear voice. "However, there is no reason to drag the class outdoors. The school department just bought a complete filmstrip series on nature. Your job is to use it." With that, she turned to a pile of papers on her desk, effectively dismissing me.

My blood boiled as I walked back to the infirmary. So much for a "meeting." I found it absurd that something as simple as providing the students with fresh air and exposure to nature was forbidden.

This was ridiculous. And I had to do something about it.

This was the late '60s after all, and education was becoming more personalized and relevant. As an undergrad at the University of Massachusetts, I'd been inspired by the educational philosophy of Dr. Dwight W. Allen, the new Dean of the School of Education. He believed that learning should be driven by an *internal* desire to acquire knowledge and not controlled by an *external* desire for a grade or ranking. He also held that recognizing each student's individual differences was paramount to successful teaching.

With every passing day at Belchertown, I'd become more and more appreciative of the philosophical crumbs I'd taken away from my time at UMass. They gave me the resolve to try to reform what seemed on every level to be broken. I tried hard to modify every lesson so it accommodated student diversity. I tried to prepare each lesson so it was uncomplicated and easy to understand, but not so simplistic that it became insulting or boring to the more advanced students. I tried to invent new ways to introduce the greater world to these cloistered students—for "show and tell," I brought in items like a vegetable peeler, a whistle, or a funnel and had them experience the object using their senses and then ask me questions about it. It was a constant effort to balance the different learning needs of my students, but it was comforting to know that even if a lesson went completely off track, a day in my classroom topped the monotony of life on the floors above. Even a little schooling was better than none.

Seeing how well my students responded to whatever novelties I was able to introduce, I remained determined to take them outdoors—my blowup with Mrs. Sharp notwithstanding. I knew a trip outside the infirmary would provide an immeasurable benefit and an exciting adventure for all of them. So despite Mrs. Sharp's objections, on a warm fall day two weeks to the day after our run-in, I held my first class in the meadow just behind the infirmary. I knew she would give me hell if she found out, but

I reasoned that just holding class outside was not the same as the nature walk I'd proposed earlier.

I knew that semantic argument wouldn't hold up, but it was the best defense I had, and the opportunity for the class to breathe fresh air was all the motivation I needed. Furthermore, no additional personnel would be needed if the usual attendants transported the kids down the elevator onto the ramp leading to the loading platform instead of all the way to the base- ment. The word "furthermore" in this case was part of my inner dialogue, in which I catalogued excuses in the event we got caught. I knew I would probably just have to ask for forgiveness, and at this point, I figured it was better to ask forgiveness than to ask permission.

As my pupils arrived that morning, they were escorted out to the patio instead of into the classroom. Ed, who had become a trusted and devoted classroom aide—and would likely remain so as long as I kept the pencils coming—helped me arrange the students roughly in a semicircle in front of a table lined with common outdoor objects, such as pinecones, stones, and clumps of grass turned brown by fall. Next to each object was a white index card on which I had written the name of the item. I anticipated the need to also represent the words for invisible things like the wind or auditory items like truck noises and swirling leaves, so I prepared posters with the headings THINGS WE CAN'T SEE and THINGS WE CAN HEAR.

Looking at the students now assembled outside the building, I was certain that the outdoors was truly the ideal place to learn about the outdoors.

"I like it much better out here," Teddy said, as he was wheeled up to the table.

"Why's that?" I asked, while pulling Ron a few feet back to get the sun- light out of his eyes.

"Because it doesn't smell," Teddy replied, "and I feel kinda free."

Ruth squealed and raised her eyes, seconding that comment.

Dennis interjected, "I feel like I've escaped this shithole!"

"Really, Dennis?" I said. Weeks ago, he had agreed to try to use less pro- fanity. "You know sentences that don't contain the word *shit*." I turned away slightly after saying this, mostly to keep myself from laughing. Despite this colorful description of the infirmary—which I actually agreed with—my mental tally of Dennis's swearwords had been on a downward trajectory.

Everyone looked happier and less stressed, and the diversion from the indoors was a perfect opportunity for my students to have some new sensory experiences. Dennis must have sensed the difficulty Wendy had seeing the items on the table because of her position in her cart, so he picked up different items and held them up for her to see.

"That one," she said. He held up a small rock flecked with mica crystals that glittered in the sunlight, and she carefully studied the sparkles. I wasn't surprised when she asked to hold that object.

Jack quickly checked out all of the items on the table. Though he showed no interest in carefully examining any of them, he settled back in his cart contentedly and became enthralled with the cumulous clouds that slowly moved east to west across the sky. Danny maneuvered himself out of his wheelchair onto the grass and dragged himself over the ground, stopping every few feet to pull out some grass and toss the cuttings into the air.

Barbara and Paula, who stayed next to each other throughout this experience, each grabbed a short branch and busied themselves with banging the ends on the table or against each other's stick. Teddy was interested in the flashcards and quickly took on the role of mentor as he showed the words to Ruth and Ron and said each one aloud. They both politely attended to Teddy's reading lesson.

While everyone remained engaged with different activities, their excitement spiked when the wind picked up and they felt it on their faces. When I heard a truck approaching the loading dock, I became silent, cupped my hand to my ear, and pointed with enthusiasm when the truck actually turned the corner. The sight of a large approaching truck was something to behold, a rare experience for some of the students. When the attendants arrived to take the students back into the building, they seemed cheerier than usual, watching my students enjoy this novel experience. Teddy looked over at them and declared, without sarcasm, cynicism, or scorn, "School was really fun today."

Ron and Ruth immediately and enthusiastically seconded, and I saw no reason not to repeat the excursion. Despite the knowledge that forces greater than me could crush the opportunity, my students and I continued to escape under the radar to the outside patio for the rest of the fall.

CHAPTER 10

It occurred to me that my classroom was like the one-room schoolhouse of old, where a single teacher had to accommodate students of all ages, temperaments, and abilities. Despite the diversity of my classroom, I still had to prepare lessons that would resonate with each student. And that's just what I tried to do in my first few months as their teacher.

I learned to introduce lessons in a way that would hold my students' attention, make the most of their curiosity, and impart skills that were actually valuable—and by valuable, I mean functional. With the goal of teasing out where the class stood, I'd introduce traditional educational categories such as current events, literacy, math, art, and music. The planned outline for every lesson would be similar. First, I would announce the topic and begin a discussion. Answers would come in the form of speech for some and nonverbal yes/no responses for others. We would explore knowledge of vocabulary about the topic, both spoken and written. Next, I'd teach the use of tools associated with the topic. For instance, if a student couldn't turn a page or use a tool such as scissors or a pencil, I'd look for alternative ways to support their use of that tool—or teach them another way to accomplish the task.

One thing that helped reveal and strengthen my students' abilities was the birthday list I started for them at the beginning of the year, based on my initial review of school records in Bernie's office. Paula's birthday came first, on September 13, the first Saturday after the beginning of the school year. On the Monday following her birthday, I placed a card behind the screen in Independence Hall and quietly encouraged each student to sign it or place some personal mark on the card. Having the students sign in Independence Hall served two purposes: I wanted to keep the card a surprise for Paula, but I also wanted to observe, for the first time, the specifics of each student's writing proficiency and what kinds of supports they might need from me.

When Teddy arrived behind the screen and learned what he was expected to do, he whispered to me that he couldn't sign the card because he didn't know how to hold a pencil.

"Teddy," I whispered back, "welcome to the very place where you can learn to write. Just wait here."

I knew Teddy could read, so I was confident he was familiar with the shapes of letters. He just needed support to hold on to a pen or pencil, as cerebral palsy had affected the strength of his grip. This difficulty seemed relatively easy to address. I pulled a strip of white medical tape from our first-aid kit and wrapped it first around the pencil, then around his hand, with the pencil resting firmly between his thumb and index finger.

With my pencil, I wrote *Teddy* on a blank sheet of white paper, then turned it to face him. "Now it's your turn."

Teddy hesitated for a moment. Then, with great care, he unmistakably and legibly printed his name on the paper.

My heart leapt. "Great job, Teddy!" I said, with a nod of approval. I knew this was probably the first time in his life that he had ever written anything. "Would you like to sign Paula's card now?"

I slid Paula's birthday card in front of him, securing it to the table with tape. He scanned back and forth between his own written sample and the birthday card, as if trying to gather the courage to begin. I heard him say to himself, "Okay."

The finished product was even neater than his first attempt. Teddy clearly liked what he saw. A bright smile stretched across his face, and I smiled back.

"I'd like to write some more tomorrow," he said.

By early November, I was beginning to see myself as an actual teacher. I was learning how to instruct students with a range of intellectual and developmental disabilities. I was learning how to spark their imagination through interesting and motivating activities. They were learning new things—and I myself was learning alongside them.

Of course, I couldn't completely control or erase the effects of a disability—but I *could* help mitigate the effects of a life spent in a mind-numbing and lifeless setting. Who wants to focus on things that are boring and monotonous? It wasn't always easy to find stimulating activities in the infirmary, but I was discovering that every moment offered an opportunity to target the goals of specific students and help them learn. Recognizing these opportunities just required some deep digging on my part.

I also concluded that when a student failed to follow or participate fully in a lesson or conversation, it was often due to an underlying misunderstanding of basic concepts. Even my students with the most severe intellectual disabilities could identify many objects or activities by name, but some students needed a primer on the most fundamental qualities or characteristics of these items. I tried to teach them, for example, that a door was so much more than just a door. This familiar item was a rectangle and was made of wood or metal, sometimes with glass inserts. A door can swing or slide open and can be left open or closed. It is hard to the touch and can be painted any color, and it can be associated with objects such as keys, doorknobs, and doorstoppers and concepts such as privacy and openness.

No two students were performing at the same level, so keeping my lessons interesting to the entire class and helping each person learn something new was a real challenge. It was a lot like juggling and never being able to drop the balls and take a break. I spent a lot of time untangling the mystery of what my students knew and what they needed in order to learn. For example, Paula, Barbara, and even Danny often needed and wanted to be exposed multiple times to the same material, so I used redundancy and multiple illustrations to leave a lasting imprint. Teddy did math problems from a legitimate math workbook nearly every day, but I also gave him word problems based on experiences from the infirmary environment that I used as a lesson for all the students. A lesson about Nancy stealing towels from another ward could be used to teach Dennis multiplication, Ron and Ruth some simple addition, and matching or color identification for Barbara.

One exercise that consistently held the interest of the entire class was what we called the Never Before Game, which involved creating a sentence that no one had ever written or spoken before in the history of mankind. This was one of our favorite activities—not only did it make the whole class erupt with screams and laughter, but it was also a great opportunity to review spelling, learn word definitions, and use words in multiple contexts. The game consisted of two groups, the word choosers and the sentence builders. The word choosers didn't need to read or speak, only to indicate a word by pointing to or moving toward a picture, object, or color in the room or in a magazine. As the words were chosen, I wrote them on the blackboard, and experienced and evolving readers alike had the chance to read them aloud. Sentence builders were exactly that: They used these chosen vocabulary words to create new sentences. The only rule was that the sentences we built needed to be grammatically correct.

Wendy especially enjoyed this game—and interestingly, she only offered adjectives like soft, furry, or one of the primary colors. Based on the homogeneity of her word choices, I surmised that her small stuffed animal collection served as a tangible foundation for her suggestions. Paula, on the other hand, always blurted out short words like "go," "stop," and "up." Eventually a sentence would evolve from their suggestions as I wrote, or sometimes Dennis sounded the words out, all the while encouraging more people to add words and say the sentence as it grew. The sentences were often silly and nonsensical, the sillier the better. One particular sentence brought the house down: *Mister Shane spilled some blue paint on his head and some feathers fell from the ceiling and he looked like a blue chicken before he yelled STOP.*

Everyone contributed in some way to the evolution of the final sentence, and each student's contribution was pointed to and praised before the final reading. Dennis often read the final sentence, and he loved the idea that he was the only person in the entire world, inside or outside the institution, who had ever said that particular sentence.

It was in great part due to Ed that we were able to do so many group activities. His first job was to push Ron into the schoolroom. Given what I'd learned of Ed's history, I wasn't sure he'd accept that responsibility, but he did it each day, albeit with little emotion. I'd expected him to be shy and withdrawn, and he initially did develop the habit of retreating to the corner of the room after pushing one or another of the boys into class and remaining there unless I asked for assistance. Ed didn't say much over the next few months, but our silent relationship matured, and I began to think he actually enjoyed the work and found pleasure in his escape from the tedium of the ward. I was determined to break him out of his isolation.

Ed's assistance quickly became essential to the functioning of the classroom. He contributed in so many ways, but most importantly, his presence allowed for the kind of personalized instruction that otherwise would have been impossible. He instinctively positioned the students in wheelchairs to allow them to better participate in a lesson, and he retrieved dropped items. He knew where most materials were kept and quietly brought them to me when asked. Ed was also strong and capable and could help with turning, lifting, and moving the students who needed physical assistance.

Initially, Ed reacted only when given specific instructions, but over time, he adapted to the rhythm of the classroom and began to offer assistance on his own or anticipate an activity and prepare or organize the appropriate materials. He carried out every assignment without complaint. I grew to rely on his help so much that I began to worry that someone from the school administration—or, more to the point, Mrs. Sharp—would arrive and ask him to leave. I had no doubt that if she were to investigate his role in the classroom, she would be able to cite some regulation (real or otherwise) that would lead to his removal.

Ed's affect was typically flat at first, but his demeanor changed as his interest in classroom activities grew over time. He smiled only occasionally, but an especially huge smile would break out on his face when he was given a compliment or praised for his assistance. He also showed a distinctly cheery, almost contented look when he received his weekly earnings—a bundle of pencils. I was willing to compensate Ed with monetary wages, but whenever I hinted at a change in the form of payment or attempted to modify the currency, he insisted on receiving only pencils. It was clear that he wanted nothing else, and given his circumstances, maybe he didn't really require anything more.

So I nurtured Ed's fascination with pencils, and they remained our form of legal tender. No doubt I supplied him with more pencils than even he could ever have imagined existed. Early in the year, I tried to delight him with pencils in colors other than the standard yellow, but I noticed he always left those back in his bed space, leading me to believe that only yellow pencils had any real value to him. Although I never actually checked, principally because it would be an invasion of his privacy not unlike opening his bankbook, I estimated that his pencil trunk would be close to full by the end of 1969.

CHAPTER 11

A s the months went by and I grew more and more comfortable in my new role, I thought often of the promise I'd made to Ron's grandmother at the beginning of the year: to help him become a better communicator. It gnawed at me, both during class time and when I was home planning lessons. Both Ron and Ruth, I knew, needed a more effective way to communicate. It wasn't that they couldn't understand or didn't have things to say—the issue was that they weren't able to use traditional speech to get their thoughts across. I viewed this as a cruel form of incarceration where their ideas, feelings, and beliefs were held hostage. I couldn't imagine the frustration that came from total dependence on others to express needs, comments, complaints, and joys. And I was determined to find a way to improve this aspect of their lives.

In some respects, both Ron and Ruth were actually good communicators. As long as their communication partners posed questions properly, Ron and Ruth could make requests and express thoughts. The "twenty questions" system was awkward, though, and it forced these bright, energetic teenagers into a dependency on others. While a competent questioner could usually get right to the issue at hand, a questioner with less skill—such as a resident with similar communication issues, or an impatient doctor or staff member—might not be successful at all. It was ironic that the two most intellectually gifted students in the class had the greatest difficulty showing it.

As a result of a lifetime of being unable to talk, both Ron and Ruth had become virtuosos of nonverbal expression. Smiles, glances, nods, and frowns were used to the maximum, including gestures for yes and no. Unfortunately, these methods offered little spontaneity and limited topics of discussion, and they produced extremely slow and labored dialogue.

I struggled to think of ways to allow them to more successfully and efficiently express a greater variety of topics and emotions. I had to devise some way for them to become initiators rather than responders, to move from dependence on others to independence.

I started with the basic premise that a good conversation was essentially a back-and-forth collaboration: one person talked while another listened, and then the roles reversed and the speaker became the listener. I took to casually eavesdropping on conversations at the supermarkets, in bars, or in line at the movie theater, which confirmed my thesis. There was nothing earthshattering about this conclusion, but it did allow me to contrast typical conversation patterns of give and take with Ron and Ruth's style.

Appreciating this communication style difference was a good beginning, but I had considerably more to learn, so I did some research. Unfortunately, there was little to be found in journals or reference books. Some articles discussed speech anomalies like stuttering, articulation, and voice disorders, but they offered virtually nothing on developing an alternative way of communicating for people who could not speak and had limited movement. There was sign language, of course, but Ron and Ruth lacked the necessary motor skills to form precise hand gestures.

At this time, most people who experienced extreme communication challenges had other severe health issues, and they either died shortly after birth or were institutionalized. And once they had been sent to places like Belchertown, they were no longer the focus of any academic research.

If I wanted to help Ruth and Ron communicate better, it was clear I would be on my own.

I began to spend more time with them after school, making more than a dozen visits to Wards 1 and 5 over the course of a few months. For these extended afternoons, I rode the elevator to either the first or second floor along with one or another of the student groups. I would casually roam the wards, talking with residents and staff and occasionally assisting with tasks that were not of a private nature. My main objective, however, was watching and listening to interactions between the staff and Ron or Ruth.

I chose to keep my project to myself, hoping to observe the teenagers and their attendants without making anyone self-conscious. Initially, my presence in the wards was somewhat uncomfortable for the staff, since they weren't used to having an observer while they carried out their routines. The more visits I made, however, the more normal it became. The few times I was asked why I was spending so much time upstairs in the wards, I simply told them I wanted to get to know my students better.

I enjoyed making these unannounced forays into the wards, visiting residents and talking with staff. It gave me the opportunity to meet residents I otherwise wouldn't have encountered, including the seniors who had spent most of their lives at Belchertown—many of whom experienced the same disabilities I observed in my students. I appreciated the chance to get to know the older residents, though it was unbearably sad to imagine Danny still requesting keys at seventy, or Dennis with a packed suitcase next to his iron bed at eighty, still waiting for his parents to reclaim him. Time could easily find a way to stand still here as the staff turned over or retired, while decades of tedium stretched on for the residents.

One day in November, just after Thanksgiving, I pushed Ruth into Ward 1, where Pauline was reading the bathing wall chart. Pauline noted our arrival with a cheerful, "Hi, Ruthie."

I directed the wheelchair toward Pauline and stopped. "Hi, Ruthie," she repeated. "So, sweetie, did you have a good day in school today?"

Eyes up.

"Did you learn any new words?"

Eyes up.

"Good for you. Did anyone give Mr. Shane here a bad time?"

Immediate pout.

"Well, that's good too. Do you need to use the potty?"

Eyes up.

"Do you mind if Jenny takes you so I can give Louise a bath and start getting ready for supper?"

Ruth gave a pouting look, signaling, "No, I don't mind." Then, as if part of the same sentence, she scanned the room, spotted Jenny, glanced back at Pauline, caught her eye, looked out at Jenny, and then looked back to Pauline. This silent exchange carried considerable meaning, as if she had actually uttered, "Sure, it would be fine for Jenny to assist me, and in case you weren't aware, she's over there."

Pauline fully understood and called out to Jenny.

I watched them leave the room, my gears turning. Ruth's ability to communicate whole sentences nonverbally felt significant, and I'd have to think more about how to use her impressive skills to help her improve her communication.

While Ruth was in the ladies' room, I took a detour to visit with Wendy, who had been absent from school due to a bad cold. She was lying on her back in her cart.

"Wendy, are you feeling better? I missed you today."

"Hi, Mr. Shane," Wendy said, shifting her gaze from the ceiling to stare into my face. After hesitating for a moment, she continued. "I forgot what your voice sounds like."

"Wendy," I said, a little choked up by the sweetness and sadness of her comment. "Oh dear, I don't want that to happen! Shall I stand here and talk and talk and talk until you're sure I sound like me?"

"You sound just like Mr. Shane."

"That's good. I wouldn't want to sound like Pauline, would I?"

"But you're not Pauline. You're Mr. Shane," she insisted.

"I am, Wendy," I repeated. "I really am Mr. Shane."

When Ruth returned from the bathroom, she seemed content to relax and observe the late afternoon routines as they unfolded. She closely observed the bustling staff rather than the residents, many of whom were silent and still. I watched as she focused on the attendants' banter, smiling and pouting appropriately along with each nuance of their interactions, whether they were speaking with each other or with residents. She was smart, curious, and engaged, and I knew these qualities would serve her well as we worked together to expand her communication skills.

Even though Ruth and Ron could be highly effective communicators if yes/no questions were asked in the proper fashion, they had limited opportunities to actually initiate a conversation with someone or keep one going. One exception was Teddy, who had a particular connection with Ron, but their interactions were more like ongoing monologues than actual conversations. Teddy was like a sportscaster or environmental reporter who described the actions that both of them could clearly observe: "Norman is puking over there." "Now the attendants are having a cigarette break." "I think Benjamin needs to go to the bathroom."

It was difficult for me to assess whether Ron or Ruth felt any invasion of privacy, given that receiving assistance with toileting and very personal hygiene care, like dealing with bowel movements and menstruation, had become routine for them. But the attendants treated them with respect, never failing to say something to them as they passed by en route to some other task. Although the affection was genuine, these remarks were frequently empty statements such as "Hey, Ron, what's up?" and "Ruthie, you're back," which didn't require any response. When a reply was needed, the conversation tended to center around personal care, and usually a yes or no answer was sufficient: "Ruth, feel like lying down now?" "Ron, do you want to be moved near your bed?" "Would you like your radio turned on?" Occasionally, the attendants found the time to indulge in the kind of small talk that everybody is familiar with: "Hey, Ron, have fun in school today?" or, "Gonna watch *Laugh In* on TV tonight?" These brief comments were important in maintaining a sense of humanity, but were not the basis of genuine conversation. This was talk on the fly in a frenetic environment.

In order to participate in rich conversation, Ron and Ruth would have to learn to become initiators as well as responders. They lacked the expressive verbal tools needed to question and initiate conversations, which made communication difficult, especially when time was of the essence. For example, if one of them had to communicate "My stomach is churning and I need to get to the bathroom immediately," they would most likely begin with a groan, followed by a "What's wrong?" from the attendant, followed by another groan, followed by, "Are you hot?" and a forehead check. "No, you're not hot. Is your stomach upset?" Eyes up! "Do you need to go to the bathroom?" Eyes up! The right question would eventually be asked... but too late.

One morning a few weeks before, I was walking in from my car. Jimmy Kearns had escaped again, and he came up and greeted me. As we walked back together, he held out his arm. At first I thought he wanted to hold my hand, but I realized he was showing me a new silver medical alert bracelet that displayed his name and medical diagnoses. After I got back to my classroom, my mind wandered back to Jimmy's bracelet, and something clicked. It was so obvious that I wondered why it had taken me so long to come to this conclusion. I realized Ron and Ruth needed written communication, just like the bracelet had communicated with me. Now my wheels were really turning, and I had a lot to think about.

Studying Ron and Ruth's methods of communication should have been part of my basic training at Belchertown—but, as was the case since my first day, I would have to figure out how to help them by myself. My bright, enthusiastic students deserved more. And I had a promise to keep.

CHAPTER 12

Although my main objective for being in the wards was to study Ruth and Ron in their natural environment and gain a better appreciation of their manner of communication, the environment itself and my presence within it was never far from my thoughts. Less than a year ago, I hadn't known Belchertown existed, and I was wrapped up in my own worries about my next step in life. Now I spent my days both haunted by the sadness of my surroundings and overwhelmed with determination to make the residents' lives better.

The wards were identical in size, furnishings, and interior decoration, but each one radiated an individuality that was largely a product of the people who lived and worked there. The ward that housed my female students ran with greater precision than the boys' quarters. The attendants for the girls carried out mundane chores with little chatter. They adhered to bathing, dressing, and toileting timetables and dealt with the everyday tasks of ward living with little emotion. Many of the girls sat silently in wheelchairs lined up at the front of the ward, facing the entrance door. Others were placed in the wooden boxes that lined the walls. Most of the sound in the room came from cleaning and bathing activities or from distressed moans or groans or sighs. The attendants didn't completely ignore the girls—they would sometimes stop to check on them, brush hair from their eyes, or straighten the body of a girl who had slid down in her wheelchair. The girls seemed to reflect the mood set by the attendants' quiet acceptance of what needed to be done. Or was it the other way around?

The boys in Ward 5, it seemed, were a product of a different environment. The noise in their ward was louder and marked by a greater level of activity, not just from the workers but from Dennis, Jack, Danny, and Teddy. Often, attendants or residents played loud music in the room, and I spent enough time there to know that their tastes ranged from rock and roll to folk and occasionally country. (The music selections generally depended on the attendant.) There also seemed to be more personal contact and communication among the residents as well as with the staff. The attendants completed their work, but it seemed to be less scheduled. I never could determine if the staff or the residents set the tone for each ward, but the chatter and motion of the boys disguised the fact that they, like the girls, were isolated in an unstimulating environment.

It was evident that many residents of both wards were loners, and considering the setting, it was easy to see why. There were no books, toys, or other materials to occupy them, so they stared into space, watched an insect fly around, pulled on a loose thread, or sometimes just sat making repetitive movements. Some residents were immobile, with little opportunity for communication or socialization while lying down.

During one visit, I was speaking with Dennis in Ward 5 about how much his math skills had improved when I heard a loud bang coming from the changing area. I looked over and saw that an attendant had tripped after kicking over a tin pail and mop. The stream of soapy water presented another hazard as she slipped, but she caught her balance en route to the commotion at a bed space near the back of the ward. Suddenly, there was motion everywhere. Every person who could walk—staff or resident—moved in that direction.

"What's going on?" Leanne, a newly hired attendant, yelled as she flew past us.

I didn't know, but I was going to find out. I stood, Dennis grabbed his crutches, and we, too, became part of the procession.

At the back of the ward, two attendants were hovering over someone, screaming, "He's choking! He's choking or something."

A man flailed on the floor, eyes wide open and his hands clutched to his neck. Another man sat beside him in a wheelchair.

"He's choking for sure!" one of the attendants yelled as she pulled a few wheelchairs back to clear the space around him.

The man on the floor was clearly in distress; his eyes panned the room, begging for assistance.

Leanne, who had moved in beside him, took charge. "Norman, what happened to him? Was he eating something?" she shouted to the man in the wheelchair.

"Ee ha-in uh sheeshah," Norman said, but just as he did, another resident a few beds away let out a shrieking cry loud enough to mask his words.

"What?" Leanne said desperately.

He calmly repeated, "Ee ha-in uh sheeshah."

I moved in closer to Norman, listening closely. "He said that he's having a seizure."

"But he's not an epileptic," Leanne shot back, her panic growing.

"Ay, ay know," Norman said.

"He said he knows," I translated.

"Are you sure? Are you sure he wasn't eating something and he choked?" she asked again.

"Yea-uh," Norman said, not backing down from his initial diagnosis.

The staff was growing more frantic, which I found somewhat surprising for a group of people accustomed to dealing with crisis in general and seizures in particular. If this was a seizure, it was affecting a person who apparently didn't have a history of epilepsy, and it would be dangerous to attempt to remove a foreign object from his throat or squeeze his stomach. This trembling man was lying on the cold tiled floor, wide-eyed and scared, looking up at the people assembled around him. I felt hopeless, looking back and forth between the man writhing on the floor and the self-appointed rescuer trying to resolve this medical crisis.

Suddenly, without any specific intervention other than the group's silent pleas for the flailing to stop and his breathing to return, the man's body went limp like a wet mop thrown on the tiled floor.

"It's okay, Hank," Leanne said in a soothing voice. "You're gonna be all right."

Bernie arrived at the scene and was quickly given the incident details. With military precision, she began giving orders. "Leanne, please call Dr. Ivanok and let him know what just happened. Someone, give me a hand over here. Let's get him into bed."

The attendants' response was instantaneous. Moments earlier, they'd acted like a regiment without its leader, but Bernie, with little fanfare, put her crew back on track.

I looked back to Norman. He had a face that showed a few days' beard growth, though his bright blue eyes were clear and his brown hair was neatly combed. He was well dressed, wearing a dark green sweatshirt and a pair of brown pants. Even while he was sitting at rest, a tremor affected his arms and head, and I could see a little twitching in his face.

"You saved him," I said.

"Ay-ee knoe-owe," he said. When Norman spoke, he cocked his head slightly to one side in a gesture that appeared to stabilize his neck.

"My name is Howard. Howard Shane."

"Ay-ee knoe-owe."

"Norman, right?"

"Ya-up."

"What do you do around here, Norman?"

"Sae-eevlie lie-ves."

"What was that? I couldn't understand what you said."

"Sae-eevlie lie-ves."

"What? Oh, save lives, you save lives," I said, before he needed to repeat his witty comment for a third time.

"Ya-up."

"Well, you do it pretty well." I paused for a moment, then asked, "Say, how long have you lived here?"

"Ther-tee fayee-v yees."

"Thirty-five years. Then, how old were you when you came to this place?"

"Foe-err."

I congratulated him on his good work with Hank and told him I'd see him again.

What stuck with me from this incident was not so much the sight of Norman as he was now but the thought of him living in this institution for all but four of his thirty-nine years. Born in 1930, he had essentially missed the Great Depression while in this facility. I wondered if the economic tumult had factored into his parents' decision to bring him here. He would have been too young to fight in World War II, but living within the walls of this institution had isolated him from that war and the Korean conflict as well. The sixties for Norman had not been marked by antiwar protests, bellbottoms, or experimentation with drugs. I wondered what he knew about any of the seminal events that had occurred while he spent his days behind these walls in a metal-barred bed. In most respects, the days—and indeed the decades—for him were pretty much the same.

Over time, I came to know Norman and found that he was a gentle man without enemies. I believe for the most part he was content with his surroundings, as deplorable as they were, because he had no sense of what he was missing. His impression of his parents was a memory of near-strangers who visited only occasionally. He had, for all intents and purposes, been raised by three shifts of attendants. When this four-year-old toddler had cried out in the middle of the night because of pain or night terrors, paid workers had held him. No doubt they cared about him. Most likely, they hadn't mistreated him and had probably provided some comfort. Some may even have loved him. But regardless of how I rationalized this experience, "home" was not a word that could be used to describe Belchertown.

Norman had grown accustomed to boredom and a lack of fresh air the way a child from the suburbs grows accustomed to soccer and baseball, dance recitals, and playgrounds. He had learned to expect little and live with little, and that was exactly what he had.

He never complained.

He was a paragon of society's silent abuse.

CHAPTER 13

"You're late," Bob stated, as I plunked myself down on the barstool next to his.

I could barely hear him over the music blaring from the jukebox. I cupped my hand around my ear. "Did you say you're looking for a mate?"

"Very funny," he said. "What's up?"

"Someone had a seizure on the ward."

"Why were you up in the ward this late?" he asked. "Do you think spending the extra time there will get you Teacher of the Year?"

I was silent for several seconds, searching for an adequate comeback. "Teacher of the Year? I'd be happy if they just thought I was a teacher."

"Seriously, why are you spending all your free time up in the wards?"

I brushed my hair back over my ears. "So you want me to be serious, right?"

"For once, yes." He must have sensed I was about to be forthcoming; his shoulders slouched a bit, and he leaned slightly toward me.

"I'll tell you, but I'm warning you: I'm dead serious about what I'm about to say, so if you laugh, I'll have to kill you. The only ones who will miss you are the women in Ward 2," I said. "Bob, I have a very simple reason for being on the ward, and it all has to do with trying to figure out a way to help Ron and Ruth communicate. It just eats at me that those two kids are going through life watching the world happen around them. If I spend enough time up there with them, I think I might come up with a good idea to help them express themselves."

Bob raised an eyebrow, took a swig. "You *are* serious, aren't you?"

"As serious as I have ever been about anything."

"So?" he asked with a grave face.

"So you want to know how I would do it?"

He nodded and sighed.

"Drink another beer," I said. "You're looking way too serious, and you're starting to scare me."

He took another swallow to humor me but never broke eye contact. "So?"

"Okay, here's what we know. They're two typical teenagers except for the fact that they can't control their movements and can't talk. They know how to bring people into conversations by first getting their attention and then responding to multiple questions with easily recognized yes/no signals. They can't initiate a topic of discussion other than by making some noise to get attention, and then they can't express themselves unless a listener guesses the topic or asks the right question. In short, they don't have a set of symbols, like words or phrases, that they can control and manipulate."

Bob sat absolutely still for about ten seconds as he thought hard about what I had just said. I wasn't sure how Bob would react to this. One of his wise-ass remarks might actually help cut the tension in the air.

"It's funny," he said. "I knew everything you said already, but I never put it together in a way that makes so much sense."

Encouraged by this, I continued. "The problem is figuring out what to do about it. But a few weeks ago, Jimmy Kearns pointed me in what I hope is a good direction."

"Jimmy Kearns who lives in the infirmary?"

I filled Bob in on the encounter with Jimmy. "And after I saw Jimmy's medical bracelet, something clicked. I realized Ron and Ruth needed written communication, just like the bracelet had communicated with me."

I paused briefly before charging ahead with the idea that had been spinning around in my mind. "So what if they can't talk?" I said. "Why not just converse by spelling words rather than speaking them? We need to substitute speech with something else, and I see the only choice being written language—spelling. Simple, isn't it? I'll just have them spell instead of talk," I concluded, leaning back in my seat with satisfaction.

"That's all very interesting," Bob replied, "but there's still one small problem: They can barely read, and they can't hold or control a pencil."

I dismissed that with a wave. "All right, so there are a few holes in my thinking, but don't bring me down. Those are just details."

"Sure, but in this case? Details matter."

"Actually, I think I know how to do it." I leaned toward him. "I'm serious here. What are they able to control now? You're the PT."

Bob's brow furrowed. I waited, and then he said with conviction, "Well, they can control their eye movement."

"Exactly! Precisely!" I said.

"Your idea is for them to spell with their eyes?" he asked.

"Yup. I'll have them pick letters and words with their eyes."

"That's all fine, but have you forgotten they can't spell either?"

"More minor details. That just gives school a whole new meaning," I said.

"I like your thought process here," he offered. "I'll be glad to help you try to think through all of this."

"I'd like that," I said, hope surging through me.

Bob held up his beer, as if to toast my developing plan. "But enough about the school for now, okay?"

It was nice to take a break with Bob, but once I got home, my enthusiasm about the communication project kept me up for most of that night. Rather than waste time in bed, I headed to work a couple hours early. The clock in Bernie's office read ten after five a.m. I peeked into Ward 1. It was completely quiet. No residents stirred, and the sparse night shift team sat at the entrance of the tub room in silence. Two were reading, and one heavyset woman sat in a rocking chair normally occupied by a resident, gazing pensively into a room filled with dozens of sleeping bodies.

Unnoticed, I turned and walked alone down the corridor and downstairs to my classroom, where I headed straight for the storage closet. I tossed a few supplies around until I found the clock I had crammed into the cabinet on the first day of school.

Using a screwdriver I'd brought from home, I pried the glass off the front of the clock and broke off the minute and hour hands, leaving only the second hand intact. Using the clock face as my guide, I traced its circumference on a sheet of white oak tag paper. Then, with a pair of sharp state-issued scissors, I cut out a donut ring and inserted it into the clock. I replaced the glass cover and then plugged the cord into the outlet again. Thankfully, the second hand still ticked.

Pleased with myself, I ran upstairs and taped an envelope with Bob's name scrawled on it to the front door of the infirmary. I assumed he wouldn't miss it unless it was removed or he was too hung over from the night before to read his own name. The note read:

Bob,

Before you begin your sadistic torture (or what you affectionately refer to as physical therapy), can you stop by my classroom?

Howard

P.S. In preparation for your visit, you might want to ready the Teacher of the Year plaque.

Just after seven o'clock, Bob stuck his head in the door and gave me a crooked grin. "All right, Shane, make it quick. I have real work to do, and it doesn't include viewing your lesson plans. Truth be told, I'm beginning to see why Mrs. Sharp questions your competence." I didn't flinch. "So... what do you have?" he asked, his expression shifting to genuine interest.

"Take a look at that," I said, pointing to the modified clock that rested on the chalk tray at the front of the room. Around the perimeter of the paper overlay, I had inscribed the names of my ten students at even intervals. "Sit here," I said, kicking a chair with my foot until I'd positioned it directly in front of the clock. I crouched next to the wall outlet to the right of the chair and plugged in the cord. The second hand began its movement around the circle. As it began to revolve, I told him, "Stare at the moving hand, and when it lines up with the name Ruth, I want you to look up just as Ruth would. That will be my signal to pull out the plug and stop the movement of the second hand."

I grabbed the cord and positioned myself in front of Bob so I couldn't see the names on the surface of the display or the movement of the second hand. I focused exclusively on Bob's eyes, waiting for him to give the signal. He didn't take his eyes off the clock face. The moment his eyes shot upward, I yanked out the cord, then stepped behind Bob to confirm that the second hand was indeed aimed right at the intended name.

"Ruth," I said quietly.

"Ruth it is." Bob put aside our characteristic sarcasm and said, "So let me be sure I understand all this. You're assuming that Ruth and Ron will follow the pointer with their eyes and indicate what they want to eat, or answer a question in class, or name the capital of Denmark by giving a signal for the pointer to stop when it lines up with an intended answer, request, and so forth?"

"Yes, exactly!" I said. "If the right vocabulary is contained on a template, they'll be able to give answers independently and not have to rely only on *yes* and *no*."

Bob stood and looked back and forth between the clock and me. "Do you think they'll be able to follow the pointer and read words and phrases on the template?"

"Eventually they'll learn to read the words, but first let's find out if they get the idea of stopping the moving second hand at the right location," I said. "I know they can recognize their own names, so this should be fun for them. And, Bob, to go back to last night—I want you to know I realize that substituting reading for speaking will be a long road. I know this is just a first step."

"Don't get so freaking modest on me," he retorted. "Seriously... this is really a great idea you've created here."

"Thank you. I have marked the moment," I said sincerely.

"Mind if I watch when you introduce this little machine? I'm very curious to see how they do."

I was pleased by his sincere interest and delighted that he wanted to participate, so I too avoided any sarcasm and promised I would wait until he returned before starting the exercise.

At eight forty that morning, when my students still hadn't arrived, I went searching for them. On the first floor, the girls were lined up in front of the elevator door, but the door was wide open, revealing the car was stuffed with dirty laundry. Bernie, who had just walked down from the second floor, told me all the boys were ready for transport and sitting in front of the elevator one floor above.

A workman from the laundry service was hitting all the buttons, but the elevator car didn't respond. "Here we go again, Bernice," he said.

"Yes, here we go again, indeed. George, why don't you empty the bags out into the corridor, and I'll go call maintenance."

Anxious to get the students down to the classroom, I asked, "How long do you suppose before the elevator is running again?"

"Oh, within the hour," she said, winking at George.

"Really? So these girls should stay here and wait?" I said, pointing to my students.

"I meant within the hour, but I didn't specify an actual day." Bernie was trying to make a joke about this, but I could tell by her clipped tone and folded arms that she was frustrated and angry. "To be honest, Howard, this old elevator could be down for the morning or for a week. I just never know. A crew will be here in the next twenty-four hours, but unless it's a fuse or something obvious, they'll have to send out for any parts, because they never seem to have them in the truck with them."

"But what about my students and getting to school?"

As the words left my mouth, I realized I'd made a mistake. Bernie's face reddened.

"I'd like nothing more than to get these children to school, Howard, but I've got a few other things to think about—like getting the soiled laundry out of the hallway, scrubbing the feces off the floor, finding a way to get food onto the second floor so all the residents can eat. You know, little details like that."

"Bernie..."

"Sorry," she said simply, before I could complete my apology. Then, she stalked into her office and slammed the door.

"What about these girls? Should they go back to the ward?" asked one of the attendants.

"Someone run upstairs and find Bob Bergquist," I said with confidence. "Tell him to come down here right away. You can leave the girls in the hallway with me."

In a few minutes, Bob's booming voice filled the stairwell. "Ah, I see the launch has been postponed."

"Oh no, we just have to do lift-off manually," I replied. "No problem now that you're here."

He looked at the now half-empty elevator car and remarked, "Could be a while."

"That's what I've been told. Let's you and me carry the chairs down the stairs to the basement."

"Would there be any *humans* in those chairs you propose to carry down two flights of stairs?"

"Yeah, all the humans in the class. I can see no other way at this moment to get them to school. Dennis and Barbara can walk down the stairs. Wendy and Jack will need the most help, because their carts will have to be carried. The big wheels on the rest of the chairs can roll down the stairs one tread at a time. You'll serve as the safety net."

"Sure, why not? Let's do it," he said—but I detected a trace of reluctance in his voice.

For the next half hour, the students screamed with delight as we transported them down the stairs. As we tilted a chair back while holding the handles, momentum allowed the wheels to easily roll from one stair tread to the next. *Bump da-da bump da-da bump!* Of course, having Bob as the spotter in front of the wheelchair added to my confidence. The kids squealed and laughed as if they were on an amusement park ride. This was an adventure for them.

"Bob," I asked, when everyone was safely in the classroom, "do you ever have those days when you just know that nothing is going to go wrong even when others think that everything will get messed up?"

He just shook his head, smiling. As we arranged the students' chairs, I said, "I hope no one reports us for violating SR 333—the Stair & Chair Transportation Act of 1966."

"What are you talking about?"

"It's in the facility handbook. Safety Regulation 333 states, and I quote, 'No employee can transport any more than eight students per day in either an ascending or descending direction over a flight of stairs.' I think we're screwed because we carried nine students."

I frequently fabricated rules and regulations like this and would spout them to anyone who would listen, including just enough plausible detail to mock the absurdity of some of the school's policies. I couldn't help chafing against the knowledge that many of these rules had the effect of denying freedom, dignity, or human rights to my students and their fellow residents.

Hauling students to school brought out a level of excitement in the students that I hadn't seen before. Unfortunately, it also brought out Mrs. Sharp, who entered my room not more than an hour after Bob and I had finished transporting Wendy—the last student—down the steps.

Dennis spotted her first. "Uh-oh."

"You can say that again, Dennis," she stated, shooting me a lethal look.

"Good morning, Mrs. Sharp," I said, returning her glare with a grin.

"Don't," she said, holding up her palm. "You know very well why I am here."

I dropped the pretense as well as the volume of my voice and said, "Maybe we should take this out in the corridor."

"Mr. Shane, that won't be necessary. I would prefer that we meet this afternoon right after school in my office."

Dennis repeated, "Uh-oh."

With that, she turned and started out the door.

"I'll be there," I offered. "In the meantime, we're about to do something extraordinary as part of our communication curriculum, and you're invited to stay and observe. Mr. Bergquist is here to watch the excitement, too."

She walked away while I was still speaking and, with her back turned, gave a curt, "I'll see you after school." She slammed the door behind her.

"Wow! Do you think she knows about SR 333?" Bob inquired.

"I bet I'm about to be exposed to a whole new set of rules and regulations."

"Seriously, what are you going to say?" he asked.

"The truth, of course. That you made me do it." Before he could react, I took out the clock I'd modified. The morning had taken an unexpected turn, and I was eager to get down to business. "Now it's on with the experiment. Okay, guys," I said, turning to address the class. "We're going to try something new today. Bob, would you mind holding the communicator clock in front of everyone?" I handed the clock to Bob.

"What's that weird thing?" Teddy asked.

"You'll see in a minute," I told him.

"Can-dee, I see candy," Paula said. Paula was correct, for I had taped a Milky Way candy bar wrapper onto the paper collar in the quadrant between twelve and one o'clock.

"Who's the candy for?" Dennis asked.

Wendy piped in. "I like candy, too, everybody."

"We'll talk about candy later," I assured them. "First, I want to see if you know how to point to the candy bar."

Before I could say more, five hands pointed toward the candy bar with sufficient accuracy. Danny, Wendy, and Barbara were not paying attention, and their hands made no attempt to signal. Ruth, Carla, and Ron attempted to move their hands, but their fingers did not point in the direction of the clock. Their eyes, of course, told a different story, because if darts could fly out of their pupils, all three would have hit a Milky-Way-bull's-eye.

I pointed toward the candy myself and explained that using my hand was one way to point at an object. I also informed the group that today we were going to learn another way to point—one that involved the help of an electronic pointer. Then, I plugged the clock into the wall outlet, and the pointer began its slow circular journey. "Everyone, look here at the end of the pointer." As I said this, I kept gliding my finger just below the tip of the second hand. "See it? Look here. Here it is. Now, when it points directly at the candy bar, I want you to tell me by yelling, blinking, or kicking your feet," I said.

My shifting finger and the pointer were approaching the twelve o'clock position. "Get ready! It's getting close!" I yelled. I was, of course, curious about Ron and Ruth's attention to the apparatus and their reaction to what was happening around them. I was delighted to see how interested they were and how their eyes, too, were glued to the moving indicator.

As the pointer reached one o'clock, noise erupted in the room from Jack, Dennis, and Teddy, the boys who could talk and who understood the game. I pulled the plug, and the second hand came to rest between the L and the K on the brown and white wrapper of the Milky Way. I observed that Ron was blinking repeatedly, but I couldn't be sure that he was acting on his own or taking his lead from the others. I couldn't be certain whether Ruth had caught on, either.

"Look at that! The electronic pointer is aimed right at the Milky Way. Does everyone see how this game is played? Now, let's try it again." I removed the tape and placed the candy bar in the vicinity of eleven o'clock. I called on Teddy to answer by himself, because I knew he wouldn't get it wrong, and I wanted to give the class another chance to figure out the new pointing system. I inserted the plug, and Teddy easily pointed out when the pointer and the candy aligned.

I left the candy bar in place and called on Ron. "All right, Mr. Benoit, do you see what to do?"

Ron quickly responded with a definitive *yes* blink.

"Want to try it by yourself?"

Strong blink.

With that, I inserted the plug into the electrical outlet, and the pointer started up. It passed the normal locations for four, five, six, and seven o'clock. All the while, Ron's eyes were frozen to it. Then, it passed eight o'clock. When the second hand pointed between nine and ten o'clock, Ron blinked, and I pulled the plug.

Bob had been looking down from over the top of the clock, watching only the movement of the second hand. When I stopped the motion based on Ron's signal, he shouted, "Yes! He got it!"

"Excellent, Ron! Great job," I said, swelling with pride and relief.

I let the others try it, knowing some of the students were still confused by the task. I wanted to keep their experience errorless, so I provided plenty of verbal help to students who needed extra support.

When I asked Ruth to give it a try, I had little doubt from her smile and confident expression that she, too, would be successful.

"Well, Ruth," I said with a grin, "you seem awfully cocky about being able to do this, so let's just up the ante a bit."

With that, I removed the paper overlay featuring the candy bar and replaced it with the one Bob had experimented with earlier that morning.

"You see this new design, Miss Sienkiewicz? Do you notice that this new template has been custom-made with your name on it? I'm going to start the clock again, but this time, when it points at your name, I want you to let me know, okay?

Eyes up.

"Here it goes," Jack barked out.

"Right you are, Jack," I said. "Here it goes. Where it stops, nobody knows."

The pointer moved around the circle. When it pointed at her name, she simultaneously smiled and looked up.

I pulled the plug, stopping the movement, and said, "Fabulous job, Ruth."

It had worked. Both Ron and Ruth had been able to successfully use the clock device as a pointer. I felt euphoric and energized. I was confident that both of them could manage this kind of assisted communication.

Although Bob probably would have been willing to hold the clock the entire time, we eventually propped it up on the chalk tray at the front of the classroom. Paula observed the switch and said, "Thanks, Bob." I was moved by her appreciation of his effort and her intuitive sense of timing.

"You're welcome," he replied. "Anytime."

For more than an hour and a half, we used the clock face with a variety of templates to identify words, numbers, and objects. Depending on each student's understanding, the same item could be used in a variety of ways. While Paula used a wooden pointer to find the number six, Jack was required to find the answer to the problem, "What is eighteen divided by three?"

Bob stayed for the entire session, enjoying the activity and the successes of the students and—I suspected—thinking about all the possibilities and opportunities this method could open up. I, too, was lost in the moment. I knew as the morning proceeded that I was experiencing what a veteran educator might consider a great teaching moment.

Later on, after the meeting I'd been dreading, I told Bob that this was truly what I called a Charles Dickens day. I reminded him of the famous line at the beginning of *A Tale of Two Cities*: "It was the best of times, it was the worst of times." That morning, I'd had the best of times. The experience with the clock communicator had been more than memorable—it had been magical. I knew this would be a game-changer for many of the students, and it could prove to be monumentally important for Ron and Ruth.

But my meeting with Mrs. Sharp—even before it began, I knew it promised to be the worst of times.

At the end of the day, I entered her office.

"Sit down, please." Mrs. Sharp gestured toward the only extra seat in the room, the same gray metal folding chair from my last visit. I sat down in front of her oversized oak desk, waiting to begin. She remained seated and continued to write as if she were alone, never once looking up. The longer she deliberately ignored me, the more uncomfortable—yet oddly amused—I became. As the neglect continued, I scrutinized her office décor. The surface of the desk was highly polished, but I suspected not by her. The walls were lined with dark wooden bookcases, but only a third of the shelves held books or stacks of papers. The other shelves were conspicuously empty. The only paper on her desk was the single sheet in front of her, which she focused on as if she were penning an amendment to the Constitution. Also on her desk was a two-tiered tray marked IN and OUT and a trifold gold picture frame displaying formal photos of a dark-haired child of about five years of age, a man wearing a light-colored suit, and a woman in a flowery summer dress. That frame was the only personal item in the entire office.

The pen hit the blotter with a thud, and she looked up over her pair of half glasses.

"Mr. Shane, do you mind telling me what that stunt you pulled this morning was all about? Do you have any idea what it means to follow rules and regulations? Are you aware that that kind of recklessness is incredibly dangerous? Those children either go down to school in the elevator or don't go to school at all. Is that clear?"

I wasn't sure she had taken a breath as she barked out that admonishment. "Yes," I started, "but I would like to try to explain. First, I was not trying to pull a stunt or trying to do anything that would harm them. I—"

"Nothing that would harm them?" she shouted, shoving her glasses up into her hair. "You thought carrying children in wheelchairs down two flights of stairs wasn't dangerous?"

"I wouldn't exactly call it dangerous, or at least the way I did it wasn't dangerous. Can I explain about the safety net?"

"No, let's talk about how ill-advised and irresponsible this was of you."

"I wasn't trying to be irresponsible. I was—I'm concerned about the children's education, and I didn't want to lose a day because that overused, old elevator broke down."

At that remark, she yanked her glasses from her head and tossed them on the desk. "That is very noble of you, but that's not an acceptable excuse. I haven't decided how I'm going to deal with this, but for now, just consider yourself on probation."

"Probation?" I felt my stomach lurch as I parroted the word back to her. "What does probation mean?"

"It means I'm going to give some serious thought as to whether you should continue to teach in this institution."

The lurch in my stomach turned into a tightness in my chest, but I wasn't about to back down. I pulled in a deep breath.

"I think you're making a mistake," I said. I sat up straight and looked her directly in the eye. "Look, I'll admit that my actions could be considered a little risky, but I did not blatantly put these children in peril. I put certain controls in place to ensure that they'd be transported safely. I'm making progress over there in that classroom, and it would *not* be fair to those kids to take that away from them."

"Maybe you should have thought about that before you broke the rules."

"There's a rule about how students in the infirmary get to school?" I asked. "I don't mean to be impertinent, but could you tell me the actual rule that I broke?" I really didn't want to be disrespectful, but I did want to know whether there was an actual regulation or if she was threatening me without any real backup.

"You're dismissed for now," she said as she put her glasses back on.

"Just like that?" I asked. When she returned to her paperwork, I knew the meeting was over. Walking out, I turned and faced her again. "Mrs. Sharp—"

She threw her pen back onto her blotter and glared at me. The anger in her expression stopped me midsentence.

"Mr. Shane, you seem to have an unusual way of looking at the residents here," she said. "Don't you understand that they need protection? Whether you want to believe it or not, they're not smart enough to think for themselves. They're retarded, period."

"I don't mean to be disrespectful," I said, softening my tone. It was dawning on me that my job was in jeopardy and all my goals for these kids would evaporate if I was fired. I was ready to grovel if I had to, just to give my kids a chance.

My kids, I thought. They had become *my kids.*

I was tempted to give Mrs. Sharp a lecture, telling her that unless we found a way to get people participating in their communities, the skills we might teach them would be useless. I wanted to tell her that if this institution was to always be the sum total of their world, then all we really needed to teach anyone here would be how to shovel food into their mouths, keep their bodies clean, and wipe themselves. I was trying to understand all sides, but the kids, their needs, and their futures were foremost in my mind.

"I may be an optimist, Mrs. Sharp," I started, carefully choosing each word, "but I'm not completely naive. I know that we label some people as 'smarter' than others, whatever that means, but I don't think putting a sticker on them to make that clear to everyone is necessary. These kids have real potential. I wish you had stayed today to see Ron and Ruth communicate in a whole new way."

"We're through, Mr. Shane," she said abruptly.

I left her office and stood outside on the school building's steps. My internal battery had been nearly drained by this exchange, and I needed a moment to collect my thoughts and recharge. I had to admit it was difficult to defend the stairway incident, because it had in fact been risky, and my spotter defense was weak at best. I did believe, however, that getting the kids to school in spite of the elevator malfunction was a symbolic statement about action and not surrendering to a dysfunctional and archaic school program. Listening to Mrs. Sharp had made it clear that she was genuinely interested in protecting the students from harm, even if it meant walling them off from any possible challenge or danger.

Our confrontation hadn't just been a discussion about carrying kids downstairs. It had been a clash of ideologies. I knew it was useless to try to change her viewpoint, and she no doubt had reached the same conclusion about altering mine. She was entrenched because she supported an ideology dedicated to the idea of difference and separation. I was entrenched because I saw my students as human beings like myself, and I rejected a policy of institutionalizing humans because it was patently inhumane.

I had come to Belchertown—this isolated, restrictive, barren, and rule-based institution—to be a teacher, and that's what I had become. I was no longer the same person I was when I first arrived. An activist had replaced the carefree, newly graduated college boy. I now burned with a mission to alter the course for the residents who were essentially prisoners within these walls. Where I'd always been easygoing, I now found it easy to be oppositional, convinced I was standing on the very highest moral ground.

The danger was that Mrs. Sharp could trump me at any time by pulling rank. She could fire me without a second thought. If I wanted to stay here and keep making a difference, I would have to put up with her and try to find a way to work with her. I would have to be outwardly diplomatic and accommodating to Mrs. Sharp, while quietly becoming more political and radical in my efforts to help my kids make progress.

It wouldn't be an easy task for a wiseass like myself. But for the sake of my students, I'd try my best to change my approach.

CHAPTER 14

O ur class transformed after that first experience with the clock communicator. Among the group was a greater sense of cohesiveness and belonging. Every day, at least one student asked to begin our daily encounter with the clock pointer, and I was grateful that the students enjoyed the excitement that surrounded the experience. And I saw its potential for Ron and Ruth grow by the day.

The gossip going around the infirmary was that something amazing had happened in my classroom. As time passed and more staff heard about the activity, the attendants, nurses, and custodians approached me to learn firsthand about the invention that allowed the kids to better communicate. The notable exception was Mrs. Sharp, who had not been back to my classroom since she'd put me on probation.

Bernie, to my disappointment, wasn't buying all the hype. She called me in to her office one afternoon and asked what had happened and what it really meant. I didn't want to overstate things or mislead her, so I explained how the clock and the pointer had come about and what had occurred so far. Then, I offered an honest appraisal: "I think it could grow into something absolutely great, but I can't claim that what I've done so far is anything more than the first step of a long journey."

"Could Ron and Ruth actually use it?" she asked. I could tell by the hope in her voice that she wanted the story to be more than just gossip.

"They absolutely understood how to use it, but they had to rely on me to pull the cord and stop the pointer. The big trick will be for them to control this on their own—to independently control the moving pointer. That's what I'm working toward."

My chat with Bernie made me wonder if the clock communicator really had been such a great success. After all, they could just gaze toward the words and essentially accomplish the same thing. In some ways, adding the electronic clock just made what they had to do more complicated. I knew in the back of my mind that true success would mean they could select from an entire alphabet all on their own. Independent control had to be the goal. I had to find a way for Ron and Ruth to control and stop the movement of the pointer. It was time for me to pull the plug on pulling the plug out of the wall.

A few days later, while my class was in session and I was talking with Wendy about the details of telling time on a clock, I noticed some commotion in the hallway just outside the classroom. Since activity was rare, except when the students arrived, any movement through the window during class generally caught my eye. On this occasion, I was drawn to the backs of two heads bobbing in obvious conversation just outside the door. I walked over to get a better look and was surprised to find Mrs. Sharp engaged in animated dialogue with two people I'd never seen before: a tall woman in a tailored suit and expensive silk scarf and a balding man in a brown tweed sport coat and red striped tie.

I walked back to Wendy, who was intent on turning the hands of the cardboard clock to show the time, one fifteen. The clock rested in her tiny lap as she fumbled with the minute and hour hands. She stopped suddenly and looked up at me. "Mr. Shane, why doesn't the clock have selectivity?"

I was standing over her cart, watching, when she asked this curious question. From my position, I watched her eyes shift from the clock up to my face. I observed her eyes doing all the work, with no assistance from a head too large to move. Despite the demand this placed on the muscles around her eyes, there wasn't the trace of a crease on the pale white skin being stretched by her forehead. "I don't know what you mean, Wendy," I answered. "What is selectivity?"

"It makes it *move*," she replied, with uncharacteristic frustration.

"She means electricity, Mr. Shane," Jack yelled out from across the room.

Wendy rephrased her question. "Where is electricity for the clock?"

I was about to respond when a forceful knock on the door startled her. All eyes turned toward it. Mrs. Sharp was now peering through the window, a sight that filled me with dread. I patted Wendy on the shoulder and told her this was a different kind of clock with no electricity, and I was proud of her for setting the time perfectly. Danny propelled his wheelchair to the door to open it, and Mrs. Sharp and the two strangers entered.

"Mr. Shane, I want you to meet Dr. Henry Peirce and Dr. Denise Ladd," Mrs. Sharp said, in a tone so amiable I wondered if the Body Snatchers had paid Belchertown a visit. "Dr. Peirce is a professor of communication disorders from the University of Massachusetts, and Dr. Ladd comes from Boston University. I am delighted that they have joined us as our educational consultants. I told them all about the wonderful work you're doing here, and they insisted on seeing it firsthand."

I blinked, shaken a bit. From her agreeable tone, I surmised that for now, all hostilities had somehow been suspended. It was peculiar, to say the least, to observe her transition from cold to congenial. I wasn't sure what to think, but I felt my anxiety around probation begin to dissipate.

"Please, call us Henry and Denise," Dr. Peirce said, extending a hand.

"Nice to meet you both." I shook his hand enthusiastically. "And thank you for the encouraging comments, Mrs. Sharp. We've been hard at work exploring ways for everyone in the class to be better communicators—regardless of whether they can talk or not. Come and meet the students, and they can demonstrate all they've learned."

Mrs. Sharp was biting her lower lip. I interpreted this as nervousness about my impending demonstration, given that she knew nothing about what we had been doing there in the basement.

"Everyone, I want you to meet Dr. Peirce and Dr. Ladd," I said. "Of course, you already know Mrs. Sharp."

Mrs. Sharp drifted away and began to read from a booklet she retrieved from her purse. I sighed a little as she distanced herself—of course, her sudden agreeability wouldn't extend to showing any interest in my students. Henry and Denise, on the other hand, warmly greeted each student as they navigated between the chairs and carts, asking for the students' names and saying something pleasant to each person. When we got to Ron and Ruth, I focused on demonstrating their twenty-questions communication style, so Henry and Denise could see the limits of their current skills and why I was trying to expand them. Without the slightest hesitation, Denise asked Ruth if she liked school and questioned her about what we did in class. I was impressed with how easily Denise learned to ask the right questions to get to the heart of a topic.

"Hey, Mr. Shane, why don't you show them the clock you made?" said Teddy.

I sought out Mrs. Sharp. Very politely, I said, "We'd love to show off what we've all been working on."

"Not today, Mr. Shane," she said. She was still trying to sweeten her tone for our visitors, but her words came out clipped. "We have to finish our tour. Maybe they can come back another time and you can show us all the things you're doing."

"Well, I wouldn't mind looking at this clock," Henry said. I got the sense that he was in full control of his calendar and not particularly concerned about keeping to her schedule.

"Mrs. Sharp," I interjected, "I can do this really quickly."

I interpreted her lack of response as tacit consent. I had won this round, and she knew it, but I was also certain this incident would have consequences. "Thank you, Mrs. Sharp," I said pleasantly. "The children have been waiting to show this to you."

She didn't smile.

"Danny," I asked, "would you mind opening the cabinet? Ed, will you get out the clock?"

Danny wheeled right over to the cabinet, proudly pulled out his key ring, and opened the cabinet door. I studied Mrs. Sharp for her reaction. If this irritated her, she didn't show it. No discernable reaction to Ed's presence in the room, either. I made a mental note never to play poker with our academic director.

Ed pulled out the modified clock and put it on the chalk tray. The class demonstrated the operation of the clock by selecting words and objects on a variety of templates we'd developed since our initial trial just over a week ago. We had graduated to more advanced work than simply pointing out a Milky Way, so our guests were observing templates that contained more difficult material. I had also developed a quieter and less conspicuous way to stop the pointer: by wiring a thumb switch between the clock and wall plug. This allowed the focus to be on the students' ability to time their signals to precisely halt the pointer.

In silence, Henry and Denise watched the first demonstration of the apparatus outside of my class and the close circle of the infirmary staff. It was also the first peek for Mrs. Sharp, who looked on stoically yet attentively. I could tell she was curious, which was highly satisfying.

Both Ron and Ruth made their selections almost perfectly. Ruth's nearly flawless execution was marred by a mistake I attributed to a mild case of performance anxiety. On this occasion, she appeared so nervous that she failed to react as the pointer passed the designated target. The expression on her face revealed exactly what ran through her mind when the indicator glided past the correct answer: "Oh, rats!" She knew she'd missed it, and we all fell silent and stared at the second hand making its way around the clock face. It was as if time itself was at a standstill for the full sixty seconds as we all willed the indicator back around the circle toward the intended word. At last, as Ruth raised her eyes at exactly the right moment, there was a collective release of breath. I moved my thumb, and the arrow stopped.

"Interesting," Mrs. Sharp finally said. I waited, hoping for more, but she simply reminded the consultants they had other places to go and stops to make. Then, she exited, leaving the door open for Henry and Denise to follow her into the hallway.

I was a little disappointed when Denise said her goodbyes and followed Mrs. Sharp out, but Henry lagged behind, telling the class that he'd enjoyed meeting them all. I tried to read his face, but his reaction was noncommittal. I had to admit, I'd been hoping for a more enthusiastic response from both him and Denise.

I began to question the wisdom of showcasing the project in its most basic and undeveloped stage. I worried that Mrs. Sharp might squash the project by suggesting it wasn't part of any approved curriculum. I knew, of course, that if she ordered me to stop I would ignore her, but it would be an unfortunate setback if I had to take the project underground.

I was deep in thought, my students having left for the day, when Henry came back to my classroom. I was at my desk reading about a Cornell experiment, the results of which indicated that children unable to speak due to cerebral palsy could still understand directions. I wasn't surprised by the findings—but, as the article stated, most theories of language development implied that the act of speaking was needed to assist the brain in learning to understand what it heard.

"That was quite a performance by your students today with that clock gadget!" Henry said.

I looked up, startled. I'd been so immersed in my reading that I hadn't noticed him entering the room. "Ron and Ruth are amazing, aren't they?" I said. "In fact, all the students are just so extraordinary."

"Mrs. Sharp tells me you just started teaching this year."

"That's right. I started in September."

"When we were touring the school, she talked about every teacher in every classroom but said almost nothing about you. She made a point of mentioning that this program was different from the other classes." He paused briefly, as if considering his next words. "She said that your classroom wasn't in the school building, and that meant she couldn't keep an eye on you."

I smiled, but I wasn't sure how to respond—or why he had come back to my classroom, for that matter. "Where is Dr. Ladd?" I asked.

"She had to drive back to Boston, but I stayed to learn more about what you're doing here." He pulled up a chair and sat down across from me. "To clarify my role, I'm a consultant to the school and not necessarily or specifically to Mrs. Sharp. I don't work for her, so you don't need to worry about this conversation going back to her."

"That hasn't been the norm around here."

"Well," he said, "I'm going to be on the grounds most weeks for the rest of the school year. How would you feel about my stopping by and watching and working with you?"

"Was this Mrs. Sharp's idea?" I asked.

"No, not her idea. Actually, after our tour, both Dr. Ladd and I thought that yours was the most interesting class we saw. If you agree to my visits, I'll tell Mrs. Sharp that I've decided to spend time in your class."

"And if she doesn't agree?"

"She'll agree, but that's my concern, not yours." He said this with a hint of a grin. I got the feeling that not only would he be back, but he would also enjoy informing Mrs. Sharp about his decision.

"I'm not trying to be flippant," I said carefully, "but what's in it for my kids and for me?"

He smiled. "The simple answer is, you'll have the chance to get my opinion on what you're doing," he said. "I could be a good sounding board for the clock project or react to other ideas you may have. You might even want to try out some of my ideas. Who knows? As farfetched as it may seem, my hanging around might just help you become a better teacher."

I was encouraged by Henry's words. With little hesitation, I said, "When do we start?"

Author Howard Shane, around 1970, at the start of his career and his Belchertown journey. Recently graduated from the University of Massachusetts, Amherst, he took to his first job the philosophy that doing something of personal interest plays a key role in learning.
(Author collection.)

An Austin FX3 Metropolitan taxi (1958), similar to the car Dr. Shane drove in 1969.
(Creative Commons - SG2012, CC BY 2.0 https://creativecommons.org/licenses/by/2.0, via Wikimedia Commons.)

The Belchertown State School administration building, the location of Superintendent Bowser's office.
(From the Donald LaBrecque Collection, courtesy of Katherine Anderson.)

The Stein and Goldstein carousel that greeted Dr. Shane on his arrival at Belchertown State School. The hand-carved horses were gifted by a local benefactor for the enjoyment of the residents.
(From the Donald LaBrecque Collection, courtesy of Katherine Anderson.)

The infirmary building at Belchertown State School during its construction. Dr. Shane's students were destined to spend the majority of their lives in the infirmary and rarely left the building.
(From the Donald LaBrecque Collection, courtesy of Katherine Anderson.)

Dr. Shane's classroom in the infirmary building before he began teaching at Belchertown State School. The classroom, located in the basement, required students to take an elevator to class.
(From the Donald LaBrecque Collection, courtesy of Katherine Anderson.)

Photo of a dance in the auditorium of the schoolhouse building at Belchertown State School.
(From the Donald LaBrecque Collection, courtesy of Katherine Anderson.)

The schoolhouse building on Belchertown State School campus, location of Mrs. Sharp's office and the spring dance. At the time, it was not wheelchair accessible.

(From the Donald LaBrecque Collection, courtesy of Katherine Anderson.)

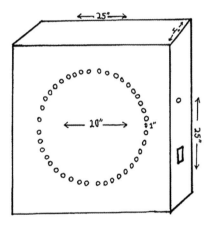

Original design drawing for the Expressor, circa 1970. Dr. Shane helped create the Expressor with two students from the engineering department at the University of Massachusetts.

(Author collection.)

Ron Benoit using an early version of the Expressor in 1970. Lights moving around the circle highlight choices. The student activates a mercury switch on his wrist to stop the lights and indicate a choice.

(Author collection.)

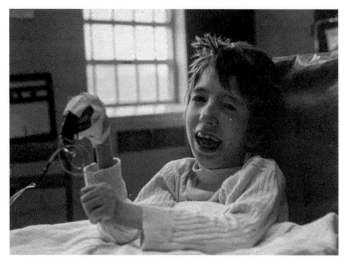

Ruth Sienkiewicz-Mercer with a mercury switch attached to her hand.
(Author collection.)

Bob Bergquist, circa 1970. Bob was a physical
therapy graduate student working at Belchertown
State School during Dr. Shane's tenure.
(Courtesy of Christopher Bergquist.)

Dr. Henry Peirce, Professor of Communication
Disorders at the University of Massachusetts,
served as mentor to Dr. Shane.
(Author collection.)

Dr. Shane speaking at a podium in 1984. Dr. Shane's year at
Belchertown State School inspired him to advocate for individuals with disabilities.
(Author collection.)

Dr. Shane at a podium with Senator John Kerry in 1988.
(Author collection.)

Professor Stephen Hawking with Dr. Shane at Boston Children's
Hospital in October 1999. Dr. Shane contributed to the development
of a computer voice for Professor Hawking.

(Author collection.)

Dr. Shane and Ron Benoit attending a baseball game at Fenway
Park in 2012. They remained friends after Dr. Shane's time at
Belchertown State School.

(Author collection.)

Ron Benoit with his son, Andy Benoit, circa 2010.
(Courtesy of Andy Benoit.)

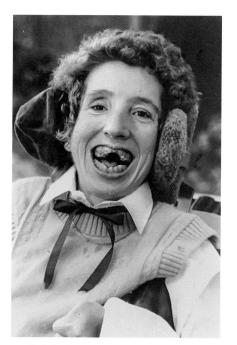

Ruth Sienkiewicz-Mercer went on to marry
Norman Mercer (another former Belchertown
resident) and write *I Raise My Eyes to Say Yes,* a
book based on her life.
(Courtesy of Steven B. Kaplan.)

Ruth Sienkiewicz-Mercer's word
board, with "Howard Shane" in the top row.
(Courtesy of Steven B. Kaplan.)

Dr. Shane accepting the Frank R. Kleffner
Lifetime Clinical Career Award, presented by the
American Speech-Language-Hearing (ASH) Foundation in 2019.
(Author collection.)

Dr. Shane on the steps of the boarded-up administration
building at Belchertown State School in Spring 2020.
(Author collection.)

After my meeting with Henry, I became intent on transitioning the clock communicator from a device that amused the entire class to its original purpose: serving as a communication aid for Ron, Ruth, and whomever else could benefit from it. We needed personalized materials that would give them the opportunity to answer questions or initiate topics. The instructional challenge was to fabricate templates that contained relevant pictures, words, and letters that reflected the content of our lessons. Templates like these would allow Ron and Ruth to participate more and rely less on my interpretation of their answers or ideas.

Thankfully, I had Ed to assist me with time-consuming tasks like cutting out large circles from heavy paper and attaching words, letters, and pictures according to my blueprints. He was glad to help, and his contributions were an enormous time saver. Before long, the clock communicator was being integrated with greater frequency into several facets of classroom life. Ron and Ruth could now answer questions by selecting words or pictures from personalized templates. Other students used it to make choices, whether for a snack or the next activity. I found that the template arrangement was fun to use but also held their focus.

Despite the improvements, I knew my clock communicator had a major drawback: as long as Ron and Ruth depended on others to stop the pointer, the validity of their accomplishments—and even their intelligence itself—might be questioned. I worried that some might believe Ron and Ruth were not communicating independently at all, just observing others' nonverbal cues. I discussed this with Henry, who was almost as enthusiastic as I was about the clock communicator as a communication and educational tool. We decided that one way to reduce the chances of this happening was for me to turn away from the template when I operated the clock for them and only watch the movement of their eyes, waiting for that upward gaze or blink. It was important to me that my fondness for these kids—and my eagerness that they succeed—wasn't somehow influencing the results in their favor. For any potential skeptics, I wanted to make sure there was no question about who was actually controlling the device.

"I'm impressed, Howard," Henry said one afternoon, after my students had left the classroom. "I think the kids—Ron and Ruth especially—are making real progress. They can communicate about so many more subjects now."

"I know," I said. "And I really am happy about that, but..." I trailed off, staring at the face of the clock communicator as if answers were lurking behind its glass.

"What's on your mind?" Henry asked, pulling up a chair.

"I know we're headed in the right direction with Ron and Ruth's communication," I said, "but the thing is, they still essentially depend on me. I want to give them real independence as communicators."

Henry nodded. "So what are you thinking, in terms of next steps?"

"I'm not sure yet. But I know I need to find a way for them to control the device without my help." I gave him a hopeful grin. "Any ideas?"

He thought for a moment. "That's a tall order," he said slowly. "But I'm with you on that, and I know some folks at the university who might have some ideas. Can I reach out to them and get back to you?"

I accepted this proposal with gratitude. As Henry left my classroom that day, I was glad I'd found myself another ally at Belchertown—and excited by the progress we might be able to make together.

CHAPTER 15

Twelve inches of snow in January was not unusual for Western Massachusetts. Because my Austin Taxicab had unusually poor traction, I tried to avoid unplowed or icy roads, but that morning the roads were clear and almost deserted. The solitude made my early, ten-mile commute rather pleasant. The roads within the institution itself were already scraped down to pavement at six forty-nine a.m., but surprisingly I did have to blaze a trail through an unplowed parking lot. I accelerated hard into deep powder and spun my wheels as the taxi's back end slipped and slid its way to the far end of the lot, nearest to where a clear path usually led to the infirmary. Just as I slammed the car door and started shuffling my way through fluffy white powder, the state plow truck rumbled into the lot. Great timing.

I noticed to my right a single set of fresh tracks leading into the thick cover of shrubbery that lined the front of the building. Clearly, one person had marched into the thicket, but no one had yet walked out. I made an educated guess.

"Jimmy Kearns, you come on out here and see me!" I hollered.

After about ten seconds, the back end of Jimmy Kearns emerged from between two leafy rhododendrons. Stepping away, he inadvertently brushed a low-hanging branch, and a clump of snow dropped onto his striking red hair and his shoulders. He was lacking not only a hat but also a coat, a scarf, and gloves; he wore only a flannel pajama top dappled with red fire trucks that had been tucked neatly into a new pair of dungarees. Because all buttons and zippers were intact, I concluded he hadn't been out in the cold for too long. I had no idea whether he had thought to put any coverings on his feet, which were buried beneath the almost knee-high snow.

"Jimmy, you must be freezing," I said through my own chattering teeth, though he didn't look the least bit cold or uncomfortable. Seeing Jimmy standing there, I could imagine the reaming-out that Jimmy and the attendants might receive after a breakout under such harsh conditions.

"I like white snow," he blurted.

"I like the snow, too, but you shouldn't go out without a coat. Come on, buddy. Let's go back inside."

With that, we tramped toward the back entrance, Jimmy trailing just behind me, sliding his feet and staring down at the snow-covered ground. The familiar squeaking noise of leather on snow assured me he was not barefoot. Without another word, we retraced his tracks, which took us (as I had suspected) directly to the back entrance from which he had escaped.

Inside the door, we stomped the snow off, and I looked him over. Jimmy had wisely put on both socks and shoes before heading out, which eased my fear of his exposure to the cold. I figured his absence wouldn't be detected for some time.

"Okay, buster," I said. "You can either go back upstairs to the ward or come down to the classroom with me." I gestured in both directions.

He paused, and I could see him weighing his alternatives. A faint smile spread across his face. "Down," he said, gesturing in hitchhiker fashion at the stairwell over his right shoulder.

When we arrived at the entrance to my classroom, Jimmy stooped down and grabbed a sheet of brown paper that was stuffed partly beneath the door. Without comment, he handed the paper to me. I took it from him, puzzled, and unfolded it.

I read the short message to myself first, then turned to Jimmy and read it aloud. "It says, 'Stop wasting your time complaining around here. Tell Jim Shanks at the *Union* when you get really good and mad.'"

There was no signature or other identifying information. I was completely in the dark as to who had left this note.

"Don't be mad at him."

"Mad at who, Jimmy?"

"Shanks," he said.

"Okay, I won't be mad at him. Maybe we should have Mr. Shanks come visit us. How would that be?" I put that out as a question, realizing I was really making a statement.

"That's nice," Jimmy responded.

With note in hand, I peeked out the classroom door and scoured the hallway, hoping the tipster might still be lingering in the hall. Finding no one, I turned to Jimmy, who was now completely focused on stuffing crayons in a box.

"Jimmy," I said aloud, not really expecting a response, "who do you think dropped off this big idea?"

Later, when Jimmy and I returned to Ward 6, an attendant whose name I didn't know yelled out to us from across the room.

"There you are, Jimmy! I've been looking for you. Now, where've you been?" She spoke to him, but I suspected she was really directing her question to me. It was almost seven thirty.

"He decided to go snowshoeing and then visited with me for a while. Not to worry, he's safe and dry. Right, Jimmy?" I said.

But Jimmy had already left my side and was heading to the dayroom at the back of the ward. I watched him go, still thinking about the mysterious note that was burning a hole in my pocket.

Rather than return directly to the basement, I stopped by to visit Ward 5, which was right next door. As always at this time, it was a very busy place, and all my boys were almost ready to head to the elevator—except one.

Dennis was still in bed with his pajamas on, staring at the ceiling with his hands interlocked and tucked beneath his head. I walked over to his bed, sensing he was in distress but knowing he might not be willing to discuss it.

"Dennis," I asked, "are you feeling well? Are you coming to school today?"

He used his elbows to prop himself up against the bars of his short metal headboard. "I think I'm going to stay here today," he said, turning his eyes from mine.

"Is there something wrong?" I asked.

He looked at me directly, and for the first time, I could see traces of light pink rings around both eyes. He had obviously been crying. "Dennis, what happened?"

"How would you like to be called a retarded moron?" he asked.

I tensed at the slur. "I wouldn't like it at all. Nice people don't use words like that. Who called you that name?" I inquired. It was all I could do to contain my anger. While most staff were considerate and caring, others saw the job as a slog and would talk derisively about the residents within their hearing. This comment was one of the most egregious affronts I'd yet heard in a setting where insults and slurs could easily become commonplace.

"That's what everyone thinks I am," Dennis continued. "That's what they call me."

"Really?" I countered. "Can't be everyone, because I've never said it or believed it, and I'm somebody."

"Then you just think it and keep it quiet."

"Nope, I've never thought it, because you're not."

"Okay, then what am I?"

"You're all kinds of things. You're helpful. You always help the other kids, and you help me in school. You're honest. You always tell me the truth. You're strong. You can do wheelies and suspend yourself on crutches." It was obvious he was appreciating these compliments, probably because he rarely heard them. "Ah, and you're brave. You challenged me on the first day of school, and only a brave warrior would dare to do that."

"But you got me, and I missed."

"So what? The battle was more important than who won or lost. You weren't afraid to do it, so you're fearless, too. And I forgot to mention that you're articulate."

"What's that?" he asked.

"It means you speak very well, and you really do. And I hear some of the girls think you're handsome, too."

"I don't like girls."

"Someday you might. And you're smart, too. You read, do math problems. You're learning how to read a map and even know the capitals of some of the states." I paused, trying to catch his gaze with mine. "Please don't get down on yourself because some jerk called you a name. You're not, you hear? Now, will you tell me who called you that?"

"Nobody."

"Did you say it to yourself, then?"

"Victor did," he admitted reluctantly.

"Who's Victor?"

"A new attendant."

"Is he here now?"

"I don't know. He might be."

"I don't think Victor knows you," I said. "If he did, he wouldn't say that about you. He made a mistake. Do you want me to speak with him?"

"What are you going to tell him?"

"The truth. I'm going to tell him all the great things I know about you. That you're articulate and helpful and smart and honest..."

"And brave," he said.

"Right, and brave, too."

He paused, his face screwed up in disbelief. I could tell he wasn't quite sure if I would actually go talk to Victor.

"Are you lying?" he asked me.

"No, Dennis," I assured him.

"You're really going to talk to him?"

"I will. I promise. But now you get ready for school." I patted his shoulder. "I haven't taught you everything yet, have I? There's still a lot left to learn."

Dennis looked up at me with the smallest of smiles on his face. "Mr. Shane, I think I feel better now." I returned his smile, relieved I could give him some small amount of comfort.

As soon as I left Dennis, I raced down the stairs to the first floor, then down the corridor leading to the front door, where I met up with several attendants leaving the building. I had a hunch about the one male in the group.

"You're Victor, aren't you?" I tried to stay calm, though I could feel my heartbeat quickening. "Do you have a minute?"

"Sure. Who are you?" His eyes were rapidly darting around, not focusing on me. The pitch of his voice was unusually low.

"I'm the teacher from downstairs. Howard," I said, extending my hand. I could see it was shaking slightly from anger. I thought of the mystery note I'd received earlier: *When you get really good and mad...*

Victor was not what I had expected. He was barely more than five feet tall. He wore a crew-cut hairstyle, and although most of his features were sharp, his eyes had a droopy, sad look.

"What's up?" he asked.

"Victor, I'm a little uncomfortable talking about this, but I promised Dennis Russell that I would. He said you called him a bad name." I repeated the slur to Victor with reluctance. "He was pretty distraught."

"Are you sure he said *I* called him that?" Victor asked. He talked slowly, as if gauging each word before he let it out of his mouth.

"Yes."

"Well, I didn't say it." He started shifting his weight from one foot to the other. "I'd never do that."

"I don't know what to say," I replied. "I'm not sure why he would say that if you didn't."

"I have no idea either. Maybe he just dreamed it up. Hey, no biggie. He probably just thought he heard it."

I took a step back and waved my arm for him to follow. "Come on, how about we go and talk with him? That might be a way to straighten it all out. It could make him feel a lot better."

"Who, you and me?" he asked, checking his watch and looking toward the front door. "I—I have to..."

"Yes, and I think Bernie should be there, too. I know she likes to work these things out right away." I'd made that part up, but I assumed she really wouldn't want something like this festering on the wards.

Victor shuffled his feet. "Forget it. I'm not going to do that."

He took a few steps away from me. I took one toward him.

"I'm not accusing you, Victor," I said calmly. "I just want to make it right."

"Look, that kid is a little shit tattletale," he blurted, his pitch rising, "and I'm not gonna let him get me in trouble!"

"Excuse me? What did you just call him?" I asked.

"Who do you believe, anyway? Me or him?"

I thought briefly of the old Chico Marx line, "Who are you going to believe, me or your own eyes?" Victor's next question removed any lingering doubt.

"Don't you think us normal guys ought to stick together?" he said.

I took a deep breath. "I don't know what to say to you," I said evenly, "except that the 'normal' guys I know wouldn't even think to say something like that to another human being."

I shook my head, walked away, and headed straight to Bernie's office to report Victor.

Bernie's initial reaction surprised me. I'd expected immediate shock and outrage, but she started off by emphasizing that she was overall very proud of her staff in the infirmary. For a while, I wasn't sure where this conversation was headed. Would I be viewed as a whistleblower? Or worse yet, would Victor actually get away with this kind of abuse?

"Occasionally, however," she went on, "there are some who shouldn't work with people because they lack compassion and kindness, and it turns out that Victor falls in that camp. Unfortunately, even staff who are verbally abusive to patients are protected by a very powerful union, and it's not easy to terminate them. But," she smiled, "I do have some control, at least, over who works in my building. Let me see what I can do."

I left Bernie's office feeling confident that Victor would not be abusing Dennis or any other resident in her infirmary again. My instincts were right: the next day I learned that he had been reassigned to another building. I could only hope his sudden transfer would cause him to rethink his attitude—or, better yet, his career path. It was only a small victory, as I was left to wonder how he would treat the residents in his new place of work. But at Belchertown, small victories were sometimes all you could hope for, and each one mattered.

CHAPTER 16

I had no idea who left the anonymous note, and as the morning wore on, I became more and more distracted. The reference to the *Union* surely meant the *Springfield Union*, the daily newspaper from Springfield, Massachusetts, located just twenty-five miles west of Belchertown. My contempt for the practice of institutionalization was common knowledge among the Belchertown staff, but to date, my grumbling and objections had yielded only a long list of sympathetic listeners and a shorter list of hostile opponents, especially Mrs. Sharp. My secret messenger might be leading me toward someone who could actually be in a position to bring about change.

By the end of morning class, I was so obsessed with the note that as soon as the students departed for lunch, I headed to the town center to place a phone call. The only pay phone close enough to get me back in time for afternoon classes was in the tavern. In my paranoia, I was convinced that in this town of six thousand people—largely supported by the very institution for which I held such contempt—a rumor about a daytime drinking habit would surface. Nevertheless, my need to find Jim Shanks outweighed that risk.

"*Springfield Union,* how may I direct your call?"

"I'd like to speak with James Shanks," I responded.

"Just one moment." The line remained open, and I could detect the sound of pages turning. Close to half a minute passed before the line was picked up.

"Shanks here." He seemed to drag out his words, as if he wasn't getting enough sleep.

"Mr. Shanks, my name is Howard, and I wondered if you had a minute to talk."

"Depends what we're talking about." He spoke in a monotone, which made me think he wasn't that interested in talking with me.

"I wanted to talk to you about Belchertown State School. I, uh..."

"Just a second. What is your last name?" he asked.

"Shane, Howard Shane, and I am—"

"Is that Shane like the movie *Shane?*" Before I could confirm, he moved on. "What about Belchertown?" His rate of speech had picked up. Maybe he was becoming more interested after all.

"I'm a teacher there, and someone at the institution suggested I contact you about..."

"Who was that?"

"I don't know," I said.

"Let me see if I have this right," he said. "Someone you don't know suggested you contact someone else you don't know?"

"Yeah, I know it sounds a little unusual," I offered, "but I suspect it's because I think innocent people shouldn't be treated like animals and someone at a newspaper should know all about—"

He interrupted me again. "Do you want to speak to me on or off the record?"

"What's the difference?" I asked, fearing that I might sound naive by asking.

"Off the record you're an unnamed source, and on the record—well, you might be identified."

"I don't think it matters to me. Should it?" I asked.

Rather than answering my question, he took the conversation to another level. "So maybe we should meet. Are you okay with that?"

"Yes, sure. Sure, I am. But before..." I paused, trying to find the right words. "Um, can you tell me how the information I share with you might be used?"

"I'm a reporter, and I write about things that others should know about. Isn't that why you called?"

"Yes... I just never talked to a reporter before, and I guess I want to be sure this leads to something."

"Do you know the diner in Northampton?" he asked.

"Sure, the Florence Diner."

"How about we meet there at seven tomorrow night? How will I know you?"

I suggested we meet in the parking lot and explained that I drove a car that was impossible to miss.

"What, do you drive a hearse or something?"

"Yeah, something like that," I responded.

Before I could clarify further, he hung up. I felt relieved that I'd had the conversation, but at the same time, I felt unsettled over the uncertainty it presented. I also thought that for a reporter, he hadn't allowed much time for me to respond before he cut me off.

The short ride back to school did nothing to reduce my anxiety. I wasn't concerned or anxious about sharing the truth, but I was concerned that such a disclosure would mean immediate termination. The reality of telling a reporter about the misery at Belchertown was exhilarating but frightening. It was obvious that I had just shoved myself in an entirely new direction. My quiet battle with Mrs. Sharp—and the administration of the school by association—was about to move off the grounds. Despite all my bravado, was I really ready for this?

Yes, I told myself. Yes, I was. I was prepared to defend what I felt so strongly about, for the sake of the residents of Belchertown.

<hr>

That night I lay awake in bed, thinking about what exactly I was going to tell Jim Shanks. The conditions in my students' wards were bad enough, but there was an even deeper horror to Belchertown, which I'd witnessed firsthand over the past few months on my visits to the other buildings. In the wards that housed residents who were considered to have the most severe disabilities, there were striking differences in the quality of care, the extent of the impersonal connections between staff and residents, and the overall condition of the buildings themselves. In many cases, the residents were treated with gruesome disregard.

I wondered how Jim Shanks would react if I told him about the nursery building, where the youngest residents lived. Diapers often went unchanged, injuries went unnoticed, and gentle human contact was rarely provided by the overworked staff. And in buildings A and K, residents with severe intellectual disabilities were packed together under the supervision of a limited number of attendants. If a resident even wore clothes, they were tattered and ill-fitting and often forced on them by the attendants. No one had been taught how to dress. They were hosed down at the end of the day for cleanliness and ate from pots with their bare hands, as they had never learned to use utensils. The walls in these buildings held no pictures or mobiles, and the rooms were bare of other objects, toys, or anything to keep the residents occupied. Whatever potential the residents had, their abilities were never fostered. Instead, they were left to wither away as days turned into weeks and weeks into years.

What would Jim Shanks say if I told him about the conditions our fellow human beings were living in? Would he react with the horror I felt— or would he believe, as most of society seemed to at the time, that people with disabilities had no hope for a better life?

I had no idea what awaited me at our meeting. But for the sake of my students and their fellow residents, I knew I had to speak out.

I arrived at the diner a few minutes early the next night and kept the motor and the taxi's feeble heater running to try to stay warm. The parking lot was crowded, and several cars along the edge were trapped under piles of snow. Ten minutes after seven, a car drove into the lot and, with little change in speed, swung into the open spot to my right. I pushed down on a lever on the passenger-side door, and the large glass window slid down its track. Freezing air and light snow blew in. The hood, roof, and trunk of the other car still held mounds of snow, suggesting the driver had scraped off just enough to be able to drive, but with a restricted view.

"You were right. You'd be hard to miss," Shanks said as he stepped from his vehicle, slipping a dark stocking cap over his ears. He asked if I wanted to go into the diner or stay in the parking lot. Standing next to the window in the cold, he quickly scanned the interior of the Austin. When he realized there was no passenger seat but instead a wall separating the driver's compartment from a luggage cubbyhole, he drew his own conclusion and headed toward the diner. "Come on," he said. "The coffee's on me."

"Great," I muttered, scrambling out of the car to keep up with him.

Even though it was dinnertime, the smell of breakfast greeted us at the door. Inside the Florence Diner, a distinctive gray granite counter ran from one end of the room to the other and was fronted by a series of round, ruby-red, swiveling vinyl stools. Along the front of the diner were several booths that looked out onto the street. Shanks and I sat down opposite one another in the corner booth, away from the counter, where our conversation wouldn't be overheard. I felt obvious and conspicuous, but no one had looked up when we entered. From our booth, we were able to view the light traffic crawling along snow-covered Main Street.

"Why is it, exactly, that you called?" Shanks asked.

With that question, we both fell silent, and I found myself staring at him. He patiently returned my look, waiting for a reply. As a reporter, he was probably used to moments like this, using the stillness to evaluate what he was dealing with while his conversation partner decided on what to say and how to say it. I had practiced an especially earnest and articulate monologue all afternoon, but now that I was actually sitting across from him, I feared I might come across as just a meddler or a rumormonger. I was also aware of my age and how he might view the reliability of someone clearly in his early twenties.

I put that thought aside for a moment. It might not make any difference what I told him, or the discussion might result in something positive for the residents. By my calculation, the worst-case scenario was that anything I said could further anger and alienate the administration and lead to my termination. I willed myself to take a calm, steady breath.

"I haven't worked at Belchertown for very long," I began, "but I've been there long enough to know that the way people live there—it's no way to treat a human being."

Jim leaned forward, his expression suggesting that nothing else in the world mattered except the words coming out of my mouth. It felt good to vent, and even better to have an eager listener.

I continued. "Someone—as I said on the phone, I don't know who—left me a note suggesting that I speak with you. I guess they did this as a way to enlarge the network of people I complain to about the conditions at the 'school.'" I made air quotes, believing he would understand the sarcasm. "I suppose you can tell that I'm vocal about my opinion, but talking with you certainly changes my audience."

"It took guts to make the call, though, and even more to actually show up tonight," he said. "A lot of people back out."

I contemplated this. "I don't know about guts, but I guess I've got less to lose than most of the other people who work there. I haven't been at this all that long, and no one in my family lives in Belchertown or works at the school. I'm the stranger who dropped in one day and is now creating a minor disturbance by breaking a few rules and talking openly about problems. And, by the way, in the middle of that, I try to do some teaching."

He smiled. "I've been working on a story about the state school for a while. I'm pretty sure the person who told you to call knows that. It hasn't been easy to get inside information. That school is a closed community. The superintendent refuses to give me access, says it's against—"

"Let me guess: state regulations."

He nodded. "Like I said, your anonymous note no doubt came from someone who's aware of what I'm preparing and thought you would be a good ally. I have to ask, what do you want to get out of this?"

"Nothing!" I said, almost before the question departed his lips. "Well, nothing but the satisfaction of knowing that more people, people beyond the walls of Belchertown, can learn about the way people live inside that closed community. I guess for me, it's about awareness—an awareness that people are being cast away and treated like animals just because they don't look or move or communicate like most other people. And all of this is sanctioned by the state."

"You should know that talking with me won't improve your popularity." As he offered this warning, he dabbed his napkin at a ring of spilled coffee left over from the waitress's first pour.

I started to tell him that I couldn't care less, but stopped talking when the waitress strolled over to check on refills. We both shook our heads without looking at her.

"I don't care about being popular," I told Shanks as the waitress walked away. "I have enough friends."

"It's fair to say that the story I intend to publish will likely shock, affront, and upset a number of people," Shanks said. "It will be as graphic and detailed as I can make it, and I hope it will get people's attention. But it won't be my life's work, and after it's published, I will move on to the next story. Don't misunderstand me. I hope it puts a stake right through the heart of the state, but it might not make any difference whatsoever."

"But it might," I offered sincerely.

"Maybe—especially if there's some public outcry. Or some politician who jumps in all outraged and decides to respond, because he calculates that he can better his career by taking this on as a cause. But from what I've learned so far, that's unlikely."

"Why do you say that?"

"Because people with disabilities don't vote, for one thing, and talking about them may not necessarily gain any voters, either. In fact, it may do just the opposite."

"So... you're saying we're just wasting our time? Or I'm wasting my time?"

"I didn't say that," he countered. "All I'm saying is that you should be realistic about what talking to me can do—or the possible outcome of any piece I might publish. If you want to tear the place down, you might be more successful with a bulldozer than a printing press."

"Have you been there? Have you seen the way people live in that place?" I asked.

"I have. I've even toured A and K buildings," he said.

"Then you certainly don't need me to tell you how horrific it is. A and K are the worst."

"They are indeed," he agreed, his expression grave. "But—before we discuss conditions in those buildings, I'm curious to know more about you. Why don't you tell me what exactly you teach and what drew you to take this job at Belchertown?"

It occurred to me that he probably needed more assurance that I was legitimate. Our waitress returned to the booth and quietly refilled our coffee cups, this time without asking. As she tidied up our table, I paused and thought about his question. Shanks looked out the window and tracked a car making its way past the diner.

I confessed that I'd gone into teaching to avoid the draft—a polarizing admission in January of 1970, but I wanted to be honest with Shanks. I told him how I'd set out to be a history teacher, was drafted anyway, and drifted into the Belchertown job when an unexpected medical problem ended my military career.

"Anyway, I found myself in a position I wasn't really trained for, but it was education, so I grabbed it. It's become clear to me that not many people want to teach those with disabilities or work in an institution like Belchertown."

I paused briefly, trying to gauge his reaction, but he just sipped at his coffee.

"Initially I hated working there," I continued, "but once I got used to the place, the students, and being a teacher, I became obsessed with the job, so now it's a main focus of my life. Actually, I'm probably a little too involved—a little too close to it, but the residents got to me, and I want more for them. I want to see change. I want the residents to live better, fuller, freer lives. And I guess just talking to you means I've become more public in my opposition to this institution and what it's doing to those who are forced to live there. On this front, I'm willing to take the extra step. I'm willing to be at the head of the protest line, carrying the biggest sign, to go way out on a limb, to sacrifice in some way—in any way." I paused, then said, "I'm even willing to lose my job."

For the next hour, our conversation became more animated and intense as I told Jim Shanks about conditions in the infirmary and the subtle and the not-so-subtle humiliations and indignities that came with living in the institution. I didn't hold back when he asked about the administration, policies and regulations, staffing, or conditions of the buildings and grounds. It wasn't all bleak, though; he was clearly amused by my stories of the residents and seemed to enjoy learning about their accomplishments, their interactions, and their lives in general. My classroom, I explained, was a safe haven and a time for learning and fun and freedom.

Shanks became silent for a moment, his eyes following a snowplow on the main road in front of the diner. "I really appreciate what you had to say tonight," he said. "You know, hearing about your classroom makes the story I want to tell even sadder. It speaks to the reality that these are human beings we're talking about, and they have to endure conditions most would consider inhumane. I just hope drawing attention to this will make the right people want to do something about it."

I nodded. I hoped so, too.

We looked around the diner and noticed that the only activity was our waitress and an aproned teenager with hair down to his waist moving about the room, clearing dishes and straightening tables. My watch read ten after ten p.m. It was hard to believe we had been talking for a solid three hours, but I was glad to have found another ally and a way to make some changes at Belchertown—even if it meant that I burned some bridges in the process.

CHAPTER 17

B ecause of the mysterious note—followed by a preoccupation with my
whistleblower experience—I had given little thought to my conversation with Henry about creating a new version of the clock communicator.
However, I was not surprised to learn that he was true to his word: he had
indeed spoken to his contacts, and he'd arranged for me to meet Allen Fitch,
a professor in the School of Engineering at UMass.

It was early February when I stood at his door for our four p.m.
appointment. Professor Fitch was sifting through a pile of papers on his
desk. I suppose the sound of my approach alerted him—without looking up,
he waved me in.

"Sit, sit," he said, his face just inches from the papers. Still not looking
up, he pointed to the only free chair in the room. "How do you spell your
name again? I can't seem to find a Shea in my class roster. What course is
it you're taking?"

Before I could clarify the reason for my visit, the phone rang, and
he grabbed the receiver on the first ring. "I'll be there in ten minutes," he
shouted and hung up.

"Professor Fitch, I'm not one of your students," I said. "I believe Henry
Peirce has spoken to you about me. I'm a teacher from Belchertown State
School."

He looked up for the first time, and I took in his thin quizzical face
and unkempt leaf-brown hair. "Ah," he said. "Yes, I do recall speaking with
Henry about this. Remind me again about the specifics."

I told Professor Fitch about Ron and Ruth, and how they were able to
comprehend but not speak. The problem, I emphasized, was that they had
no way to independently express themselves. As I spoke, he ran his fingers
through his disheveled hair, and his arms and torso seemed to be in constant motion. I could tell he was listening intently, though.

I told him what I had done to date with the clock pointer and speculated that a real solution might be an electronic device that my students
could manage by themselves. "I believe an engineering solution is the key
to solving the problem," I said.

"Fascinating, just fascinating," he said. "I would like to come out there and see how I might help."

"That would be great." I was stunned and delighted that it had taken so little effort to get this distinguished UMass professor involved.

He grabbed his jacket and headed toward the door. "Let's go! Time's a-wasting!"

"Great!" I responded, getting up quickly to follow. "But... don't you have another meeting or something?"

"Actually, when I thought you were one of my students, I pushed a button that I installed under my desk. It makes my phone ring. I do it to shorten meetings I think are going to be uninteresting." He smiled at me. "This meeting was far from uninteresting."

On one hand, I thought his electronic solution to what he perceived as an irritating human problem was ingenious, but on the other, I was relieved I wasn't one of his students. Maybe while he was at Belchertown, he could help devise a device that would warn me when Mrs. Sharp was near.

Professor Fitch assured me it would be no trouble to drive me back to retrieve my car from campus after his visit to Belchertown, so we agreed to travel together. The black V8 Ford Mustang we climbed into was not the vehicle I had expected the professor to drive. I liked the guy more with every passing minute.

On our trip, the muffled growl of the 289-horse engine played background to my lengthy description of Ron and Ruth's difficulty with accomplishing purposeful movement. I told him that to gain control over a communication device, we would have to find a movement that Ron and Ruth could exercise consistently, repeatedly, and with control. He started asking questions: Can they point by hand or foot to a target on a table? Could they control the movement of their head from side to side or move a knee left or right? I explained that they were able to make these movements, except for pointing, but could do so only inconsistently and with great effort. I added that the harder they tried to perform a specific movement, the more flustered they seemed to get and the harder it became.

When we turned left out of the center of Amherst onto rural Route 9 west toward Belchertown, the questioning stopped and the professor and the car both heated up. Without warning, he zigzagged past several cars, gaining speed as he passed each one. Adding to the drama, his lips moved slightly, and I actually heard him say as we passed a car, "Screw him!"

I was shocked but mostly scared. "You don't need to be in any hurry, Professor Fitch. Everyone will still be there when we arrive. No one ever leaves Belchertown."

He just smiled.

It was a little after five p.m. when I unlocked the front door of the infirmary—just two hours since I had left for the day for my meeting at the university. Rather than launch into any rants about horrid conditions and how inhumane it was to imprison innocent people, I simply ushered him in. He covered his mouth with the sleeve of his wool sport jacket and stared at me, wide-eyed and speechless. Knowing his senses were in free-fall, I offered my personal remedy.

"Mouth breathe!" I whispered, as we left the fresh outdoor air behind. "You'll get used to it."

We worked our way down the upstairs corridor to meet with Ron and Ruth. Attendants wheeled stainless steel food carts to the different wards, preparing to feed the building's two hundred residents. A few residents walked along the hall as they made their way to the small dining room. I rarely saw this much activity in the corridor, but then again, I was hardly ever there this late in the day.

At the entrance to the girls' ward, I held open the swinging door. The color drained from Allen's face as he stood there openmouthed, seemingly paralyzed, just peering into the room. I had forgotten what Belchertown did to the unprepared visitor. From simple daily exposure, I was becoming accustomed to the sights and sounds of this setting—the children left alone in beds or on tables, the smell of diapers and dirty laundry, the stark surroundings, the occasional moans. I would never consider it acceptable, but I'd grown used to it on some level.

I pointed to Ruth, who sat alone by her bed. Allen didn't budge from the doorway.

"No way," he whispered. "No way."

"I know it's awful, but let's go over and meet Ruth so we can head back out."

"I can't go in there," he said under his breath. "I mean it!"

Thinking quickly, I suggested we go downstairs to the classroom and away from all of this.

At first I was a little taken aback by the professor's inability to deal with the sensory experience of the girls' ward, but I reminded myself how shocked I had been on my first visit here.

"Sure, sure, just not here," he insisted, and quickly headed back down the corridor. I followed him out, and when I caught up to him, he was waiting to be released through the locked main door.

On the sidewalk outside the building, I had an idea and asked if he minded waiting for me. I rushed back into the building and turned right toward Wards 3 and 4, where the older women lived, and approached an attendant named Grace. "I need a huge favor, and I'll understand if you can't do it," I said.

"Okay, I can't do it," she said, without concealing her smile. "What's the favor?"

"I'd like you to escort Ruth Sienkiewicz from Ward 1 and Ron Benoit from Ward 5 to my classroom."

"When, *now*? Before or after I feed, bathe, and then tuck twenty people into bed?"

"I know this is a lot to..."

"Give me ten minutes," she said, and hurried off into the ward.

I found Allen standing in the same spot, staring at the ground. He had gained his composure.

"Sorry," he said. "I just couldn't."

"It's my fault," I said. "I forgot how awful it is to see all this for the first time. Before we give it up entirely today, I might have a less stressful solution."

Professor Fitch walked beside me to the back door—which, to my astonishment, was unlocked. The first unlocked door I'd encountered in all these months. It felt like a sign. After locking it behind us, we went to the classroom. He seemed fine in this quieter part of the building.

My classroom looked strangely different—not because there were no students, for I was often alone in the room. Dusk gave the room a sullen and cheerless look. I quickly turned on the light and led Professor Fitch to the corner where I kept the clock. Attached to its face was a template with several letters left over from a lesson I'd led earlier that day.

"So, this is it?" he asked earnestly.

"I sit here," I said, pointing down at the seat I was already occupying, "and the moment they give the signal, I activate this switch." I pointed to the switch I had installed on the electric cord connected to the clock and the wall plug.

A commotion in the corridor briefly interrupted us. Moments later, Grace pushed Ruth into the room, followed by another attendant pushing Ron's chair.

"Right there is fine," I said, "and thank you so much. I know this wasn't easy."

Grace grinned. "Anything for these two, but you'll have to get them upstairs yourself. We have to help finish with dinner."

"Do they know upstairs that these two hellions are down here?"

Ruth looked up sharply before either of them could respond.

"Guess they do," I said, smiling at Ruth. I looked over at Ron, and he flashed a quick blink that signaled he, too, was in the clear.

Professor Fitch appeared to be a different person from the traumatized man who had gone nearly boneless upstairs. "My name is Allen," he said, looking back and forth between Ron and Ruth. "Mr. Shane has asked me to come meet you to see if I can help find a way for you to control that clock over there."

"Okay, guys." I pulled up a chair to face them. "I want you to show Professor Fitch how you control the clock pointer. All set?" I began with a series of general informational questions, with Ruth and Ron answering almost simultaneously.

"Can you guys look at the door and then blink three times?"

Both complied without hesitation or error.

"Is three bigger than two?"

Ruth looked back at me as if to say, "Give me a break." Ron blinked, and Ruth gazed up.

"Is my name Richard Nixon?" I asked.

Ruth squealed. Both indicated no, Ron by turning his head to the right and Ruth by pursing her lips.

I gave this brief quiz not only so Fitch could observe how they responded, but also to reinforce the idea that their comprehension was not compromised by cerebral palsy.

Then, I turned to the real reason for our early-evening visit: namely, to identify consistent body movements that might facilitate their ability to independently operate the device.

I asked both Ron and Ruth to move parts of their body to figure out whether they could execute any movements other than eye-rolling and blinking with ease and consistency.

Fitch's intense focus shifted between Ron and Ruth as they tried desperately to comply. Although a few movements were performed with relative accuracy, other attempts resulted in little—if any—of the movements I asked them to complete. We saw the desire to complete the tasks in their eyes, but they couldn't will their muscles into action. Professor Fitch looked sad but thoughtful while tracking their movements and the anguish that accompanied each attempt. He didn't utter a sound, just slowly tapped his right index finger against his chin.

Next, I tried to look more closely at the movements each student had shown the most promise of controlling. For Ron, that meant moving his head from side to side or moving his wrist. When I asked him to turn his wrist as though looking at a watch, Ron surprised me by rolling his arm successfully. Ruth's attempt at that was less successful, so it was clear that this movement would not work for her. She performed more accurately, however, when I asked her to pretend she was lowering her arm in and out of a bucket of water.

I moved between them and said, "Now try to elbow me in the stomach." They tried to extend their elbows to reach my belly. "Come on, Ron," I kidded. "You wouldn't hurt an old man, would you, Ruth?" I was happy to see they were enjoying themselves despite the tremendous effort I knew they were making. I tried to imagine what it would feel like if I couldn't reach immediately for something I needed, scratch an itch, or remove a seed from between my teeth.

I tried one more exercise with them: I waved my watch and asked them to track it with their eyes as I moved the timepiece in a circle. As I did this, Fitch said, "You're getting sleepier, sleepier." I asked him to be quiet, but both Ruth and Ron laughed energetically.

"Okay, kids," I said. "One last question: Do you like school?"

It was heartwarming to see Ruth's immediate eye shifts and the intensity of Ron's blinks.

At this point, we'd been at this for about forty-five minutes, and everyone looked tired, including Professor Fitch. I knew it was time to wrap things up. "Allen, can you wait here with Ron while I take Ruth upstairs? I'll be right back for him."

Fitch interjected immediately: "I can push my new friend myself, if you don't mind. I can handle that job just fine."

I learned a great deal in the infirmary that evening. I was reminded that walking into a reeking ward that housed forty human beings in metal beds and cribs that were not unlike cages was paralyzing for a first-time visitor. It had been no less so for me—I had just tried to cover my dismay with humor. The shocking and disturbing images, and the associated sounds, smells, and restraints, were so foreign to those of us who lived in the world outside those locked doors. As uncomfortable as Professor Fitch had been at first, he was relaxed, gracious, and comfortable after he'd spent a little time getting to know Ron and Ruth.

I knew he completely understood the urgency of our task ahead: giving these bright teenagers control over their communication.

Two weeks to the day after Professor Fitch's visit to the infirmary, Bernie came to my classroom to inform me that there was a telephone call for me in the office. "It's a professor from the university," she said with an encouraging smile. She volunteered to hang out in the classroom while I took the call upstairs.

"Hello?"

"Howard, Allen here."

"Hi, Professor Fitch. How—"

"Can you be on campus at three p.m. tomorrow?" he said.

"Uhh, sure. See you then—" The line went dead. "Yes, I'm fine, and you?" I said to no one at all. Then, I hung up the receiver and headed back down to my classroom, feeling curious and optimistic.

The next afternoon, after leaving Belchertown a bit earlier than usual to make it to the campus, I discovered two guys—presumably students—standing next to the entrance to Professor Fitch's office. They were pressed against the wall, one looking half asleep and the other just bored. The taller of the two, a guy with dirty-blond hair and wireframe glasses, dressed in jeans and a wrinkled plaid shirt, did awaken enough to acknowledge me by nodding. The bottom of his shoe rested on a white wall that contained scores of scuffmarks, no doubt the product of indifferent poses by many other daydreaming students. I asked if Professor Fitch was inside. The bored guy, without dropping his straightforward stare, answered, "I think so."

I went ahead and knocked. No answer. After about thirty seconds, I gave the door two more solid hits, waited, and still got no response.

I was turning to leave when the door opened slowly to reveal Professor Fitch, who was pressing a phone receiver to his ear and signaling for us to be quiet. When he was certain we understood how we were to behave, he motioned for us to come in. Dutifully, all three of us marched in, stopped in front of his desk, and awaited his next instruction. The hand doing all the gesturing pointed first at me and then to the one empty chair none of us had felt comfortable sitting in. I obeyed and sat. The other two folded their hands and stared passively at the floor in front of them.

Allen continued to hold the phone to his ear, occasionally muttering, "Uh-huh," and, "Yes," and rolling his eyes as if to say, "Can you believe this?" Had it been anyone else besides a guy who conveniently dialed his own number to circumvent face-to-face encounters, I wouldn't be so suspicious that this was nothing more than a two-way conversation with himself. Eventually I heard him say, "Good, good, glad you have one. Could you mail that to me at the university?" Then, he hung up without saying goodbye. "Have you boys had a chance to talk together about any of this?" he said to the three of us.

"Professor Fitch, we haven't really met," was my reply.

"Then why don't you introduce yourselves while I go see about a bigger room with a blackboard?" he said.

It occurred to me that removing himself from the introductions would enable him to avoid the embarrassment of not recalling names he should know. It also gave him a convenient way to minimize human interaction. He disappeared out the door, and Bill, Thomas, and I made our introductions. We all seemed more at ease now, as if Professor Fitch's instructions to become acquainted had been permission to act naturally.

Thomas was the one who had acknowledged me earlier in the hallway. Bill had a dark complexion, wavy brown hair, and brown eyes, and he was dressed casually in jeans and a plain maroon UMass t-shirt. It turned out they were students in the engineering department and had volunteered to work on a special project that Professor Fitch had announced in class.

Allen beckoned us to a conference room down the hall, where he wasted little time assuming the role of professor. "What we have before us," he began, "is what I consider a complex applied human factors engineering problem. And by that, I mean we have a circumstance in which people are unable to perform a certain task that many other humans perform quite easily, like kicking a ball, squeezing toothpaste, turning on a light switch, or talking. Now, Howard here has been trying to find a way for his students who have cerebral palsy to be able to express themselves when they can't talk. He has come up with part of the answer by using an electrical alternative, the second hand of a clock, as a way of pointing to desired information. As clever as this approach might be, the students still can't stop or start the clock by themselves, so the role of engineering—the human factors problem—is to find a way for the students to operate the pointer independently."

I was spellbound by how effectively he had delivered his overview of the problem, captured the advantages of the current approach, and then pointed out what still needed to be accomplished.

After a brief pause, he continued. "So, on one side of the equation we have human beings with a very real human predicament, and on the other side we have the need to discover a viable engineering solution. I want you to think like engineers in order to design and build the remedy." As he made this last point, he pointed to Bill and Thomas with a piece of chalk.

Suddenly, I was nervous. I didn't doubt they were intelligent and eager, but I did worry that a complex problem was about to be assigned to rookies. Once again, I was in for a surprise.

Professor Fitch then turned to the chalkboard and, without uttering a word, proceeded to create a three-part drawing. First, he drew a clock face, including the numbers one through twelve, and in the middle of the circle he placed a line with a pointer to signify the second hand. About a foot to the right of the clock, he drew a rectangular box and wrote the letters *ICB* inside the rectangle. About a foot from the box, he sketched a stick figure.

"This represents the existing display, which lets the kids indicate what they want to say," he stated, pointing to the clock face illustration. "And this, of course, symbolizes the kids." He pointed to the stick figure. When he pointed to the rectangular box, he said, "ICB stands for independent control box." Finally, he drew a line connecting the clock to the box and another connecting the box to the arm of the stick figure. "Here is where we come in," he explained, pointing again to the ICB rectangle. "This box is going to take a signal that comes from a movement made by a student, which starts the pointer moving. The movement by the student back in the opposite direction causes the pointer to stop."

"But how is the ICB box going to know that the student has moved?" I asked.

"Good question. If Ron or Ruth could simply push a switch like the button on a doorbell, they would press the button, and instead of the doorbell ringing, the pointer would move. It does this because the control box interprets when the button is pushed or not pushed, and it sends that message directly to the moving pointer. But as we know, we need to be more creative and take advantage of movements Ron and Ruth can make to control the switch, right?"

"Right," I said, eager to hear what he was proposing.

"When I observed them, I realized that although they both have the same condition—cerebral palsy," he clarified, as an aside for Bill and Thomas's benefit, "they don't move in the same way. Ruth moves very slowly, and Ron's movements are jerky. We need a switch that both can operate. What I thought might work is a switch called a mercury tube signaling device, or simply a mercury switch. It's a small glass tube filled with liquid mercury. When the tube is tilted to one side, the liquid mercury rolls down the tube and completes a circuit. When the circuit is closed, the arrow moves. When moving the tube back to its starting position, the mercury streams back, the circuit breaks, and the arrow stops."

"How would that work for Ron and Ruth?" I asked.

"Well, imagine one of these mercury switches placed on the kid's arm, leg, or head," he said. "Instead of pointing at a button to control the pointer, they would have to change the position of their arm, leg, or head, and that would cause the mercury to run and the pointer to move. Just think of all this as an indirect way to link a student to the clock face. By moving the body part containing the mercury switch, they'd be able to independently stop or start the pointer and indicate what they want to say."

I was getting excited. "So how would we go about getting one of these switches?"

"We'll have one shortly," he said. "That call I was on when you came in? I was talking with a supplier to the department who just happens to have a mercury switch and will ship it here in a few days."

Allen clarified the design of the ICB for his students—who, to my delight, seemed to comprehend his instructions and to speak the same technical language.

"Professor Fitch," Thomas asked, "does it matter if the power for the system is direct or alternating current?"

"Good question," said Fitch. "I think that as inconvenient as it might be to use alternating power and have to plug the system into a wall outlet, a battery-powered system might run out of energy right when one of the kids is in the middle of making a choice."

Thomas nodded his head throughout Professor Fitch's answer. I could tell he was genuinely pleased with the response and not just being obsequious.

Before we departed, Allen indicated that the interface box was part one of a greater engineering adventure. He suggested that the interface box circuitry would eventually be transferred to another device he had in mind that one day would replace the clock. "But enough for one day. I'll be more specific about the new device at another time." He left the room without looking at us again or saying goodbye.

The up-and-coming young engineers left in the room with me had not yet adopted Allen's impolite manner. They stood to shake hands with me and exchange goodbyes. I didn't hold back my enthusiasm for what they were about to do on behalf of my students and invited them to visit the classroom anytime.

It was just after five when everyone had finally left the room. I learned the time from reading the clock that hung over the chalkboard. It was another round-faced clock, nearly identical to the partially dismantled one that now sat in the corner of my basement classroom. Both clocks had started their mechanical lives with an identical purpose: simply show-ing the time of day. This clock had stayed true to its original goal, just like

I thought I would back when I'd entertained thoughts of becoming a history teacher. But my classroom's version of the clock had, like me, taken on a much more unlikely role. We were both a little battered and disheveled, but we were serving a higher purpose now, and that made me smile as I clicked off the lights and closed the door behind me.

CHAPTER 18

As the school year passed, Dr. Henry Peirce continued to visit the class and participate in whatever activity was on the schedule. It didn't matter whether we were engaged in math, reading, or another kind of lesson: he was always up to the challenge of discovering ways to accommodate each student's level of understanding and unique style of learning. After the students left each day, he offered insightful suggestions about teaching techniques and strategies. At first, I'd felt self-conscious having someone observe my teaching, but I was getting used to having Henry hang out in the class, and I came to enjoy and appreciate his presence. That was also true of the students, who seemed to welcome his friendly participatory and observational style. I noticed that over time, Henry too revealed his growing comfort by removing his sport coat or loosening his tie during class.

One afternoon in mid-February, just after everyone was out the door, Henry said, "I've been wondering about that poster." Pointing to a sheet of oak tag above the entry door, he said, "What are those slogans all about?"

> **STUFF TO THINK ABOUT**
> 1. *Self-determination—make your own decisions!*
> 2. *Be as self-sufficient as you can be!*
> 3. *Self-respect yourself!*

I explained that the clubhouse where I'd played sports in high school had a slogan board, too. "Our coach had two sayings over the door going out to the field. The first one was 'when the going gets rough, the rough get going,' and the second was 'winners never quit and quitters never win.' Now, I know those sayings weren't the most original, and I'm not sure they actually affected the outcome of any games, but I did think about those words back then, and I never forgot them."

Henry smiled. "So you put up your own catchphrases there to pump up your team."

Henry had a way of focusing on what I was saying that made me think my ideas were meaningful and really mattered. It startled me to realize how much I had come to value Henry's opinion of my goals, lessons, and approaches. I smiled back at him—but a part of me also wondered if Henry thought my slogans were trivial or simplistic. I decided he wasn't trying to embarrass me; he was just interested in why I had displayed them.

I felt shy talking about my teaching philosophy, but the slogans were up on the wall for all to see, and I wanted Henry to understand my thinking. "These three slogans all have to do with the same thing: self," I said. "As I added to the list, I began to realize that the focus of my teaching was on developing the students' sense of self. Because there's so little room for the development of individuality at Belchertown, I had to try to create a space for it."

I paused to gauge Henry's interest. He seemed engaged, so I pressed on. "In this place, so much of the students' days is predetermined by routine. With their disabilities, they're often dependent on others for even the simplest tasks. Here in the classroom, I want my students to learn to make decisions on their own as much as possible and see the consequences of those decisions, good or bad."

Henry gestured to the third slogan. "Tell me about this one."

"'Self-respect yourself!' I know it's not grammatically correct, but getting these students to believe in their own dignity and worth is likely my most difficult, but most important, assignment."

Henry was still for a moment and looked lost in thought. I tensed, wondering what he was about to say.

"Good, yes, very good," he finally murmured. "I think you should write down what you just told me. I think this will make for a very powerful essay."

I was taken aback. "What would I do with an essay?"

"You should apply for graduate school for the fall. As good a teacher as you are, you have plenty to learn. You should think about moving on and getting an advanced degree."

"And leave my kids?"

"Temporarily," he said, putting on his blue blazer. "You could come back and teach here, but you probably would do something else after finishing school."

"Not interested," I said immediately. "I don't think that would be the best thing for me right now, and it certainly wouldn't be for them. We're finally starting to make progress with the communicator, and I'm not ready to walk away from that."

"There are others you will help, and perhaps to a greater degree, if you go on to graduate school," he insisted.

"Henry, don't think I'm not flattered by your suggestion," I countered, "but right now this job feels just right to me."

I could tell Henry considered arguing with me, but instead he extended his hand and said, "Thanks for sharing your viewpoint. I believe it forms the foundation of a rather sound philosophy. I'm sure we'll have more opportunities to discuss educational matters another time."

I shook Henry's hand, relieved that he didn't see my rejection of graduate school as a rebuff of him or a denial of his importance to me as a person or as a teacher. I was changing as a person because of these students and this setting, and I was hopeful that Henry might continue to be a mentor during this critical time in my personal and professional development. While he may not have been pleased with my quick decision, I hoped he understood my intentions were good. I genuinely worried that an untimely departure from their teacher and ally would be traumatic for my students.

Henry began organizing his papers and sliding them into his bulging briefcase. I'd noticed that he was always taking notes while I was teaching. I asked him what he did with all the notes.

"Why, I hand them to Mrs. Sharp," he said with a grin. "She's hoping to adopt your educational approach throughout the school."

I was fluent in sarcasm, so this remark made me burst out laughing.

Henry continued: "You must know that I believe in what you're doing. Building lessons around a student's interest or trying to find new activities to excite them and augment learning—that *should* pervade the entire institution. It is unfortunate that it's not part of this school's philosophy."

I was thrilled to hear him confirm that my way of teaching resonated with him. Words failed me, so I nodded fast.

"Look," he added. "You're a pretty good teacher who could become a great one. I can see that you don't want to go to graduate school, but you've got things to learn. If you're ever going to get the chance to become a better teacher, you'll have to learn a little bit of old-fashioned diplomacy. For example, I'll bet you don't care at all about what that woman thinks of you. But by the same token, do you think she gives a damn whether you're over here teaching or not?" He raised his hand to keep me from answering. "Allow me to answer that question for you: definitely not. Just remember, her life, her job, her credibility will not suffer at all if you're over here teaching or if you're working in a pet store in Springfield, selling canaries."

"What's the difference? Caged animals, caged people," I said. My anger at all of it had crept into my tone.

I sensed that Henry was becoming frustrated with me. "You're awfully smart for someone who's just barely reached puberty. And that, my young friend, is precisely your problem. You have a wisecrack for everything. For some reason, you want to give off the impression that you don't care about anything—except your kids, that is. Well, you know, and now I know, that your problem is that you care *too* much about everything. And that's not a bad thing. But if I were you, I would try to lose some of that attitude and think about the bigger picture."

"The big picture being...?"

"The future of these students, for one. Your own future as a teacher, for two." He waved the conversation away. "This is probably much more than you bargained for today. I'll run along and stop by next week after you've had a chance to think about what I've said." He paused and glanced down at his worn briefcase. "Fair enough?"

I nodded, my mood having soured, and Henry left.

I thunked down in my desk chair and sighed, combing over the words my mentor and I had just exchanged. I was resentful that he'd had the nerve to insult me in my own classroom, but I was also pleased that someone whose opinion I valued so much had taken the time to say something constructive to me. And he was right about one thing. I needed to watch my big mouth, for the sake of my students and their future progress. My conversation with Henry had just reinforced what I'd known all along: that I'd lose much more than my paycheck if I talked myself out of my job.

CHAPTER 19

A month had passed since my meeting with the journalist Jim Shanks, and I hadn't heard anything more from him. So I was shocked on Sunday morning, March 15, 1970, when I picked up the paper I typically read on weekends and this headline jumped out at me: "The Tragedy of Belchertown."

It was on the front page of the *Springfield Union*, stacked right next to the *Boston Globe* at the little general store I frequented.

I stared at the headline for a moment before grabbing the paper and retreating to my car. I dug into the article with trepidation, hoping it would capture Belchertown accurately and wondering if I would be named as a source. I soon became spellbound as I read about this place that had become so central to my life. A voice in my head kept repeating, "Yes, that's true!" or "Can you believe that?"

When I finished the article, I folded the paper carefully and set it on my lap. I had a feeling of complete satisfaction, because of the depth of the content and because of the skillful way Jim Shanks had presented it. I was also relieved that my name had not been mentioned, with no clues pointing to me as an informant.

Over the next five days, five equally powerful and equally sickening articles appeared in the paper. This multi-part exposé was a damning portrait of the school—including details I was familiar with in the infirmary— but it also turned a spotlight on life for residents in the other buildings, whom I rarely saw. Shanks focused on the back wards of the overcrowded men's and women's dormitories. He described scenes that I had glimpsed myself: grown men and women, some naked, sometimes sitting in pools of their own filth, rocking and staring blankly into space or at televisions, the only source of stimulation available. If they were uncooperative, attendants would restrain them by tying them to benches or chairs. At one point, Shanks quoted M. Phillip Wakstein, a regional administrator for the state's Department of Mental Health, as saying, "The only difference between Belchertown and Auschwitz is the lack of gas chambers."

Shanks did distinguish between the horrors of the back wards and the slightly better conditions in other buildings. In the nurseries where the younger children lived, he acknowledged that the physical conditions weren't quite as deplorable, but that the older children still spent most of their time unsupervised in a day room, watching TV and playing with plastic bottles since few toys were available. They had a teacher, but she—like me—was on her own in a basement classroom. I was gratified to see that Shanks had highlighted some of the achievements of my students in the infirmary, adding some bright spots to an otherwise bleak and disturbing condemnation of the institution.

Reading each article was like watching a movie; I could visualize most of the scenes based on my own observations. For the places I hadn't observed firsthand, Shanks's descriptive writing style filled in the missing imagery. Each article brought me searing reminders of the horror I had struggled not to get used to, and fresh hope that Belchertown's exposure would somehow lead to change.

I bought multiple copies of each of the six articles and shared them with friends and relatives who didn't live in the area. I guess I could have been embarrassed that I worked in such a place, but because I made my rejection of everything Belchertown—except the residents—known to anyone who would listen, I felt a certain amount of pride in my public condemnation.

Unsurprisingly, the administration was furious and defensive, going so far as to call the series "irresponsible sensationalism." In April, the school issued a report called *An Objective Review of Belchertown State School*, which responded to many of Shanks's accusations point by point. It also admitted that understaffing was a serious problem and promised some reforms. Among the suggested changes from the State Mental Retardation Commission were expedited building repair and cleanup, more sanitary food handling procedures, individualized plans or programming for each resident, expanded volunteer programs, and more opportunities for residents to walk and exercise. The report also revealed that by housing residents in big group wards, the school wasn't keeping up with the current state policy of unitization, which required residents of similar ages and abilities to live together in smaller units.

When I arrived at work the Monday after the first article appeared, I had a folded copy of the newspaper tucked under my elbow. I didn't have to start a conversation about the exposé, because it was naturally on everyone's mind. The mood among the staff was mixed. Everyone knew there were problems—and I wasn't the only person who complained about them—but the staff also felt under attack, accused of indifference, negligence, and worse. I suspected that because the infirmary was not incriminated as an abusive or neglectful environment, per se, the tone of the infirmary staff wasn't as defensive. And Shanks did have some positive things to say about the staff, pointing out that "the staff itself can't be blamed for the conditions at the institution. Most are dedicated to the children. Some have performed near miracles with the youth." Instead, he blamed state officials who refused to fund the school sufficiently. But even with Shanks's attempt to deflect blame from the employees, I didn't get the feeling that any of my colleagues were particularly delighted that the cat was publicly out of the bag.

Though Jim Shanks had warned me at our meeting that the article might not trigger any changes, the Massachusetts legislature actually took up the cause. Within weeks they established a joint committee, chaired by Senator Philip Quinn, to investigate conditions at Belchertown and a state hospital, about twelve miles to the south. This oversight committee also included Representative John Olver, who had just begun serving that previous January in the Massachusetts House of Representatives. Another member of the investigating committee was the president of the Belchertown State School Friends Association, a group made up of mostly parents and family members who volunteered their time and raised funds to improve the lives of residents. I soon came to realize that the Belchertown Friends group was steadfastly committed to improving conditions at the institution. However, their intention was to create more humane segregated environments for their children rather than to commit to moving the residents into the community.

A few weeks after the articles were published, the snow was gone, and the crocuses were popping up between the bushes in the front of the building—the first signs of spring started appearing on the Belchertown campus. Things were starting to percolate, and I could feel change in the air. The staff buzzed with surprise at the sudden attention from the outside world. Although conditions hadn't visibly changed yet, I would occasionally see small groups of visitors in suits peering into wards or huddling in conference in hallways. Sometimes they would request interviews with

Bernie, and I could only imagine how busy the administration was as they tried to keep the indignation from escalating in the outside world.

One afternoon, I stopped in to chat with Bernie. We were enjoying our usual banter, Bernie slyly funny and me making my usual sarcastic quips. When I stood to leave, Bernie asked, "Would you sit for just another minute? I want to ask you something. I've been meaning to ask you for some time now."

My stomach clenched. Had she found out I'd talked to Jim Shanks? Would she ask me, point blank, if I'd had anything to do with the articles?

Bernie paused, pinning me with her gaze. She got up from behind her desk and came around to perch on the edge of it, right in front of me.

"Why are you still here?" she finally asked. "I didn't think you would make it a week, based on the color—or lack of color—you turned on your first day in this building."

"So you noticed," I said, in a quiet voice that begged her to leave that incident in the past.

"I am a nurse, remember? I'm trained to recognize when someone is about to die. But now that more time has gone by, a better question is: Why are you getting in so deep?"

I didn't hesitate. "Because it makes me feel useful—really useful."

"But that's not enough of a reason," she countered. "There's got to be more to it than that."

"You're entirely right," I conceded. "I was taken aback when I first arrived, and, to be honest, I didn't think I would be able to work in this building."

"So why did you stick it out? You practically had a fistfight with Dorothy Sharp in the middle of Ward 1 during your orientation tour. You must've known this wouldn't be easy work."

"Believe me," I said, sighing and running my hand over my face. "I wondered if I could actually work in a place that was this far removed from anything I had ever known or seen before. The buildings, the wards, the people—just all of it. But when I realized that larger forces outside the institution had created this whole mess, I came back. And just kept coming back."

"To change it?"

"Not at first. Originally, I'd just thought I would come to work and leave," I admitted. "Then, I wanted to become a better teacher. And eventually, yes:

I did begin to think about how to change it. I decided I'm not going to avoid the important things anymore. If something is worth doing, then it's worth fighting for."

We both sat in silence for a moment, lost in our thoughts. Finally, I said, "You know, I originally decided to become a teacher because I wanted to avoid the draft. But I've changed, and I'm not running anymore. I intend to stay and fight."

"And what does 'fight' mean?" she asked me. Her brow furrowed, as if she'd wondered about the answer to this question for quite some time and was fairly sure she wouldn't like it.

"Bernie," I said, "I just mean that if I see all this as horrific, and you and the others do too, and even the newspapers and the state legislature are investigating us, then why don't we do something about it?"

"Like what?"

"Like, strike! Like make a big stink. A protest. At the very least, stand outside with placards proclaiming that we won't work here because of the inhumane treatment of our fellow humans. What better time than while people are paying attention to how things are done here?"

"And who is going to keep the residents alive while we're all out there saving them?"

That stopped me in my tracks. "Good point."

"We'd need to organize better and keep a skeleton crew on hand to keep things safe while others are protesting."

"We could do that! I know we could." I nodded fast, hoping she was catching some of my enthusiasm. "You have me all worked up now. What do you say, Bernie? Let's start to protest the conditions ourselves."

Bernie fixed her eyes on mine and rhythmically tapped a fingernail on her desk for several seconds. When she spoke, her voice was noticeably louder than it had been moments before. "No, I won't go on strike, and I doubt you'll find many others who will, either. Look at you. You're young, talented, educated, smart, and passionate. Face it: for you, this place is just a distraction. A temporary detour from whatever your life will become."

"Bernie—"

"You'll find some business to run or some law firm on the top floor of some building in Boston or New York. Belchertown State School will still exist for you, but only as an unpleasant recollection. It will become a memory for you, like Little League baseball and summer camp. You might see a wheelchair and think of someone back here."

I tried to interrupt her again, but she extended her palm to silence me.

"Howard, for the majority of us here, this is our life. We have families to feed and mortgages to pay. We can't just put all that on the line, even if we allow ourselves to comprehend what it means to work here. And you know what else?" She leaned in, as if sharing a weighty secret with me. "There will come a time when you, too, will have commitments like these— big ones that will weigh you down, pesky little responsibilities like kids and dogs and car payments. Right now, you're thinking with your heart. You're young, you *should* do that, but as time goes on, you, too, will begin to think with your brain, and then your idealism will fade, if not disappear. That's just the way it is. I'm not saying it *should* be that way. I'm just saying that it *is*."

I was paralyzed, my mouth agape. I stood, poised to offer one of my curt responses, but I was hard pressed to conjure up any kind of response at all. When I did speak, my words squeezed out of my throat in a raspy whisper: "I hope not!"

From the silence that followed, I think we both knew it was time for this conversation to end. Bernie turned her attention from me and fumbled with a short stack of mail on her desk. I stood and walked out the door, closing it quietly behind me.

CHAPTER 20

When Ron next rolled into the classroom in early April, he did so in a woefully undersized wheelchair pushed by Bob Bergquist. My initial thought was that this was a prank, but the pained look on Ron's face told a different story.

Bob positioned Ron next to Teddy and pulled me aside to explain. He revealed that Ron's regular chair, already a tight fit for a growing teenager, was now beyond repair and could no longer be wheeled in a straight line. He then informed me, in a tone that was equal parts exasperation and despair, that Ron would not get a new chair for at least six months and that this was his "interim" chair. Bob made it clear that extended time in an undersized seat not only inflicted pain but often led to skin breakdowns and sores and contributed to muscle atrophy.

I was at a loss for words. The list of injustices that affected the residents of Belchertown was extensive, and now I could add this to my list. I burned with anger at the thought of Ron spending all of his waking hours in an undersized chair that caused endless discomfort and pain.

I thought the simplest temporary solution, of course, would be to borrow a larger chair until a more appropriate one could be ordered. Bob agreed, but he had learned that the undersized chair Ron had been assigned was the only one available. It was indefensible that a building housing two hundred people with various disabilities had only one backup wheelchair, and it was built for a small child. The expectation that Ron should use this tiny wheelchair for another half a year was absurd, not to mention cruel.

"Bob, if you have any plans for the weekend, you'd better cancel them. I'm going to need your help with my next invention." Bob allowed himself a chuckle, thinking I was joking, but I wasn't. I was sick and tired of the kids—my kids—having to live with such indignities. I was tired of all the rules and regulations that dictated their lives. No new wheelchair for six months... really? If Belchertown wouldn't come through for Ron, then I would. I'd spend the next few days building him a wheelchair myself.

"I'm in," said Bob, when I told him my plan. "What time are you picking me up?"

Every so often, it startled me to realize how dramatically my weekend plans had changed since I began teaching at Belchertown. On this chilly, bright Saturday morning, I set out to locate the small junkyard that Milton, the school custodian, had told me about. He said the salvage yard had been around since the 1940s and that we'd probably find what we needed.

Bob had agreed to come along, but he was plainly annoyed by our seven a.m. start time. He sat in the back of my cab clutching a large cup of black coffee like a hand warmer, silently staring straight ahead. I slid back the divider window that separated the driver from the passengers so we could interact, but he was in no mood for small talk. I turned the dial on the radio, attempting to find some fitting music. With no success, I finally settled for the local news and kept quiet. About ten minutes out of Belchertown Center, I was thrilled and frankly surprised to discover a large metal sign, its faded letters indicating that the Granby Salvage Yard was just two hundred yards ahead.

We pulled up to the entrance. I leaned out the window and spoke to the proprietor, who was standing behind a chain-link gate. A large man with a ruddy complexion, he wore overalls, black work boots, and a ball cap that sported the UMass football team logo.

"We're looking for a bucket seat," I yelled out.

"I don't have any foreign parts," he answered in a distinct gravelly voice, eyeing my black Austin taxi. "What the hell is that, anyway?

"It's not for this car," I said. "It's not going into a car."

He paused. "Come on in," he said, rather reluctantly, then lumbered over and slid back the gate. "What kind of bucket seat do you want, then?"

"We just want to be sure that it's a real comfortable seat that isn't ripped."

"And one with real leather," Bob insisted, finally coming out of his coma.

"If you don't mind my asking," the man said, "what are you planning on doing with it?"

"We're going to put it on a rolling platform and use it like a wheelchair," I said with conviction, trying to give the impression that we did this all the time.

"I'd want a T-bird seat if I had to sit in it all day long," the man offered.

"Why's that?" Bob asked.

"Well, because I got one, for one thing—and it's a beauty, too... genuine red leather, no rips, no tears, no cigarette burns. It'll be cheaper because the other one got destroyed in the accident. People usually want both seats."

"Was anyone killed?" I asked. I wasn't superstitious, exactly, but I'd feel a little uneasy knowing Ron was riding in a passenger seat salvaged from a fatal wreck.

"Nah! The gal just got herself banged up pretty bad. The rest of the car is still here if you want to see it."

Bob and I hauled the seat out of the shed and placed it on the rough gravel-surfaced ground. The owner followed along and pulled a rag out of his pants pocket. He snapped the cloth several times to release the dust and then wiped down the red leather, which was indeed in perfect condition.

"Well?" he asked. "Just what I said, right?"

"That depends on the price," I said with a smile, but I was already pulling out my wallet.

"Give me twelve dollars, and I won't tell anyone you stole it."

After handing the man his money, I thanked him earnestly, and the three of us packed it into the expansive back seat of my taxi.

"Good luck building that wheelchair," the man said. "Can I get a picture of it when it's all done? Like to put it in the office, if you think of it."

The kindness of the request struck an emotional chord in me. "No problem; I'll do that," I said. I grinned all the way out through the gate.

Since construction of the chair base would require real carpentry tools, which neither Bob nor I had, I'd called Henry a few days prior to our trip to the salvage yard, confident that anyone who lived in a house would have some tools. At first, Henry thought the idea of building a wheeled seat was peculiar—especially for a teacher and physical therapist. However, after witnessing Ron nearly falling out of his current chair and hearing about the bureaucratic stalemate that barred him from getting another one any time soon, he agreed that it made sense for us to intervene.

Henry wasn't home when I motored the Austin up his driveway with Bob and the leather T-bird seat in the rear compartment. He must have remembered we were coming, however, because he'd left the garage door open, exposing a rather substantial collection of tools—few of which either of us knew how to use. I searched for the materials I had purchased and left at Henry's a few days before: two-by-fours, wooden planks, and an assortment of screws and nails. Instead, I spied in the corner a completely assembled square platform resting on four operational wheels. The platform base looked sturdy enough to hold a person weighing up to five hundred pounds.

"Well, this makes our job a lot easier," I said. "Can you believe he did this? Now all we need to do is join this gorgeous red leather seat with that handsome, homemade wooden base."

As we dragged the seat out of the back of my car and rolled the wooden base out of the garage, Henry arrived. He bounded out of the car, patted me on the back, and shook hands with Bob.

Henry gazed at the two components. "Boys, I expected you would have had this project completed by now," he teased.

"We would have," I said, "but for this phase of the construction, Bob and I needed someone who knew how to use an electric drill for more than mixing cocktails."

"That's quite a seat," Henry remarked as he circled around it, closely inspecting it and stroking the red leather. "It does look really comfortable, doesn't it?"

After placing the seat in the middle of the platform, Bob set it at just the right angle, using his expert knowledge of seating and positioning. Now Ron would be able to sit comfortably for extended periods. The three of us then discussed how to attach the seat to the platform and fashion a handle for pushing. Two hours, many laughs, and—thankfully—no injuries later, we backed away and gawked at our final product. The three of us circled the wheelchair without a word, admiring our handiwork. I envisioned Ron, comfortable at last, sitting back in that big bucket seat with a big bright grin on his youthful face. I was thrilled that he would finally be sitting comfortably, and very proud that I'd had something to do with it.

I arrived at Henry's early on Monday in a borrowed pickup truck with a cargo bed large enough to transport the chair to the infirmary. Henry must have heard me backing in, because he was standing beside the chair in the front of the garage when I climbed out of the cab. The wooden platform was now a glistening white.

"Morning, Henry," I said. "I see the chair has had a little facelift since Saturday. It looks terrific."

"Oh, I had a can of white paint just crying out to be matched to that gorgeous red leather, so I slopped on a few coats. I think it looks pretty good, if I do say so myself."

"I wouldn't argue with that. Do you have time to follow me out to the school for the unveiling?"

"That's nice of you to offer, but I have a class to teach."

"When will you be out again?"

"Probably on Thursday morning, but don't worry. The way this chair is fastened together, it's not falling apart anytime soon. Besides, this project belongs to you and Bob—I'm just the painter."

"Yeah, right. I'll let Ron know you gave the chair its special look. And just so we're clear, you did a heck of a lot more than paint. All of this would still be a pile of two-by-fours with four wheels lying on top if it weren't for you."

In quintessential Henry style, he simply said, "See you Thursday."

I drove into the grounds and headed to the infirmary, planning to off-load the chair at the loading dock before moving it to the second floor. For my timing to be right, I needed to get the chair into the ward before Ron was assisted out of his bed and into his temporary chair. I arrived at the building and quickly backed the truck into the loading dock, then rolled the chair onto the elevator. I was relieved to find it functioning this morning.

I left the chair outside the entrance to Ward 5 and opened the door. The room was buzzing with activity as the attendants got residents out of bed and ready for the day. I spied Ron still lying on his back in bed, looking straight up at the ceiling. He didn't notice me as I approached. It looked like he was next in line to be dressed, and when the nearest attendant spotted me, I touched my finger to my lips to signal him to be silent. Ron was now lying on his stomach while a nurse and attendant studied something on his bare back. I was afraid to ask, but I figured that if a bedsore was forming, using the new chair would help to resolve it.

Bob walked in as the two male attendants were about to turn Ron over, and lift him into his chair. Ron looked at the uncomfortable interim chair and moaned. "Too small?" Bob asked.

Ron blinked definitively, without hesitation.

"Why don't we try another chair, then?" I said.

With that, I retrieved the chair from the hallway and wheeled it to Ron's bedside. Bob swung Ron around so he could see the new chair, and he exploded with excitement.

"Feast your eyes on this work of art!" I said, circling the chair.

"Like what you see?" Bob asked.

Ron's entire body reacted. His legs attempted to extend and the muscles in his back went rigid. The body tension was definite and distinct—another way for Ron to communicate an unmistakable yes.

Bob and I deposited him gently into the bucket seat. I snapped the T-bird's seat belt, and we both stood back. Everything looked right, including the seat angle Bob had calculated. "Not bad for three amateurs," Bob confirmed.

Ron forced his head against the back of the seat and turned it from side to side, looking bewildered.

"Hey, tough guy," I said. "Does that seat feel comfortable or what?"

Ron blinked to indicate yes, but I knew him well enough to know that he was confused by all this activity.

"You're wondering where it came from, right?" I asked.

He shot back a yes with no hesitation.

"Would you believe that Bob and I made this chair with the help of Dr. Peirce?" I asked.

He blinked.

"So you do believe that we made it?"

Another blink.

"Is it comfortable?"

He blinked again. This time he added repeated glances from us to the floor, from us to the floor, us to the floor.

"Is there something wrong with the chair?"

"No," he indicated as his faced tensed, expressing that he was frustrated with not being understood.

"Okay, let's try this again," Bob interjected. "You like the chair, you're comfortable, but you want to get out of it. Is that right?"

Thrilled that we understood, he blinked, punctuating his response with a piercing shriek.

"You want to take a look at the chair and be put back in. Is that what you want to do?" I asked.

His eyes blinked an undeniable yes.

Bob and I looked at each another and simultaneously moved to either side of Ron. Each of us put a hand under one of his thighs and the other against his shoulder blade. "All right, lift," Bob said, and out of the chair Ron came. We held him securely and walked around the chair, letting him admire every inch of it. Then, we carefully lowered him back onto the leather seat.

"Ron, enjoy your new ride," I said. "I'll see you in school later."

I was swelling with pride—but more importantly, with happiness for Ron. I made eye contact with his attendant, who had watched all this with a smile on her face. She came over and pushed Ron back into the ward, where he'd be greeted with a bit of a hero's welcome.

News of Ron's stylish vehicle traveled quickly throughout the infirmary that day. Every attendant came to check out his new chair, and the excitement of the other residents was palpable. Ron seemed to enjoy the celebrity that came with rolling through the corridors of the building in his custom vehicle.

The day Ron took possession of his new ride was, in most respects, like most other days at Belchertown: The students came to class, we worked on the day's lessons and activities, and everyone departed at the usual time. But Ron's comings and goings took on a whole new dimension. I knew he was more comfortable. I saw it in his demeanor. Before, he had been in constant motion during the day, searching for a position that wouldn't cause him discomfort. But now he sat peacefully during class, engaged and focused on the day's lessons.

Ron's new chair was so much more than just a chair. It was a gateway to learning.

CHAPTER 21

For a few days, I was riding high on the success of Ron's wheelchair. Every glimpse of him in his new chair buoyed my spirits. I had no way of knowing that just one week later, I was in for my worst day yet as a state worker for the Commonwealth of Massachusetts.

My Monday began innocently enough. I had just spent a rare weekend completely free of work-related concerns. This meant that I made no Saturday or Sunday visits to the school and hadn't built any wheelchairs, created any lesson plans, talked to any reporters, or worked on any other materials or activities related to my students. I'd needed the break, and I felt refreshed.

"Morning, Bernie," I exclaimed, peeking into her office before heading down to my classroom.

Bernie looked up from her desk and waved me into her office. She avoided eye contact as she fidgeted with papers on her desk.

"Okay, what's wrong?" I asked. "What did I do now?"

"This time you didn't do anything wrong," she retorted, still not looking at me directly.

"Now that's a backhanded compliment if ever I've heard one. Well, what's up, then?"

Bernie turned and stared out the window. I walked between her and the window in an effort to get an answer. She glanced down at her desk.

My entire body began to fizz with anxiety. I felt unsteady on my feet. I knew that what Bernie was about to reveal would not be good news.

"Nothing happened to one of my students, did it?" I asked. *Please, please let them be okay.*

"No, they're fine. It's just that, well..." She took a deep breath. "Ron's chair has been confiscated, Howard. He didn't have it all weekend."

My anxiety ebbed, and anger and confusion rose up in its place. "What do you mean, confiscated? Who took it? For what reason?"

She made eye contact with me, finally. In a soft monotone, she tried to explain: "Apparently, all medical equipment, including wheelchairs, in any state facility has to conform to some established code. Also, all of this equipment has to be purchased from a state-approved vendor. Since the chair was actually homemade in your basement or wherever, it didn't come from one of the approved vendors for medical equipment. From what I was told, it was against the rules to even bring the chair onto the grounds."

"Bernie!" I shouted. "Do you remember what that boy was sitting in before we made him that chair?"

"Of course I do," she spat out, meeting my frustration with her own. "I made it clear that I thought taking his chair was unwarranted, but there was nothing I could do! I had no choice but to follow orders."

"Bernie," I said in a calmer voice. "I'm not blaming you. Where's the chair now?"

"Friday afternoon, right after you left, a couple of the guys from the maintenance shop came over with orders to get the chair. I asked them to wait until Monday so I could look into it further, but they said they had to do what they were told right away."

"Was Mrs. Sharp behind this?" I asked. "Did she take the chair away from that boy to spite me? She wanted to get at me, so she thought she'd make Ron suffer?"

"That's what I thought, too, but I don't know for sure. I'm not certain how to find that out, either."

"Can I use your phone?" I said, my hand already moving for the receiver. "I'd like to see if I can find out what happened. Don't worry—I'll do it discreetly and quietly. I don't want to ruffle any feathers."

"Be my guest," she said, gesturing to her desk with a full arm sweep.

I picked up the phone and dialed the number from memory.

"Mrs. Sharp!" I barked when I heard her pick up. Hearing my own voice, I reminded myself to rein in my anger a bit. "What do you know about Ron Benoit losing his new wheelchair last Friday?" I said, in a tone as restrained as I could manage.

"Mr. Shane," she answered with infuriating calm, "you will need to take that up with the superintendent. Don't you be wasting your day on this matter. You have classes to teach, and it really is none of your affair. Good-bye." She hung up the phone before I could respond.

When I dropped the phone back in its cradle, Bernie looked at me with a question on her face. I didn't have to answer—my face said it all. We sat for a moment in grim silence.

"Well," she offered. "I will say, it was refreshing to see how discreetly and quietly you did that."

"Bernie, what is Bowser's number?" I asked.

"As in Superintendent Bowser? That might not be such a good idea."

"Mrs. Sharp recommended I speak with him directly if I had any questions, and that's what I plan to do."

Bernie glanced at a typed list she had posted on her wall, then sighed and read the number out to me while I dialed.

"Good morning. I'd like to speak with Dr. Bowser, please," I said to the receptionist who answered. "It's Howard Shane. Tell him that Mrs. Sharp suggested I speak with him right away. Yes, I can wait, but tell him the purpose is to discuss the matter of Mr. Benoit's new wheelchair being stolen."

Across the room, Bernie locked eyes with me; her brows were raised and her mouth slightly ajar. She wasn't even pretending to be doing something else. After a few minutes, the receptionist came back on the line to inform me that Dr. Bowser would be in meetings all day and wouldn't be able to speak with me. I kept my anger under control and asked her to relay a message: that despite my own busy schedule, I'd be at his office within the hour, accompanied by Ron Benoit, and we'd wait until the superintendent had a moment to talk with us.

"And please be sure that Dr. Bowser is aware that if he can't meet with us, I will have to report the stolen wheelchair to the state police," I added.

"I—I'll notify him," she assured me.

I hung up the phone and glanced over at Bernie, who was studying me intently.

"You aren't really thinking of calling the police, are you?" she asked.

"Yes, I am. That was the first thing that went through my head when you told me what happened. When someone takes something that doesn't belong to them, what do you normally do?" Before she could respond, I said, "You call the police. That chair didn't belong to the men who took it. It belongs to Ron. It was his. I gave it to him. It was a present."

"But you can't really blame the guys who came to get the chair," she said. "After all, they were told to do it."

"I have no doubt that someone instructed them to do it, but that doesn't exonerate them. That's one of the problems around here: bad things, inhumane things, are carried out on behalf of someone else—or, more dangerously, on behalf of the state or the government." Though our last conversation had ended poorly, I still hoped Bernie would help me. I looked at her, sensing that desperation was coming off me in waves. "Bernie, *please* do me one other favor," I said. "Let the attendants on both floors know that today's class will be starting a little later while I introduce Ron to Dr. Bowser. Okay?"

She nodded. I was glad to know she was still willing to help, if only in small ways.

I found Ron sitting in the undersized chair we had replaced. His chin was tucked against his chest, and he appeared lifeless. Sadness and anger washed over me, but I knew I'd have to push my feelings aside for his sake.

"Straighten up, Ron!" I said, as jovially as I could manage. He startled and then came to life again, struggling to adjust his position. "You and I are taking a little trip across campus. Are you up for that?"

Ron looked baffled. He offered a slow blink that I interpreted to mean "sure, but why?"

I explained my plan to him as I pushed his chair to the elevator, rolled him down the ramp in the rear of the building, and wheeled him along the paved road to the administration building. I told him we needed to find out why his new chair had been removed, and explained that Mr. Bowser might help us figure out how to get it back. Ron must have been taking this all in and trying to figure out what was in store for us, because he didn't make a sound or move during our trip to Dr. Bowser's office.

I introduced us both to the woman who greeted us in the foyer of the administration building and restated our purpose for meeting with Dr. Bowser. Her face clearly showed disbelief, but she knocked on a door marked *Superintendent* and disappeared inside. Moments later, she returned and announced, "Dr. Bowser has had an unexpected cancellation, and he will see you now."

I pushed Ron into the office. The room was spacious and neatly appointed, its hardwood floors gleaming and its shelves filled with leather-bound books arranged by size. A bank of tall windows afforded a deceptively pretty view of the grounds of the institution.

Ron sat uncomfortably in his old chair, glancing around the room. Dr. Bowser was behind an imposing mahogany desk, easing back in an expensive-looking leather chair. In contrast to Ron, whose body spilled over the sides of his seat, Dr. Bowser had ample room in his. The cruel irony of that was not lost on me.

Once we settled in front of his desk and I made introductions, I noticed Dr. Bowser's eyes darting over to catch glimpses of Ron. I had no doubt he recognized the gross inadequacy of Ron's wheelchair, so I let him take it in without adding commentary.

"Now," Dr. Bowser began. "My secretary tells me that you have a complaint about a wheelchair. I have looked into this matter, and it appears that the youngster was in a chair that violated our safety requirements. For that reason, and for his safety and wellbeing, we had to remove the chair and place it in storage. I can assure you that no one is stealing anything that belongs to this boy."

"I see," I stated calmly. "And, for his safety and wellbeing, he will now have to sit in this chair? In your medical opinion, Dr. Bowser, do you feel that this chair is adequate?"

Bowser cleared his throat. "It appears that this chair may be a little small, and perhaps some adjustments will need to be made. I will look into that, as well, but there really is little else I can do at the moment."

Despite the seeming dismissal, I pressed on. "I have one last question for you before I go. Sir, I'm guessing here, but I would say you're wearing a suit coat that's about a size forty-two long, correct?"

"I beg your pardon?" he said.

"This boy is sitting in a chair made for a child half his size. Now imagine spending your day in a size thirty-eight short suit. Then, you might get a slightly better idea of what it's like for him to exist in this chair. It looks all wrong, it feels all wrong, and we both know that it *is* all wrong!"

"Young man," Bowser said, his voice rising with anger, "I understand your analogy, but this meeting is over."

I was being totally obnoxious, and I didn't care. I knew that this was the last chance I would have to talk with this man. There was no question that I would never be invited back, so I kept at it: "But we haven't resolved the problem of Ron's chair yet."

"I don't know what else to tell you!" he shouted.

"You can start by telling Ron that he can have the chair we built for him back until he gets a new and proper one."

"I can't do that. That homemade version doesn't meet state safety guidelines, and I just can't, for his own good, allow him to sit in it."

I stood and pointed at Ron. "Look at this boy. Does he look safe and stable hanging over the sides of this seat?" I addressed Ron directly now, aware of the importance of involving him in this conversation. "Ron," I said. "Are you uncomfortable in this chair? Do you feel unsafe?"

Without hesitation, Ron blinked in the affirmative.

"That means yes," I told Dr. Bowser. "That's how Ron says yes, by blinking."

Dr. Bowser ignored that. "I am certain this chair meets basic safety guidelines."

"Okay, forget the safety issue. What about the health problem? You're a medical doctor. Do you think this can be good for his health, to be scrunched up in a chair of this size all day?"

Bowser stood abruptly. "There is nothing I can do about it right now. This meeting is over. I have a full schedule, and I need to get on with my day."

"Fine," I said. "Get on with your day, but if you can't think of anything you can do to help this boy's seating situation, I will."

"Meaning what, exactly?"

I rested my palms on the polished surface of his desk. "I am going to wait until three o'clock this afternoon, because I think that should give a man with your authority enough time to rectify this situation," I said evenly. "However, if by three o'clock we have no satisfactory resolution, I am going to do three things. First, I am going to call Ron's grandmother and ask her to call everyone and anyone she knows who could help him get a comfortable chair. Come to think of it, that's a call I should have already made. Second, I'm going to call Congressman Olver. I'm certain that his investigating committee would want to know about how this boy was stripped of a chair that actually fit, even if it didn't meet the regulations. Third, I'm going to call Jim Shanks at the *Springfield Union*. A tidbit like this—a teenage boy stuck with a child-sized wheelchair!—will fit in nicely with that pesky exposé that appeared on the front page. Don't you agree that the readers of Western Massachusetts ought to know about things like this? And after all, since you aren't able to fix the problem, perhaps you would welcome the help from someone else who can."

Bowser held up his hand. "Mr. Shane, I've had enough..."

I rolled Ron right over to him. "Now, I said I would do three things, but I'm actually going to do four. The fourth one will make all of this especially interesting, because I am going to call the state police and let them know that a wheelchair that belongs to Ron—not a state-owned or state-issued chair, but one that is his personal property—has been stolen. Ron, let's get going. Dr. Bowser has a lot to do today, and we've taken up enough of his time."

My heart hammered in my chest, and I could feel the dampness in my armpits as I pushed Ron out of the office and into the building foyer. Truth be told, as I'd laid out my intentions to Dr. Bowser, I'd had to keep reminding myself to sound and appear confident and unwavering. Only the belief that this was the best way to bring the chair back had emboldened me to carry on.

"Don't go anywhere, okay?" I told Ron. "I'll be right back."

I went outside to look for the same two groundskeepers who had helped lift Ron into the building when we first arrived. The men were still trimming the bushes but quickly agreed to give me a hand getting Ron out of the building. As we carried Ron down the steps, one of the workers observed, "You'd think that a place that has so many people in wheelchairs would have a way for them to get into the main administration building."

His colleague agreed. "You can't get a wheelchair into many of the buildings here."

I stayed silent. I had said enough already today to stir the pot, and it wasn't even nine o'clock yet. The adrenaline pumping through my system had me on edge. I wondered whether my assertive—some would argue disrespectful—behavior with Dr. Bowser would quicken the process of getting Ron a chair, or whether the only thing my three o'clock deadline would herald was my termination.

When Ron and I reached the infirmary, Bernie and Nancy were waiting for us. "Fine day for a walk," I said, as I retrieved my keys and locked the door behind me. "All together now, 'If you open it, lock it.'"

"Blah, blah, blah. All right, what happened?" Nancy asked, unable to hide her curiosity. I just lifted an eyebrow. Nancy leaned over to Ron and asked, "So? Did you see him?"

Ron knew I was teasing them by dragging this out, and he wanted to be part of the ribbing, so he remained noncommittal.

"I will just say that when Dr. Bowser realized that Ron Benoit was there to see him, we glided right in—right, Ron?"

Ron blinked immediately.

"Well, what did he say?" Bernie asked.

"The guy is a *real* sweetheart," I said. Leaning into my sarcasm helped me ignore the exhaustion overcoming my body as the adrenaline rush faded. "He's hoping to get this all figured out by three o'clock today. He apologized to Ron for any inconvenience this miniature wheelchair might have caused, and that's pretty much the gist of it. Right, Ron?"

Ron blinked again.

I questioned for a moment whether I should convey some details of my visit with Dr. Bowser to Nancy, but I reminded myself that the rumors would immediately start to fly around the building. I decided that such gossip might not be in Ron's best interest. "Nancy, would you mind taking Ron up and getting him ready for school?" I asked.

When they were out of earshot, I turned to Bernie. "Bowser's a complete ass. He tried to pull the 'I really care but what can I do?' routine."

"So how did the meeting end?"

"It wasn't pretty," I admitted. "I threatened to leak this story to virtually everyone in America—the press, the government, the Benoit family, the police, his mother, and his tailor. I know he's furious at me for threatening to divulge the secrets of the kingdom, but I'm hoping he'll see the downside of me bringing my grievance outside the institution. Especially with the exposé still fresh in everyone's mind."

"How do you think he'll handle it?" she said.

I'd already turned to head toward my classroom. I stopped at her question, not wanting to ponder it for too long.

"That's anyone's guess," I said.

I returned to the classroom telling myself that something positive would occur for Ron—but the confidence I tried to nurture lessened with each passing hour. By noon, I began to question what I would do if the superintendent took no action. By two o'clock, I had decided that I would carry out every revolutionary act that I had promised earlier in the day, regardless of the consequences for my career.

At three p.m., the regular attendants arrived to accompany the students back to the wards. As I watched Ron go, I was seized with the sudden fear that I'd completely mishandled our morning meeting. Why had I been so abrasive? Had I made too many threats? What if I was terminated that very afternoon, and I'd just seen my kids for the last time? I hung around the classroom, cleaning things that didn't need to be cleaned, wondering what on earth I was going to do next.

It was nearly four o'clock when Ed came in and handed me a note saying that Ron's grandmother was upstairs.

I walked into Ward 5 and headed for Ron's bed space. It was deserted, so I tracked down the only available attendant in the washroom. "Do you know where I can find Ron Benoit?"

"I think he went next door to Ward 6 to show off his new wheelchair," she said.

"He has a new chair?" I asked, astonished. I didn't wait for her to respond—I ran out of the room.

I found Ron with Norman, who wasn't feeling well that day and was still in bed. Several others were gathered around his area, including Bob, Ed, and Ron's grandmother. Ron was now sitting in a properly sized chair—one that clearly wasn't new but was clean and by all appearances in good working order. When Ron spotted me, his gaze and reaction turned everyone else in my direction.

"Hey, what's this, a new chair?" I asked, a broad smile on my face.

"Hello, Mr. Shane."

"And hello to you, Mrs. Chapman," I said, shaking his grandmother's hand. "It's nice to see you again. Ron's always so happy when you visit."

"Well, I got a call this morning from the school, and they said that the superintendent arranged personally for a replacement chair for Ron. Said it was coming from another institution near Boston. They said I might want to come and see it, so here I am." She smiled, touching the handle of Ron's wheelchair. "Oh, oh, and then they told me that this is just a loaner chair! He'll be getting his own new chair in about six weeks. But for now, don't you think he looks swell in this chair?"

"I do think he looks swell. It seems to fit him pretty good," I said. "What do you think, Bob? You're the chair expert. Does it do the trick?"

Bob, who'd remained quiet, now offered his expert opinion. "I think he's sitting pretty well. In the morning, I'll make a few adjustments, and it will be just what the doctor ordered."

It helps when the doctor is also the superintendent, I thought. "It's nice to know that when a fine man like Dr. Bowser puts in an order for a new chair, the state takes that order seriously, and presto, a fine boy like Ron gets to sit high in the saddle. Isn't it, Bob?" I looked at Ron. He stared into my eyes and smiled. I said my goodbyes and headed home, relieved that I still had my job.

The next morning, I was sitting at my desk in the classroom before the kids arrived when my door swung open—not preceded by a knock—and Dr. Bowser himself entered the room. He shut the door and stalked directly to my desk.

Stay calm, I told myself. *You did what you had to do.*

I placed my pen on the desk blotter. "Would you like to sit down?" I asked.

"You were very convincing yesterday," he blustered, "and by now you must know that Mr. Benoit will have his chair, but I don't want you to think that I'll forget your behavior any time soon. You might have won this battle—but your behavior, young man, will prove to be a very big mistake. Let's get one thing perfectly clear." He extended his index finger and pointed it at me five times, once for each of the next five words he spoke: "Don't. Ever. Threaten. Me. Again."

He turned on his heel and walked off, but at the door he paused and delivered one last warning: "For you there is no next time. Am I clear?"

"Dr. Bowser..."

"Am I *clear*?" he repeated.

"Yes. Perfectly."

"Good. Then our business is over."

He marched out, slamming the door behind him, and I watched him march swiftly down the corridor. I realized with some relief that I hadn't been too injured by his visit—or his threats. Still, it was unsettling, and I quietly reflected on the entire wheelchair affair, knowing I had made a powerful enemy.

But given the final outcome, I didn't really care.

CHAPTER 22

I found a note from Bernie taped to the classroom door. Although a week had passed since my run-in with Dr. Bowser, the memory of that confrontation was still fresh, so I was relieved to discover that the note had nothing to do with him. It was only to inform me that Professor Allen Fitch from the Engineering Department at UMass had called, inviting me to his office for a meeting.

We agreed to meet the next day after work. This time his door was open when I arrived a little after four p.m., and I found him seated at his desk. His greeting was uncharacteristically cheery as he waved me into his office. He told me that Thomas and Bill, the volunteer electrical engineering students, would join us shortly, but first he wanted a few minutes with me alone.

In my experience of late, a request for a private meeting meant something negative would likely follow. Fortunately, Allen—as I now thought of him, since he'd asked me to call him by his first name—had no interest in reaming me out. He asked me first about Ron and Ruth's communication progress, and I told him that they relished the opportunity to learn and better express themselves and that they were making remarkable progress every day. Then, looking slightly uncomfortable, he asked me if I'd share more of my views on life in the institution. I could only assume he had read the damning exposé and was trying to fill in some of the blanks for himself.

I gave Allen my candid thoughts about life at Belchertown, and he listened intently. He commented on how incredible it was that Ron and Ruth were as intellectually talented as they were, given their environment.

"After all," he said, "it's amazing that these kids can be so capable of understanding when they've been so educationally neglected—so culturally deprived, if you will. It's as if the expected intellectual delays due to institutional neglect have simply passed over those two. And probably many others who haven't yet been assessed."

I could tell he'd been researching this topic and had thought a great deal about his personal inability to tolerate what he had seen, heard, and smelled in Ward 1. I could only hope that his engineering students had become just as fascinated with Ron and Ruth's lives and what they might be able to accomplish with the aid of creative engineering projects.

As if on cue, Thomas and Bill stuck their heads in the doorway. Allen sent them directly to the conference room and told them we'd join them soon. "Let's continue this conversation later, shall we?" he said to me.

When Allen and I arrived, the guys had already drawn a diagram on the chalkboard showing a three-dimensional box. On the front of it, they had drawn forty small circles around the circumference of a larger circle. Each small circle represented a miniature light bulb. On the side of the box, they'd drawn a small rectangle to mark the on/off switch, and above it was a small black dot to designate the port where a switch could be plugged in. I immediately recognized the drawing as the blueprint for the communication device that I had discussed with them.

Allen and I sat facing the blackboard. He looked at the drawing, then shifted his focus to his students. "Well?" he said. "Why don't you tell us how it works?"

Thomas jumped in to explain the device. "So, this sketch is a diagram of the prototype we intend to build out of plywood. The power for the device would be alternating current supplied by a standard wall plug, and the person communicating would control the device with a switch plugged into the side of the box. We also knew that it was critical for the communication device to have a pointer—like the second hand of a clock or some other design that indicates the selection that has been made." He paused briefly and looked at me, and I nodded my encouragement. "We decided," he went on, "that it might be more effective to place a template marked with letters, numbers, words, or pictures within a circle of lights such as this." He pointed to the illustration on the board. "Activating the switch causes each small light to illuminate, one at a time, in succession."

"Do you mean that once the switch is activated, the light will move around the circle in a stepping motion to each of the forty lights in turn?" I asked.

"Exactly," Thomas answered with authority.

Next, Bill jumped in and described in more technical terms the mercury switch Allen had mentioned during our earlier meeting. "The mercury switch comprises liquid mercury inside a small sealed glass tube with a contact pole at each end. The flow of the mercury in the tube completes an electric circuit, causing the light to start or stop the sequential movement around the circle—something like an hourglass being tipped over and back again."

The plan was to place a tube of mercury on the wrist. By turning the wrist one way, Ron or Ruth would start the light moving around the circle. When they brought their wrist back to its starting point or original position, the mercury in the tube would shift again and cause the light to stop instantly.

Thomas sat and stared at the sketch he had drawn on the blackboard. Bill glanced hesitantly at Allen. Everyone was silent for a moment before the professor asked the first question: "What should we call the prototype?"

Thomas and Bill looked to one another, but neither spoke.

While I hadn't given a moment's thought to naming the device, an idea simply popped into my head, and without hesitation I blurted it out: "I think it should be called the Expressor."

"I like that," Allen called out.

"Fine with me." Thomas smiled, and Bill nodded approvingly.

Allen leaned back, locking his hands behind his neck, and studied the sketch on the board. "What problems do you anticipate in building the Expressor, and when do you think this model of the Expressor will be ready for a trial run in the classroom?" he asked.

Again, the young engineers exchanged glances. Bill responded with confidence. "We believe we can complete a prototype version within a month. We've checked, and all parts are available, so we don't anticipate any major roadblocks."

Allen looked to me. "You have the last word. What do you think? Does this design make sense to you?"

"I think this is fantastic. It's remarkable. If it's a go, I'll start preparing Ron and Ruth for this new way of indicating the target first thing tomorrow. And I'll start refining their wrist movements so they can operate the switch."

Allen clapped his hands together. "Wonderful design work, guys. Now build something equally impressive and you'll make us all very proud. And let me give you a little advice: don't hesitate to come to me if you run into any problems. This work is too important for your egos to get in the way of meeting your deadline. Finally, I have noted the anticipated

May 1st date of completion. Earlier is fine, but do not miss the date you just announced. Any questions?"

"No, sir," Thomas said.

"No, Professor Fitch," Bill seconded.

Allen, his hands still linked behind his neck, turned to me. "Howard, any issues, questions, concerns?"

"No—well, one. It's not a question but a suggestion. If you guys want to come out to the school and meet with the kids, just let me know." With the silence that followed, I assumed they needed to think about it, so I let the idea pass.

Allen rested his hands on the table and thanked the students for their work. Nodding their goodbyes, they left.

"Allen, they've done some really good thinking about this," I said. "I'm thrilled that we're building something entirely new."

"I agree. This is a great opportunity for these students, and I think those two recognize that. As an engineer, you don't always have an opportunity to do something this worthwhile. That applies to me as well, but I guess you know that already." He leaned a little closer to me. "I figure that even though I'd never be able to work in the infirmary building, I can still do something from fifteen miles away."

"I couldn't appreciate it more," I said. "And I can't think of anything more important for Ron and Ruth than having this working prototype. Here's to the Expressor!"

He raised his imaginary glass to mine. "To the Expressor."

CHAPTER 23

A ll my students were progressing both educationally and physically during the spring of 1970. But sometimes, despite hard work and the best intentions, things go wrong.

I was pleased that we were making real advances in Ruth and Ron's lives, both with the original clock communicator and with Ron's new wheelchair. The skirmish over Ron's homegrown wheels had affected me in several ways, one of which was a heightened sensitivity to how important proper positioning was for a person who spent two-thirds of each day in a wheelchair or cart. So when Wendy came to class one morning in a cart that wasn't hers, I noticed right away. The difference was obvious, as this one was missing its wooden sides.

"Did you get a new cart, Wendy?" I asked.

Wendy lay on her back and moved her head back and forth as she inspected the inner edges of the cart. "My sides are all gone," she exclaimed.

I made a mental note to find out at the end of the school day why she was riding around in this new cart, but in the meantime, I didn't think the design of this cart would affect her performance in our class routines. In fact, I suspected it might even give her clearer visibility without the wooden border obstructing her view.

What I didn't anticipate or even conceive of, however, was how a change in Wendy's everyday equipment could result in a life-threatening event.

It all happened so fast that I still feel breathless when I think about it. It started with Jack's signature statement at three o'clock: "The 'tendants are here!" He announced this at the end of each school day, setting in motion the students and the attendants who were lingering outside the door. His words also cued Barbara to assume her usual standing position behind Paula's wheelchair and head toward the door with her. This time, however, she lightly bumped the front of Paula's chair into the right side of Wendy's cart just as Wendy was turning her head to the left.

The force of this minor collision was enough to cause Wendy's heavy head to continue to rotate, a movement that flipped her small body over. Newton's First Law of Motion says that a body in motion stays in motion unless acted on by a force—and on another, better day, Wendy's body would have been stopped by the sides of her regular cart. But there were no sides to catch her today, and she fell out of the cart and onto the classroom's cement floor.

Wendy landed flat on her back, looking straight up at the ceiling. I rushed to her side, cold with a fear I have rarely felt in my lifetime. She slowly rolled her head to the right to look at me. Casually, she said, "Mr. Shane, I think I fell out of my cart."

"You did fall, Wendy," I said, trying to steady my voice. Two attendants joined me as I kneeled over her. The three of us inspected her head and could see no visible scratches or bruises. The attendants then asked that I take myself and the other students out to the hallway so they could check her body for cuts or marks. After a few agonizing minutes, they called me back and reported that, fortunately, they had found no abrasions or bruises. I asked Wendy to count to ten and sing "Happy Birthday." She performed both flawlessly. I'm not sure what I would have done if she hadn't been able to carry out those tasks, but a memory exercise seemed prudent at the time.

After I sent Ed to retrieve Bernie, I asked the attendants to escort the rest of the students back to the elevator and upstairs. I lifted Wendy into her cart, being careful not to tilt her head, and placed her as gently as I could onto her back. For the next five minutes, I entertained her with knock-knock jokes. Her favorite was the old standby about the orange and the banana, and relief flooded me when it coaxed a delighted giggle from her.

Bernie arrived within a few minutes, and after chiding me for moving Wendy off the floor, she examined my student more thoroughly in her cart. Satisfied that there seemed to be no obvious problems, she suggested we get Wendy back up to the ward. As we navigated the hallway toward the elevator, Wendy seemed to be in good spirits. When the elevator stopped on the first floor, I wheeled her out the elevator door and turned right. Bernie followed but went left. As she hurried down the hall, she yelled back that she would call Dr. Ivanok, the chief medical doctor, and bring him back to the ward to see Wendy.

"Bernie," I hollered, already incredulous at the words that were about to leave my lips. After all, dealing with her was the last thing I wanted to do, but I knew she needed to know what had happened.

"While you're at it, I think you should contact Mrs. Sharp."

When Dr. Ivanok arrived ten minutes later, the ward became noticeably quieter. I retreated to Ruth's bed area, where she was sitting and observing everything from her wheelchair. When Wendy saw me, she waved hello and said, "Hi, Mr. Shane, I'm glad you came to see me." I smiled back at her, lowered the iron railing, and sat on Ruth's bed as the doctor examined Wendy's head. A few minutes into the examination, Mrs. Sharp stepped into the room, searched me out, and beckoned for me to join her. I heard Teddy McNeil's voice in my mind: *Oh shit.*

Mrs. Sharp waited for me outside the entrance to the ward. "How are you doing?" she asked, when I came through the door. It was jarring to hear the genuine concern in her voice.

"It all happened so fast," I told her. "I just hope she's okay."

"Why don't we go to Bernie's office to discuss this?" she suggested.

Bernie was sitting behind her desk when we entered. She looked worried, but I wasn't sure whether her concern was for Wendy, me, or herself—maybe it was all three. Mrs. Sharp greeted her in an uncharacteristically warm manner and then asked me to describe exactly what had occurred. I retold the story, trying to remember every step but leaving out the detail about her new cart having no sides. I thought that fact might cause a bigger headache for Bernie and the staff. Mrs. Sharp was especially focused when I explained that I thought this unusual event was caused by an extraordinary alignment of circumstances. She even smiled warmly when I described how Wendy had commented, "I think I fell out of my cart" in an offhand way while lying on the cold, hard cement of the classroom floor.

As I was completing my review, Dr. Ivanok walked up and interrupted us.

"Is it true," he asked, "that the floor in the classroom is really made of cement?"

Bernie answered that it was indeed true.

He shook his head several times. "Today we witnessed a true miracle. For all intents and purposes, that fragile head falling on that hard surface from that distance should have split open like a watermelon. My God, we were lucky today! That child does not have a scratch on her. She is perfectly fine. I'm telling you, this is a miracle."

Mrs. Sharp asked if there was anything further that needed to be done. Dr. I, as he was more commonly referred to, responded that his only advice was to be sure she did not fall out of her cart again. We all laughed nervously along with him.

After he left, Mrs. Sharp returned to the incident and asked how Wendy could possibly have fallen out of her cart. "Aren't all the carts we make in the shop constructed to prevent just that from happening?"

"Not all of them, Dorothy," Bernie said. "We have a few without sides that allow for easier care of the resident, but these aren't supposed to be used out of the ward. Dorothy, I'm afraid she was in one of those carts that didn't have any rails today. It was a mistake that can't happen again."

Mrs. Sharp stared out the window, her expression inscrutable. I wondered with trepidation what was in store for Bernie, and whether Mrs. Sharp would try to pin the blame on me. When she finally turned back to us, I was unprepared for her response.

"Well," she said. "Since we experienced a miracle today, and we certainly don't have many of those, I don't think we need to confuse the good spirits that shined on us today by trying to find someone to blame. I'm satisfied just knowing our little friend isn't hurt. Are you both okay with that?"

Bernie and I glanced at each other.

"Works for me," I said.

Neither Bernie nor I spoke for a minute or so after Mrs. Sharp left.

"Two miracles in one day are more than I'm used to," I finally said.

"Two?"

"Well, Wendy being spared a serious injury, for one, and me being spared a serious reprimand."

"But you didn't do anything." She paused and then added, "This time."

"Ah, a third miracle."

Bernie fiddled with a pen, turning it in a slow circle on her desk. "Howard, I noticed you intentionally didn't mention that flawed cart when you were going over the details," she said.

"That's true," I acknowledged.

"I appreciate that you didn't. But it would have been all right to mention it, too. After all, we made a mistake."

Her jaw tensed, and her eyes glistened slightly. I could tell she'd be replaying today's events—and thinking about what she could have done differently—for a long time. I'd been there myself, and I knew how it felt.

"Hey. It turned out all right." I reached out and placed a tentative hand on her shoulder. "Don't beat yourself up."

We stood there together in silence, reflecting on what we'd been spared that day. In a place like Belchertown, where so many things could break your heart and so much was out of our control, we took our miracles where we could find them.

CHAPTER 24

Three weeks had passed since Wendy's spill. Although it had seemed like a big deal at the time, I heard no further mention of it by the staff, the students, or Wendy. I knew I would never forget that tumble, but I didn't see the need to keep the memory fresh by rehashing it. Instead, I tried to stay focused on the looming May 1st deadline for the Expressor prototype, as I continued to introduce skills that would make the introduction of the new device as smooth and productive as possible.

It was just after four o'clock when I walked past Bernie's office and out the front door of the infirmary. I couldn't have been more than ten yards up the path when Ginger, the head nurse for the three-to-eleven shift, yelled that I had a phone call. I ran back to the office she shared with Bernie to take it.

"Allen here," was what I heard the instant I put the phone to my ear.

"How did you do that, Allen? I haven't said hello yet."

"Telepathy," he answered. "Just trying to save you the trouble."

"What's up? How are Thomas and Bill progressing?"

"They're doing some final testing this weekend, and the Communicator should be ready for delivery early next week."

"Expressor," I gently corrected.

"What? Oh yes, the Expressor. Well, the Expressor will be ready for field testing next week."

I could feel my heart pounding. "Have you seen it?" I inquired. "Do they have it connected up to the mercury switch yet?"

"Yes, I've seen it, and no, they haven't finished wiring the switch yet, but that's trivial compared to building the device."

"So, what should I do?"

"Tell us where and when we can deliver it," he answered. "I think it will be important for the boys to meet Ron and Ruth. It'll help them understand the magnitude of what they will have accomplished."

"You know, Allen, for a guy who can make his phone ring at will as a way to get rid of his students, you sure are being mighty considerate of these two."

I could hear quiet laughter on the other end of the line. "Well, between you and me, these two guys turned out to be exceptional, and they have worked nights and weekends to meet their deadline. I thought their time-line was overly ambitious when they announced it, but here we are, right on the mark. Isn't next Wednesday exactly a month since the design meeting?"

The blotter on Bernie's desk was a calendar, and I calculated the time as Allen talked. "Yes," I confirmed. "May 1st is exactly one month."

With that, we set the delivery date for the following Thursday after-noon, at two p.m. sharp.

On delivery day, my excitement and anticipation had me a bit unfo-cused as I worked in the classroom with my students, waiting for the Expressor to arrive. Bill and Thomas planned to come in through the back door of the infirmary, and I was on the lookout. A bank of windows high on the west wall filled my classroom with some welcome natural light, but they also allowed me to keep an eye out and know when anyone was within twenty yards of the back of the building. Since I could see only up to the waist of a passerby on foot, I never knew for sure who was out there unless I recognized their pants or the individuality of their gait. If someone rolled by in a wheelchair, I could see their face in profile.

On one occasion, Carla had shrieked and startled all of us when she noticed Jimmy Kearns on hands and knees, peering into the room. I didn't know how long he had been watching, but he stayed there: waving, mak-ing faces, and utterly distracting the entire class. The students enjoyed his look-in so much that I had let it continue for nearly half an hour until he was apparently spotted and whisked away. I saw no reason to terminate the wonderful interruption, especially since the children experienced so few serendipitous opportunities to laugh and have fun.

It was thrilling to finally see three sets of legs pass by the classroom windows around two o'clock. Handing Ed my key to the rear door, I asked him to open it. Without a word, Ed was on the move.

The students were all facing the door when Allen entered the room, followed by the Expressor, which was carried by Bill and Thomas. The trio were greeted by the unfettered applause and hollering we had rehearsed earlier that day in anticipation of their arrival.

"Hey, everyone, please welcome Professor Fitch, Thomas, and Bill."

As the group ramped up their cheering again, Allen told us that the Expressor was in good working order, and it was especially impressive that it only took a month to build a working prototype that functions well enough to explore its effectiveness. I directed Thomas and Bill to set the Expressor down on my desk for the time being. As the group ramped up their cheering again, I took in the new device, a large, shallow plywood box with a circular white face ringed in white light bulbs. Even though I had looked at the design they sketched on the blackboard very carefully, as a real thing in three-dimensional form it looked bigger and even more impressive than I had imagined. Then, I herded them over to Ron and Ruth, who sat next to each other to the left side of the larger group.

"Ron, Ruth, here they are! And there it is," I said, pointing to my desk. "After the rest of the class leaves, I'm hoping Thomas and Bill will teach us all about the Expressor." Turning to the rest of the class, I said, "Tomorrow everyone's going to get to see how the Expressor works and maybe even try it, but first I want to give Ron and Ruth a little training after class today on how to use it. So tonight, you all have to get a good night's sleep!"

Thomas nodded enthusiastically at this suggestion, but Bill, looking stiff and uncomfortable, didn't react at all. I surmised he was still overwhelmed by what must have been his first experience with a person, or in this case many persons, with disabilities. I thought it best not to draw attention to his unease for a while and let him get used to everyone.

At three o'clock, the attendants arrived, and the rest of the class left. With Ron and Ruth positioned in front of the Expressor and Ed standing off to the side but paying careful attention, Allen asked me how I wanted to proceed. I suggested they provide a brief overview of how to operate the device—from connecting it to the power source to adjusting the speed and attaching the switch.

As Allen discussed how to bring electricity to the Expressor, I thought back to the first trial with the clock communicator, in which I'd had to pull the plug out of the wall to stop the progression of the second hand. Now, the movement of the indicator—in this case the illuminated light—was controlled by a switch, and a dial was available to adjust the speed at which the light moved around the circle of lights. I was over the moon at how much progress had been made in such a relatively short period of time.

"Let's discuss the switch," Thomas interjected. At the mention of the word "switch," Bill searched his pocket and pulled out a glass tube affixed to a standard brown watchband. A long wire extended from the glass tube.

"This is the switch," Bill began, holding out the tube attached to the watchband. He seemed to have lost his discomfort, for he told us confidently about the switch and how it worked. He held it in the air in front of him and then suspended it before Ruth and then Ron, giving them each ample time to inspect it.

Bill and Thomas were obviously proud of their accomplishment, and this satisfaction was reflected in the elaborate detail they used to describe every part of the device. No doubt it had taken them hundreds of hours to create this masterpiece, while still balancing their schoolwork and social lives, but the way they spoke about it made every minute sound like a labor of love.

Finally, we came to the demonstration. The Expressor connected to the power source and turned on, and one light was illuminated on the face of the device. Thomas inserted one end of the switch's cable into the side port of the apparatus while he held the glass tube exactly parallel to the floor. The light remained still. "Watch this," he said as he tilted the wristband, causing each light in succession to turn on and then off as the succeeding light became lit. As the light moved about the circle, Bill turned a small dial on the side of the Expressor, and the speed of the moving light accelerated. He showed off a little by making it move at its maximum speed and then turning the dial all the way in the opposite direction, causing the light to dramatically lose speed as if brakes had been applied. Seeing that we were sufficiently dazzled, Thomas brought the mercury tube switch back to its original position, and the light became still once again.

"Gentlemen," I finally said, "what can I say except that what you've built is absolutely spectacular?" I took the watchband containing the mercury switch from Thomas and held it out in front of me. "I think it's now time to turn the Expressor over to Ron and Ruth."

Allen leaned forward and pointed to the Expressor. "What do you think about that?" he asked, looking back and forth between Ron and Ruth.

Ron studied Allen for a few seconds and then blinked repeatedly, his best version of an enthusiastic yes. He was clearly elated. Ruth stared straight up and tensed her body, a clear signal that she too was thrilled.

I told the engineers that now Ron and Ruth wanted to show their gratitude for building the communication machine. Ruth stared at Ed until she caught his eye and then looked toward the cabinet in the corner of the classroom. Ed, now the budding master of subtle nonverbal exchanges, sauntered to the cupboard and found the circular template we had practiced with all week for just this occasion. Our visitors seemed awed by this silent conversation, by the fact that a directed glance could be just as effective as a verbal request to retrieve a particular template.

I suggested to Ed that he set the template inside the circle of lights. I tried not to show my relief, but I was delighted that the template fit exactly.

The close-friction fit of the white cardboard template within the circle of lights meant that no tacks or pins were needed to secure it to the Expressor. On the display before us were words and symbols, handprinted in black permanent marker, that I had gone over with Ron and Ruth throughout the week. The names Allen, Thomas, and Bill, of course, were placed at the top of the template, and distributed over the rest of the display were five other functional word options: "Thank you," "Yes," "No," "Amazing," and "Cool." Also on the display were happy face and thumbs-up symbols. When selected, these words and symbols of gratitude and excitement would hopefully convey Ron and Ruth's joy to Allen and his team.

The words and symbols were spaced at equal locations around the circle so that four lights aligned with each word. I watched the engineers scan the word list and noticed Thomas's eyes lingering longer on his own name, prominently displayed where it belonged at the pinnacle or twelve o'clock position.

Still holding the switch, I turned to Ron and asked if he had anything he wanted to express. When he blinked, I said, "For now I'll operate the switch. I want you to blink when the light lines up with what you want to say." With that, I rotated the switch, and the light started to move around the circle. He stared at the word that he wanted and waited patiently for the corresponding light to illuminate. Everyone in the room was spellbound by the light's maiden voyage around the template, and I felt a collective intake of breath when Ron raised his eyes with perfect timing, signaling me to stop the light.

Ed spoke just then, for the first time that day. In a clear and confident voice, he reported the message that Ron had chosen: "Thank you!" I warmed with pride. Ron had successfully located those words of gratitude, a lesson he'd been working on with diligence for the past few days.

Bill wasted no time in answering, "You're welcome!"

"Ruth, do you know who made this fine piece of equipment?" I asked next. She immediately looked toward the ceiling to signal yes, and then her eyes went to the Expressor. I started the light progression as she watched its movement intently. When the light approached the nine o'clock position, I saw anticipation rising throughout her entire body. At the eleven o'clock position, her eyes shot upward to signal the arrival of the light at her location of choice: Allen. I then returned the switch to its starting position, where she next selected Thomas and then Bill. As each name was highlighted, both Ron and Ruth glanced at the corresponding person, confirming that they could correctly link each written name with the man it belonged to. While the selection of these names may have seemed trivial, it was a major triumph for a couple of kids who had been unable to identify any sight words just a few months earlier.

Our visitors stayed for another half hour or so, chatting and asking me questions about my work with the students. I could tell that Thomas and Bill were proud of the work they'd accomplished, and Allen—in his own quiet way—was proud of them. After they'd left and Ron and Ruth had returned to the wards, I sat at my desk and gazed at the Expressor: a beautiful device, an emblem of progress, creativity, and determination.

The new machine held great promise. Despite it being a prototype, it was solidly built, with a surface area that allowed many more symbols or words than the original clock face system. Allen's team had delivered, and it was a terrific start—but I knew there were still some important next steps to be made. Although Ron and Ruth could now enjoy a wider range of expression, they still needed a way to control the Expressor without my assistance.

My mantra for Ron and Ruth was "independent control," and I sensed that the key rested in the small tube of mercury attached to the watchband I still clutched in my right hand. I knew that simply strapping the mercury switch to Ron or Ruth's wrist was not the answer: for two people who had little control over their movements, that would likely be a recipe for frustration. Independent operation would require careful guidance and considerable practice.

The real work of teaching my students to control the lights independently would begin soon enough. Today had been a day to celebrate kindness and ingenuity—and to give Ron and Ruth a first glimpse of the independence I wanted for them so very much.

CHAPTER 25

I generally avoided Mrs. Sharp's office in the school building, mainly to stay clear of the onerous nine-word request, "Mr. Shane, could you please stop by my office?" I was nearly out a side door with a load of supplies when my eye caught a large green poster tacked next to the exit. The message, written freehand, announced the annual spring dance.

The building janitor, a man who had worked at the institution for years, was sweeping up nearby.

"What's this about a dance, Milton?" I pointed to the poster.

He laughed as he spoke, and I noticed he had a slight gap between his two front teeth that gave the impression he had a piece of spinach lodged between them. "Mr. Shane, I mean Howard, you're over in the infirmary building too much. There's a dance every spring, put on by volunteers from the Friends Association. The whole gym is decorated. It always looks great."

I remembered the Belchertown Friends Association from the investigation committee formed in the wake of the exposé. "So, do you go to the dance?"

"Sure, I go. One of the janitors has to be there in case there are any accidents. I like it so much I always volunteer. I even take my wife. Everyone gets all dressed up, and the kids really have fun."

"You know, it's curious. I haven't heard anyone mention the dance until this very moment."

"Well, your folks don't come to the dance anyway."

"What do you mean, they don't come to the dance?" I was afraid I knew where this conversation was headed.

"I guess it's because you can't push wheelchairs up the stairs," Milton said matter-of-factly.

"Well, that's...." I started to protest and then stopped. Milton didn't need to hear one of my tirades on the inequities of this place and how they affected my students in particular. He was just doing his job.

"Thanks, Milton. I need to head back to the infirmary." I turned to leave, then paused, glancing back at him. "I'll see you at the dance."

My mind was racing as I descended the granite steps leading out of the school building where the dance would be held. It was a slow rate of descent as I counted each tread that would need to be scaled for a person who resided in the infirmary to attend the dance. When I reached the infirmary, my first stop was a small room on the first floor that contained three small cubicles set aside for physical therapy and nursing student interns. I found Bob muddling through some paperwork at the cubicle closest to the door, and I pulled up a seat to join him, relaying the news about the big dance.

"So?" he asked.

"So... wouldn't it be a hoot for the infirmary kids to attend?" I asked.

"Why? Besides, I don't see how this dance fits into your global agenda of world peace and the total ruination of this institution."

"I'm all for world peace and freedom of expression, but especially the freedom to dance. Isn't it discriminatory that the people who live in this building can't attend the one festive event in this place? We take this one bright night that might actually be distracting, if not downright fun for these folks, and we exclude them from it? Are you kidding? It's unfair, it's inequitable, and it's—"

"Hey, save the sermon for Mrs. Sharp. You'll need it when you try to convince her she should 'let your people go.'" He gave me a crooked grin and tapped his pen on the papers in front of him. "When she learns that H. Shane, teacher and Gandhi-wannabe, is promoting the idea of an integrated dance hall, she'll turn you down faster than all the girls you invited to your senior prom."

"You know, Bob, for once I think you're absolutely right," I said. "If I ask for permission for my students to go to the dance, the request will be denied. You know the old saying about asking for forgiveness... blah, blah, blah. Once the crime is committed, we'll have to deal with her outrage. We'll just need to act dumb, plead guilty, ask for mercy, and then get down on our knees and beg her forgiveness."

"What's with the 'we'?"

"Bob, where's your sense of public responsibility? Or are you resisting because of your awkwardness on the dance floor?"

I left Bob's cubicle and found Bernie sitting in her office, sifting paper clips between her fingers while talking on the telephone. I tapped softly on the widow. She waved me in and pointed at an empty chair in front of her desk.

"I need to go. We can figure this out later," she said into the phone before hanging up. She leaned back in her chair and let out a long sigh. "This better be good. I need something cheerful right now."

"Bernie, let's just suppose..."

"Here we go," she said, but a smile was already tugging at her lips, and I knew I could continue.

"Let's just suppose you had a chance to bring some of the folks who live in this building to a special function. And let's just suppose that this get-together would require that certain residents and even some attendants be away from the infirmary for, say, two to three hours. Given those parameters, which residents of this building would you think would be best suited for and thus gain the most from such an evening? Let's assume 'suited' means they would be healthy enough to go, could tolerate time away from the building, and would not freak out in a novel and busy environment."

Bernie cocked her head at me. "Do you want to tell me what you have in mind," she asked, "or do you want me to take part in this sort of espionage without knowing exactly what you're planning?"

I thought for a brief moment. "You really don't want to know what I have in mind, but trust me, it will not harm any resident in any way. They will not leave the grounds. I'm just asking you to trust me. This may sound a little convoluted, but I'm here asking you for a list instead of just blundering ahead without checking with you. I'm asking you to create a roster and close your eyes."

"I can't just give you a list like that," she said. "And we never go to any events in the school building, so I'm sure that has nothing to do with this. But in any event, there's a good chance that those same names would appear on my field trip list."

"You have an actual field trip list?"

"Well, no," she admitted, "but I should, and I've been meaning to make one. I suppose if there *were* such a list, it would hang on my wall over there for a few hours at the end of the day. If someone were to copy it, I would see no harm in that. But before you go through all this trouble, have you thought about the repercussions from your boss when she learns you're the ringleader of whatever it is you're planning?"

"Of course I've thought it through," I said with a smile. "Like everything I do, it is methodical down to the last detail."

Bernie spread her hands in the air and looked at me with a blend of fondness and resignation. "Well, it's your funeral."

The next day, I ducked into Bernie's office and snagged the list of names she had, as promised, placed on the clipboard hanging on her office wall. The heading read RESIDENTS IN NEED OF DANCE LESSONS. So much for me putting one over on Bernie. I inspected the roster of fifteen names—most of which, like Norman's, I recognized even though not all of them were my students. Almost all of my students plus Ed were included, with the exceptions of Jack and Wendy.

I sat down in Bernie's guest chair and thought about how difficult this would be: leaving two of my students behind for their safety while their classmates got to experience the dance. My brain knew it made perfect sense that moving wheelchairs from the infirmary to the school building was as far as Bernie could go, but my heart wanted us all there together. I wrestled with this for a long moment—wishing I didn't have to compromise, hoping I could come up with a creative solution. In the end, I had to admit that I didn't see a way to transport Jack and Wendy safely to the dance; after Wendy's tumble, I myself wouldn't want to risk carrying a cart up the school steps. I resolved to explain the situation to them with care and sensitivity, and try to make it up to them in some special way.

I decided to talk to Jack first, before word leaked out about my plan. Jack was the most academically advanced in the class and also more low-key than most of the others; I probably hadn't given him as much attention as other students because he was more capable. He came to class each day and paid careful attention to classroom activities. He was the one who had his finger on the pulse of the classroom, always with an eye on the ebb and flow of the class. Most often, he was the first to point out when another student needed assistance or when the attendants had arrived at the end of the school day. I knew he would understand the implications of being left behind while the others went to the dance, and I had to see how he felt about it.

I went straight to Ward 4 from Bernie's office. I found Jack alone in the day room, watching television. He was lying on his side with his head resting on his hand, propped up by a few pillows. In this side-lying position with a blanket over his body, he gave the impression of a typical teenager resting on the couch. I approached, and he lifted his head off his hand and smiled.

"Do you have a minute to talk?" I asked him. I realized with regret that this was the first time I had spoken to him in private away from the interested ears of his classmates.

His smile disappeared, and he nodded.

"Jack," I started, "there's going to be a dance over at the school building next month, and I think it would be good if some of the kids in our class could go to it. Unfortunately, for a few reasons, I don't think everyone would be able to go. Some of the residents wouldn't be able to go because of safety reasons. Some wouldn't be able to tolerate the loud noise, or the crowds of people. And some—"

"I can't go, right?" he interrupted.

My shoulders slumped; this was going to be even harder than I'd thought. "Here's the thing, Jack. You remember what happened to Wendy when she fell out of her cart? That was the scariest day for everyone—for me, for the attendants, for Wendy, too." I watched his face, but he just stared at me. "And we can't take a chance that you could fall out of your cart and get hurt. I've thought about it a lot, and I think it will be just too dangerous to bring you all the way over to the school in this."

"Okay," he said and continued to stare at me.

"I'm so sorry about this," I said. "Can you think of some way I can make it up to you?"

"Okay," he repeated.

He kept looking at me, and I realized he probably didn't understand what I meant by "making it up to him." Despite his relatively strong language skills, he wasn't familiar with much figurative language, or with the back-and-forth of personal relationships.

"What I mean is, let's do something together, since you won't be able to go to the dance," I suggested. "Can you tell me your favorite things to do?"

He didn't hesitate. "I like to go outside."

"Tell you what, how about you and I find some time to go outside?"

"Okay. I'd like to go outside anytime with you."

"All right. How about you and I head outside on some Wednesdays after school, just the two of us. We'll just go and hang out. Let's go outside for twice as long as the two-hour dance. How does that sound?"

"Okay, we'll go out for four hours," he said.

"Good. We'll go out enough times to make up for the time of the dance times two. Does that sound fair to you?"

Jack gave me a small smile. "Yeah."

I paid Wendy a visit in her ward next, preparing myself for another difficult, sensitive conversation.

"Hi, Wendy," I said, my voice gentle as I approached. "I want to talk to you about a dance that some of the kids are going to go to."

"I want to go to a dance, too," she said.

"Do you know what a dance is, Wendy?" I inquired.

"No. Are Carla and Ruth going to the dance?"

"Yes, they are. But I'm not sure you would like a dance if you went, and that's what I wanted to talk to you about today."

"I would too like it. Why wouldn't I like it?"

"Well, the dance happens in a big room where there are hundreds of people who are jumping around and bumping into each other. Would you like it if people were bumping into you?"

She shook her head.

"You like music, don't you?"

She nodded. "I like the Beatles."

"I do, too. But the thing is, the music at the dance is really loud. I mean, *really* loud."

She covered her ears and scrunched up her face. I tried to contain a grin.

"Now, does that sound like a lot of fun to you?" I asked.

"I don't like it when the noise is loud," she said emphatically.

"I know you don't," I said. "See, not going to the dance maybe isn't so bad after all, is it?"

"Yes. Maybe I won't like the dance if it's loud."

"You know something? I have a really great idea." She fixed her eyes attentively on mine. "Instead of going to the dance, how about you get all dressed up and listen to dance music right here instead. But this dance music won't be loud, so you won't have to cover your ears. How does that sound?"

"Can I listen to some Beatles music?"

"Yup, I promise there will be lots and lots of Beatles music," I said. "I'll talk to the attendants, and we'll make that happen for you, okay?"

"Okay, Mr. Shane."

Before I left, I leaned over and whispered in Wendy's ear that she was a really sweet girl.

———————

Much relieved about Jack and Wendy, I started to plan dance night. The employees I approached agreed that it was unjust to exclude the infirmary residents. Convincing them, however, that attending the function was really worth fighting for—or, as some reasoned, risking or forfeiting their jobs for—was an entirely different matter. When I tried to promote the dance as a statement about breaking down barriers for those residents who had faced so many restrictions and inequalities, I learned that most regarded it as just a dance, so I conceded that there probably wasn't some greater purpose and instead concentrated on just making it a fun evening.

With some prodding, I managed to round up three essential groups of volunteers from among the attendants and nurses in the building. The first group was responsible for gathering the evening attire for the dance. The second group of co-conspirators, the dressers, would bathe, dress, and apply makeup for the group that would attend the dance. The last group was a small band of hearty workers who agreed to help lift any resident in a wheelchair up the stone steps of the school building and into the dance. This group was mostly male volunteers, including Bob and a few other physical therapy interns that he'd rounded up.

I worried that the first group's clothing hunt could really gum up the works. How could we locate suits and dresses for fifteen to twenty residents? As it turned out, however, there were several employees who not only knew the location of clothing storage areas on the grounds but were also willing to raid them and bring the pilfered clothes back to the infirmary. Some of these storage rooms, I was told, contained rows of formalwear, including suits, tuxedoes, and sport coats for men and boys and evening gowns and special occasion dresses for women. I wondered when formal clothes like these were worn and learned that they were brought out for occasions like this dance or when a resident needed to attend a special event, usually a family function like a funeral or a wedding.

I had to wonder about the style of the clothes these volunteers would come up with when they looted the clothing depots. I was told to expect a kaleidoscope of colors and a hodgepodge of stripes, checks, and polka dots. All the clothes would be out of style and would span several decades of fashion. I was reminded, though, that the residents would be having too much fun at the event to worry about their outfits.

Collecting the clothes from the storage rooms might put the staff at greatest risk, so I told the first group about my concern that borrowing clothes was "teetering on the edge of acceptable behavior," which was really a euphemism for job loss. I wanted to be sure they undertook the risk willingly and knowingly; Bernie's recent lecture, in which she'd implied that I had less to lose than the rest of the staff in the building, had weighed heavily on me for weeks. In her view, I had no ties to the community, and my job was a transitional assignment, a way station on the path to something better. I knew that Bernie had meant no harm, but her remarks had struck at the core of the person I wanted to be. Was I just brash and carefree and willing to throw caution to the wind—and if so, to what end? Worst of all, I had to question whether I was doing all this simply for personal fulfillment and not for the welfare of the residents.

I knew these were the right questions, but I also realized the answer fell somewhere in between. Although my actions weren't entirely altruistic, I knew I had better motives than Bernie had given me credit for. Of course I gained personal satisfaction from standing up on behalf of the residents and speaking out about the terrible conditions, but I did care, intensely, about the wellbeing of these people. And my job as a teacher in the infirmary might have been a pathway to something else, but I didn't yet know what that other thing was, and I hadn't spent enough time trying to figure that out. The one thing that was abundantly clear around the matter of the dance was that regardless of my intentions, I intended to take full responsibility for the residents' attendance, thus shielding my volunteers from Mrs. Sharp's wrath. I knew she would have no problem reserving her rage and punishment for me alone.

It was refreshing to learn that no one who had volunteered to plunder the clothing storage areas had changed their minds and backed out. Perhaps they didn't expect to be apprehended or didn't view this as a major infraction. Regardless, everyone in the infirmary realized that if our plan to crash the dance leaked out, countermeasures would swiftly be taken to stop us. There was a tacit agreement among everyone, staff and residents, to keep our activity covert. The plan did not become public knowledge, and that was quite remarkable in light of the speed with which confidential information generally spread through the school.

Although family security and survival may have prevented these workers from putting their jobs on the line to protest the abhorrent conditions at Belchertown, the selfless acts of kindness, generosity, and daring they displayed during this dance caper did show me a depth of caring that I hadn't appreciated before. I realized that there are multiple ways of demonstrating empathy and a sense of commitment to others.

The afternoon of the dance was extraordinarily hectic. The action began in earnest at the end of school that Friday. After my students departed, the classroom was transformed into a command center for final preparations—bundles of clothing and accessories were sorted, gathered up, and delivered to the waiting residents. The corridors and wards were noticeably busier than usual, with nurses and attendants not only tending to their daily assignments but also managing to ready the residents for the night's activities. I was delighted to observe a remarkable level of cooperation between attendants, therapists, and others who normally wouldn't have joined forces. As I walked through the building, it felt as if the entire place was in motion; the air buzzed with excitement, the way it does before a prom or a wedding. I was so happy to know that for a few hours tonight, the residents would get a respite from their everyday routines.

By six o' clock, my classroom was in complete disarray, like campaign headquarters the morning after the votes had been cast. The space had served its purpose, and now it was time to shut it down. I wandered upstairs to check on preparations and help tie up any loose ends. On the first floor, the girls in Ward 1 were already wearing their dresses, but the application of makeup and other final touches was just getting underway. The noise level was high, as in a lively, crowded sorority house. The girls giggled, and so did the attendants. Everyone was in the mood to party. Many of the day shift staff had remained to help the girls get ready and chaperone the event, and they gave the ward a homey appearance as they bustled about in their civilian clothes.

In all the commotion, I thought of Wendy and went searching for her. A second-shift nurse tapped me on the back and pointed at Pauline and Wendy, who was lying in her cart in a quiet corner of the ward. Wendy was wearing a lovely green velour dress with a white ruffled collar. Pauline was smiling in a flowery dress that was just right for the season. "And why are you two all dressed up?" I asked, winking at Pauline.

"I'm going to a Beatles Music Party with Pauline!"

"We are indeed," Pauline answered. "And the best thing about this party is that the music isn't going to be too loud."

"I don't like music when it's loud, Mr. Shane. It hurts my ears, and I go like this."

When her hands reached up and covered her ears, I smiled and told myself I could never get tired of watching her perform that adorable gesture.

"Wendy, you are such a lucky girl," I said, "and I know the Beatles music is your favorite."

I knew that for the rest of the night, I'd be replaying Wendy's cheerful narrative. It was a relief to see her so happy, and it removed any remaining guilt about her not going to the dance. And with that weight lifted, my own enthusiasm soared.

As the fateful hour approached and it was time to leave, our operation shifted to the transit phase. It would be no simple task to commandeer our fifteen selected residents, who were not accustomed to moving very far or very fast from one building to another. While I may have joked about a lot of things, I wasn't cavalier about their safety. My biggest concern wasn't the hundred-yard stroll between the infirmary and the school building but the forty-foot incline from the walkway in front of the school to the top of the granite steps that led to the gymnasium entrance. The biggest safety concern was hauling wheelchairs up those front steps, and our plan to do so consisted of a six-person team with designated lifters and spotters. We successfully practiced lifting an empty wheelchair and then a wheelchair with an occupant up the infirmary steps, and we were satisfied the residents would be safe.

It was a perfect early-May evening, seventy degrees, with clear skies and a gorgeous quarter moon. The grass had been cut that day, so the air was filled with the fresh smell of spring. The beauty of the evening bolstered our confidence that everything would be all right.

I suggested we keep the noise low and march together. As we proceeded across the lawn, I heard the residents' shrieks of joy and the staff members' admonishments: *watch your step, keep up, stay in line.* If this had been meant as a sneak attack, we'd all have failed miserably.

Once underway, the group moved as a single entity in a steady forward direction. The long line of residents dressed in colorful formalwear stretched from the infirmary building almost to the school building—in fact, the first resident arrived at the front steps of the school just as Teddy, who was last in line, began his journey. This group was so unlike the group I had seen on my first day, when I had spotted the line of men in bland, disheveled clothing marching to the carousel. I stood in awe, with some self-reflection and a bit of satisfaction. There was Ruth, glowing in a powder-blue gown with ruffles on the skirt. There was Dennis, dapper in a dark blue suit that was only a little too big for his slight frame. There was Barbara, proud in polka dots, with her hair shaped into neat curls. I was seized with a feeling of accomplishment and camaraderie with both the residents and the staff. We had made this happen!

As residents began to arrive at the front steps, we moved immediately into a lift-and-climb mode. The first wave of infirmary partygoers to reach the entrance were met by residents from other buildings who were hanging around the door to the gymnasium dance hall. Of course, they didn't know any of the infirmary residents, nor did they have any inkling as to where these people had come from.

I strolled into the hall ahead of my group, scanning the crowd for administration personnel. No Mrs. Sharp yet, thank goodness. Maybe she wouldn't show up. I smiled and waved at a few teachers I recognized, acting like I was enjoying my role as just another chaperone. They waved back, paying little attention to me or to the growing number of infirmary residents entering the hall, many in wheelchairs and on crutches. I walked back and forth in front of the entry doors with one burning desire—to get everyone into the room before our presence was noticed. With everyone inside the gym, our guides would be able to encourage everyone to mingle and spread out, to either dance or eat. I figured that once our folks were firmly entrenched in the crowd, it would be much harder to send them back.

The sight of Teddy propelling himself through the double doors meant that every infirmary resident had arrived safely. I spotted Bob near the entrance. I had checked the large wall clock when I first walked in and made a mental note of the time. We had hoisted, lifted, and assisted the fifteen residents in less than eight minutes—maybe a new world record, or at least an institution record. When our eyes met, he broke into a broad grin and gave me two thumbs up.

As my students settled in and began to enjoy themselves, I stood on the sidelines and surveyed the whole festive setting. Pastel pink and white streamers crisscrossed the entire ceiling and dangled just above the heads of the crowd. The clothing styles spanned several decades, and the array of dresses and suits created a living rainbow of colors and patterns: stripes, polka dots, paisley, tweed.

The sights and sounds were nothing like those of any dance I had ever attended. The music was turned up extremely high, but that accounted for just a trace of the noise. Shouts and screeches of unbridled joy emanated from people who weren't concerned about what others might think. On the dance floor, torsos turned, arms flailed, heads bobbed, and legs kicked. Some of the dancers moved with wild exuberance, while others moved in a slow, deliberate manner. A few residents rocked alone to the sound of the music, while others were happy to wander the perimeter of the room.

As I scanned the auditorium, I spotted Ruth and Norman sitting in their wheelchairs side by side at the edge of the dance floor. Both were intently watching a large group of dancers when I approached.

"Why aren't the two of you out on the dance floor?" I asked, approaching them. "Would you like to get out there and dance?"

Ruth's eyes shot up in a *yes*, and Norman added his affirmation.

"I think we can make that happen," I said.

As if on cue, we were greeted by the lively opening riff of "Bad Moon Rising" by Creedence Clearwater Revival. I gestured to two infirmary chaperones standing nearby. "These two want to dance!"

Moments later, Norman and Ruth took part in what was likely the first wheelchair dance in the history of the institution. Both of them seemed to enjoy the rhythmic shuffling of their chairs, and the chaperones' grins never faded as they shimmied my students around the dance floor. At the end of the song, one of the chaperones leaned in to say something to Norman and Ruth—it must've been something along the lines of "want to keep going?" because when "Lola" by The Kinks blasted through the hall, Ruth and Norman's chairs started dancing once again.

As the music shifted gears with "Bridge Over Troubled Water," I spotted Dennis Russell in the middle of the floor, slow-dancing with a pretty teenage girl in a white blouse and a red and white plaid skirt. I was impressed at his ability to maneuver his crutches while still holding on to his dance partner. I had seen him do it in the safety of our rehearsals earlier that week, but truthfully, I didn't think he would get a chance to apply this newfound skill at the dance. When the song ended, Dennis walked by me on his way to get some punch for his dance partner. As he passed by, I leaned over and whispered, "You're a real gentleman." His broad grin was enough to confirm my observation.

I kept circling the dance floor, searching out the folks from the infirmary to be sure they were not only having fun but also staying safe. I noticed Dr. Bowser speaking to one of the older residents, and I ducked back into the crowd, not wanting to start a conversation about my students' presence. I caught several glimpses of Danny, too, zooming his wheelchair around the perimeter of the room. Thankfully, he was skillful enough to avoid any collisions. The atmosphere only seemed to heighten his already high level of activity. He wasn't talking to anyone yet, but he seemed to be having a great time nonetheless.

Ron, I noticed, was sitting alone with Carla, which didn't seem to bother Carla at all—quite the contrary. It was the second instance of puppy love I'd observed in less than twenty minutes. When the Creedence Clearwater Revival hit "Who'll Stop the Rain?" started playing, I asked Ron if he liked the song. He blinked while looking at Carla, and she said, "Yes!"

"Oh, brother," I teased. "What's next, Ron? She's already speaking for you."

Carla let out a loud squeal of emotion. Then, she said, quite distinctly, "Yes, I am."

"So long, lovebirds!" I winked and moved along, wondering idly if there was a policy about resident relationships. I suspected it was forbidden, but fortunately Mrs. Sharp wasn't here yet.

Teddy seemed to have little interest in the dance part of the evening; he was way too busy entertaining the teachers. I joined him while he was speaking with a couple of the teachers whom, until that night, I had interacted with only during our weekly school department meeting. When I approached, one of them stopped laughing long enough to ask him, "So how long was it that you were in the CIA?"

Ed had been invited to attend the dance, too, and he seemed to be enjoying himself in his own way. After being an extraordinary help in getting the rest of the residents up the stairs and into the dance, he retreated into a corner of the vast room, turned his back to the crowd, and retrieved a bundle of pencils from his suit coat, closely examining each one in turn.

"Ed, are you enjoying the dance?" I asked, loudly enough to be heard over the Jackson 5's "I Want You Back." When Ed failed to react, I reformulated my question: "How do you like the dance, Ed?"

He took two steps away from me. "Good, good. I am okay."

"Would you like to walk with me?" I asked. "Do you want go see Teddy and Ron and Paula?"

"I'm okay," he repeated, taking a few more steps away and returning his focus to his pencils.

It was obvious that this was not a comfortable venue for Ed, so I left him in peace to retreat to the place where he was most at ease. I hoped that more frequent opportunities for social encounters might help ease him into more peer interactions eventually, but for now I was just glad he was here.

We were now more than an hour into the party, and almost everyone was successfully mingling. I was chatting with Milton and his wife by the punch bowl when something caught my attention in the doorway: an emerald green dress, an impeccable French twist.

Mrs. Sharp.

She walked in with an imperious air, holding the arm of a man I didn't know but assumed to be Mr. Sharp. As she prowled the edges of the dance floor, scrutinizing the rowdy crowd, I kept a close eye on her. I saw her spot them, one by one: Ed. Dennis. Ron and Carla. Teddy. My stomach clenched as her laser-gaze searched the room and locked on me.

"Uh-oh," said Milton. "You're in trouble."

Mrs. Sharp dropped her husband's arm and set a direct course for me. Up close, I noticed that her eyes were rimmed with a thin line of black eyeliner, and she wore a deeper shade of lipstick than I was accustomed to. If we had a more cordial relationship, I would have pointed out how lovely she looked.

Instead I took a breath to steady myself, extended my hand, and said, "Good evening, Mrs. Sharp."

She grabbed me by my elbow and dragged me away from Milton. When we were out of earshot, she started right in: "Who—who *are* these people?" Flustered, she swept her arm out in front of her.

"Well, that's Teddy McNeil slowly making his way..."

"I know who they are! I want to know what they're *doing* here."

She had lobbed me a soft ball, and I couldn't resist hitting her question out of the park. "They're here to enjoy the festivities, just like everyone else who's here tonight." I spoke slowly, emphasizing the words *just like everyone else.*

"But how did they get here? Oh, never mind," she snapped. "I suppose this was your idea."

I threw myself on that grenade with no hesitation. "Yes, it was my idea—just mine and mine alone. I thought it was the perfect opportunity for people who have never been to a social function to attend this dance." As I spoke the word "people," it was my turn to use an arm, and I swung it in a slow arc. "Wouldn't you say they look pretty happy?"

"That's not the point," she spat. "They've never come to this dance before, and there's a reason for that. First of all, most of them can't dance. How can they dance if they're in wheelchairs?"

"Actually, you just missed Norman and Ruth cutting a rug. With a little help, of course." I tried a grin. "And besides, I've gone to plenty of dances where I didn't dance. I was content to just listen to the music and watch my friends make fools of themselves on the dance floor."

She ignored that argument. "Well, it's not safe."

"What's not safe?" I asked.

"Having all these wheelchairs near the dance floor, for one thing."

I shook my head in utter exasperation.

"Let me repeat, Mr. Shane: I am concerned about *safety.*"

"Me, too," I countered.

"What about getting them into this building? How is that safe?"

Throwing all caution to the wind, I said, "Mrs. Sharp, you know very well how we got my students into the building. We carried them! Well, some of them. We had to, because there isn't a ramp or an elevator. There was no other way to provide them with an equal opportunity to enjoy this function."

"But by *carrying* them up the front stairs?" She glared at me.

"Please let me finish," I said. "You'll recall that when students were carried up and down the stairwell in the infirmary, I made sure people were there to offer security. It was a safety net. Tonight, again, we put safety first. We had a legion of strong and able people who volunteered to do all the heavy lifting, and—"

"I've heard enough. We'll discuss this first thing Monday morning."

I reminded myself that another visit to her woodshed was the best possible outcome here. I had only hoped she wouldn't order the infirmary residents to leave—and surprisingly, she didn't seem to have that in mind. My students would stay at the dance. And I'd count tonight as another small Belchertown miracle.

"Okay, then," I told Mrs. Sharp. "I'll see you on Monday."

With that, I turned and retreated to Milton and his wife, who hadn't moved an inch since I had been pulled away.

As the dance drew to a close, and mild chaos reigned at the end of the last song, the infirmary chaperones managed to round up our entire contingent without incident. We brought our group together and waited for all the other attendees to leave so the stairs would be clear for our watchful descent. The afterglow of the evening was still on every face—resident and chaperone alike. Teddy spoke up and asked if he could say something.

Bob patted him on the shoulder. "Sure, but please, no more jokes, and no more singing."

Teddy looked up at Bob and laughed. He then turned to the group and said, "You know, dances can get awfully hot, but it sure is worth it!"

Teddy had said it all. No matter what happened on Monday morning, it sure was worth it.

CHAPTER 26

O
n Monday—just before noon, when the students would leave for their lunch break—there was a knock on the door to my classroom. It was one of the female residents, who was helping Bernie deliver messages throughout the building. She handed me a note, avoiding my gaze, and made a quick exit. I held the note in my hand for a moment, wondering if I should wait to read it later, away from the students. I had a hunch I knew who it was from.

On impulse, I opened it, scanned it quickly, then crumpled it and chucked it in the trash.

"Oh, shit!" Teddy yelled out. "You're in trouble now, aren't you?"

"Hey, listen here, garbage mouth. I'm not in as much trouble as you are," I said.

"For what, using a swear word? You said I could swear if I want to."

"First, I didn't say you could swear anytime you want—but forget about that for now. You're in trouble for minding other people's business." I was sure Teddy knew that he would never really be in hot water with me, but I believed it was important that he develop a language filter. Truth be told, I found his now-occasional use of expletives entertaining, but knowing when to avoid certain words in certain circumstances was crucial, and still a work in progress for him.

Bob entered the room, carrying a note that looked suspiciously similar to the one I had just tossed in the garbage. He waved his note and proclaimed, "I guess we're in trouble now!"

I looked over at Teddy and noticed that the color had drained from his face. Now he seemed more concerned than amused. "Teddy, don't worry," I said. "My note said that I've won the Nobel Peace Prize."

"What's a Nobel Peace Prize?" Teddy asked.

"Teddy, we are just joking around. I'll be fine. We'll be fine," I assured him. "You go have some lunch, and don't worry about Mr. Bergquist and me. You know we can handle any situation."

Both notes from Mrs. Sharp requested the honor of our presence at a four p.m. meeting in the conference room of the school building. When Bob and I arrived that afternoon, we took our seats, looking sufficiently repentant and somber as we awaited the arrival of our host. When Bernie walked in, I felt sick at the thought that I might have dragged her down, too.

Mrs. Sharp marched into the room, taking her place on one side of the table, confirming her role as judge and jury. On the opposite side of the table, the three of us—the purported felons—sat speechless and humble. As the four of us waited together in silence, I noticed something odd: Bob, Bernie, and I were all staring at the tabletop with appropriately grim expressions, but so was Mrs. Sharp.

The unexpected arrival of Superintendent Bowser went a long way to explain her curious behavior. Since my other two encounters with him had not been very pleasant, I assumed this meeting would be no different.

Dr. Bowser had clear, penetrating blue eyes, and today he was looking younger than his years, probably because of his perfect posture. Although his solid blue suit and red striped tie were clearly of another era, the way he carried himself made him look more contemporary.

He addressed the group. "I want to thank you all for coming so late in the day. I know how busy everyone is. As you may know, there has been a great deal of criticism lately about our institution."

I reflexively nodded, until I realized I was the only one conspicuously agreeing.

"The biggest complaint seems to be that there is not enough activity for the residents, so I have been trying, with the help of Mrs. Sharp and other members of the senior administrative staff, to create some new and interesting programs." He glanced at Mrs. Sharp, and her frown morphed into a smile. "The farm is now officially closed, but we have instituted a greenhouse program. Students from the university are now spending more time in the nursery with our young residents. Last Friday evening, we held another of our spring dances. And that is what I wanted to speak with you about today."

"Uh-oh," I whispered to Bob. "Here it comes."

"Shh," was all Mrs. Sharp said.

"When I returned home after the event and thought about what had made this year's dance so wonderful," he continued, "I realized it was the addition of the infirmary residents. So, when I was writing my report for the Department of Mental Retardation early this morning, I wrote a note on this addition and then called Dorothy to thank her for her great planning. I know it wasn't easy to safely include residents in wheelchairs, and I'm impressed."

I could not have been more surprised had antlers sprouted from his head. I glanced at Bob and Bernie. They were staring at Dr. Bowser, too, disbelief on both their faces.

Dr. Bowser clapped his hands together. "So then I told Dorothy that I needed to find some time to visit the building and see just how much the residents liked the dance."

Only Mrs. Sharp nodded in agreement. Because she hadn't cracked a smile or worn a frown since entering the room, it was unclear to me how she felt. Was she relieved that she wasn't being blamed, or upset that we (make that I) weren't being chastised (or more likely, in my case, fired)?

"She suggested that I meet with the three of you because you helped to make it happen. So here we are." He paused and spread his arms wide. When none of us ran up to embrace him, he continued: "So, once again, many, many thanks to you all."

The three of us looked at each other, astonished. Given the tone of our last encounter, I was especially shocked that Dr. Bowser showed no hint of animosity toward me.

When the meeting ended, Bernie, Bob, and I walked out of the room together, feeling stunned but vindicated. Mrs. Sharp followed behind us, leaving the superintendent alone in the room. We'd more than dodged the chopping block—we'd actually been praised for a job well done.

Maybe, just maybe, we were making progress at the institution.

———

I had made good on my promise to Wendy with the help of Pauline, who informed me that she and Wendy had enjoyed a very special evening while the other students were at the dance. Not surprisingly, Wendy had never seemed to tire of listening to Beatles music—she and Pauline had listened to the records all night, playing their favorite songs over and over (Pauline loved "A Hard Day's Night" the best, while Wendy was a "Yellow Submarine" kind of girl).

I hadn't forgotten my promise to Jack to take him outside. So the following week, on a Wednesday afternoon in mid-May, we embarked on our first adventure. Early spring was chilly in Western Massachusetts, so before we left the ward, I made certain Jack had heavy clothing and an extra blanket. We took the elevator to the loading dock level and then to the road, and from there I wheeled him to the meadow behind the building, an old pair of binoculars around my neck. I parked his cart next to a picnic table that was still covered with twigs and other debris left over from the winter, and I sat down on the bench.

Jack was quiet. I searched his face, but I couldn't tell how or what he was feeling.

"Let me know if you're cold," I said. "Are you cold?"

"No." Jack seemed almost bothered by my verbal intrusion. He paid little attention to me as he slowly moved his head to and fro, taking in the view and feeling the breeze on his face.

"Want to look through these?" I asked, holding out the binoculars.

He glanced down at them but quickly resumed his observation of the meadow. "No, thanks."

I stood up and started to pick sticks and leaves off the table. I tried to engage Jack by showing him a stick shaped roughly like a person and an interesting leaf that had curled in on itself, but Jack kept quiet, only offering one-word answers. I busied myself with the table for as long as I could stand it, and then asked again if he was cold.

"No, fine," he answered, in a tone that indicated he wasn't up for more conversation.

I sat back down, a little disappointed. I'd hoped to have some overdue bonding time with Jack; I'd pictured him smiling at the things I would show him, maybe even pointing something out to me. I tried to adjust my expectations and go with the flow. Lifting the binoculars to my face, I scanned the tree line, hoping to spot something interesting. No runaways, no wild animals, no residents on picnics or walks—all I saw were trees.

"Want to go for a walk on the road?" I asked Jack about twenty minutes later.

"No, thanks."

"What are you looking at, Jack?" I finally asked. We had been there for nearly an hour and hadn't had any real conversation. He just sat there peacefully staring, taking in his surroundings.

"What?" he said. "What did you say?"

I repeated my question.

"Oh." He tipped his face up with a look of contentment I had rarely seen on any human face. "I'm looking at the trees and the sky, that's all."

In that moment, I saw our ordinary surroundings through the eyes of my student. To me, this was a boring place to sit in silence for any length of time: just trees and grass and a bunch of debris. To Jack, this was a playground for the senses. The breeze ruffled his hair and caressed his face. Clouds drifted by in a slow parade, changing shape before his eyes. The scents of spring were everywhere—budding trees and fresh-mowed grass and flowers newly unfurled from their winter beds. Though the air was chilly, the sun peeked through the clouds at regular intervals, casting its warmth on his skin.

For the rest of our outdoor time, I happily occupied myself by tossing rocks, picking up litter, and letting my mind wander. I knew Jack was doing exactly what he wanted to do: enjoying his day in the sun.

I promised four trips in all, and Jack and I did indeed make four outings. The only difference between our first excursion and the subsequent ones was where we parked ourselves and what I brought as a way to entertain myself. Jack was no more talkative during the other trips, despite my occasional overtures. During outing number three, an attendant from the first floor came out and tried to engage him in a conversation, and though he was polite, he clearly wanted to get back to his solitude. And that was okay. Jack just loved the very essence of the outdoors, and he didn't want any intrusions.

Most people could sit outside like this any time they wanted, but for Jack it was truly a rare occasion, one he savored from the moment he arrived to the moment the experience was over. As a symbol of the limits placed on his life, his reaction to the outdoors made me a little sad. But there was something wonderful about it too, his ability to see the true beauty in ordinary sights, sounds, and smells that most of us take for granted. What would I give—what would any of us give—to able to find such joy in a view of trees and a light spring breeze?

CHAPTER 27

As I slipped back into the routine of the school days, my excitement over the arrival of the Expressor was offset by my private fear that genuine independent communication might not be possible. I had placed considerable weight on the relationship between mastery of the machine and overall independence. I was terrified that—despite the fact that Ron and Ruth could easily comprehend—they would be unable to perform the correct physical actions to make the machine work. If that turned out to be the case, it would be a colossal disappointment: not just for me but also for these two motivated students, for the engineers, and for the other students in our class, who were so excited to see Ron and Ruth succeed.

All along, I'd recognized that Ron and Ruth had conquered incredible educational challenges just in learning to read. They had come to reading and spelling so late in life but had made great strides over the past few months, breaking the complex code that paired sounds to letters and words. I knew they could overcome linguistic and intellectual challenges—but could they get past the physical challenges required to control the device? In hindsight, I questioned the wisdom of offering such a promise and began to wonder whether I should have tackled the control issue before elevating hopes and expectations.

A few days after the dance and our surprising meeting with the superintendent, Bob stopped by my classroom before school. I shared my concerns with him, and he listened empathetically.

"It's not like anyone's done this before," he admitted. "We're flying without instruments here. You just head out hoping you won't encounter problems that can't be fixed. I think the key word here is 'relax.'"

"Relax!" My voice rose slightly. "How can I relax?"

"No, no," Bob said. "I don't mean *you* need to relax. What I mean is that Ron and Ruth have to have less overall muscle tension. They need to loosen up in order to be successful. The less tension in their muscles, the more likely they'll be able to operate the switch."

"I hate to admit it," I told him, "but you've actually said something that makes sense."

He shook his head and smiled. "Every now and then, I do that."

Bob's words had a profound effect on my thinking. I had little direct influence on how tense Ruth and Ron would be, but I might be able to help by controlling external conditions. While I couldn't reduce the specific strain of a muscle, I could concentrate on finding ways to engineer the room to make them feel more at ease.

Knowing that the presence of other people could affect the outcome, I began to conduct Ron and Ruth's instruction behind the screen in Independence Hall to reduce the chance of interruptions and interference from the other students. Because I couldn't be sure what impact they could have on each other, I worked individually with Ron and Ruth to avoid the natural stress that could result from watching each other's progress. Realizing that even the physical sensation of wearing something foreign like the wrist strap might require some getting used to, I had them both wear leather watchbands for part of each day, hoping this would familiarize them with the sensation of having something strapped to their body.

The Expressor required a motor or physical movement as well as a conceptual act. In other words, it was one thing to stop or start the light in a timely manner, but it was still another to determine which item on the display represented a particular thought or responded to a particular inquiry. During the initial introduction of the switch and the new device, I separated the task of physically controlling the machine from ones that involved mental processing. I began to use the Expressor in the way I had previously used the clock communicator—with me holding the mercury switch to stop and start the light. As before, I watched their faces and not the machine to know when to tilt the watchband and stop the light. Not surprisingly, they had little difficulty transitioning to the new and larger surface for daily lessons and the novel way of using a light and not a pointer to indicate a correct response.

Unfortunately, the motor training did not go as smoothly. I tried to make it as simple as possible. With distractions controlled as well as I could manage, and with the rest of the students engaged in other projects, I brought first Ron and then Ruth to Independence Hall and positioned them in front of the device. The template on the Expressor was divided initially in two halves, with twenty lights assigned to each. Rather than use written words that might not be recognized and could potentially interfere with performance, I used drawings of familiar objects or ideas, such as a television, a toilet, or a happy face, within separate sections of the divided template. Teaching Ron and Ruth to spell would be a future goal; for now, I focused on selecting familiar words, photos, or symbols that stood for an entire object or idea.

I replaced the watchband they had been wearing with the one containing the mercury switch. For Ron, the switch was on his left wrist, as he seemed to have better control of the left side of his body. Ruth, however, nearly always held her arms bent at the elbows and had difficulty rotating her wrists. Her performance seemed to improve when the band was placed between her wrist and elbow and set so that the mercury tilted as she extended and retracted her arm.

With the speed dial set to its slowest pace, the light moved from one bulb to the next about every second and a half. At this rate, the progression around the entire circle took about a minute. Ron and Ruth's first task was to halt the light within one of the twenty bulbs that made up half a circle. To my delight, neither of them had any difficulty tilting the mercury when they had about thirty seconds to make the necessary movement. I gave instructions like *Find the happy picture. Stop it on the television. Can you find the radio?* They both demonstrated this level of control right away, so I divided the circle into four quadrants, each with ten lights. Again, they were both successful.

After that week, I hoped complete control of the Expressor would occur in short order for Ron and Ruth. But after only a few trials with more selections on the template, I began to see troubled expressions on their faces and telltale drops of sweat. It became clear pretty quickly that the fewer bulbs there were, and the faster the light sped around the circle, the more difficult it was for Ron and Ruth to stop it. And it was also clear that the extension of an arm or the rotation of a wrist, the actual movements required to stop the light, demanded an enormous amount of effort from them. Despite the obvious difficulty, they opted to keep working even after being given the opportunity to take a break.

After about a week of practice, their performance improved, and I introduced a new template with eight sections. This meant that there would be five light bulbs within each target area. In each of these eight target areas, I placed a photograph of a common object. With the photographs in place, Ron and Ruth could see that any one of the five lights in a target area was aligned with and could signal a particular photo.

Now that we were down to just five lights and up to eight photos, Ron and Ruth's struggles intensified. I sensed I was beginning to push the limits of their motor systems.

"You know, this is a really hard thing to do," I said to them both. "Let's rest for today and take this up again tomorrow."

Ron's body thrust forward, and he shook his head forcefully. Ruth made similar movements of protest. Point made: these two were not ready to stop.

"Try this," I said to Ron. "Just stare at the picture, and don't look at anything else until any one of the five lightbulbs in that target area lights up." Then, I said it again. "Remember, do not watch the movement of the light as it moves around the circle." I made this suggestion because I'd been noticing that Ron would tense up with anticipation as the light got closer to the target; most people can use that type of anticipation to their advantage, but in Ron's case, it became his enemy. I did find that this slight shift in concentration led to some improvement, to the point where he could make correct selections fifty percent of the time.

The same strategy of staring at the desired item and not watching the moving light helped Ruth as well, but not to the same extent. As much as I encouraged her and as hard as she tried, her eyes constantly shifted from the target picture back to the approaching light. With each successive failure, her frustration and disappointment were palpable. But she didn't give up, and after a week of practice, she had noticeably improved her skill: she was now able to stop the light accurately about forty percent of the time.

I imagined that learning how to twist the wrist or extend the arm with accuracy was a lot like learning how to throw or kick a ball with greater precision. The more the motor system has an opportunity to rehearse, the better the outcome. After about another week of daily practice, Ron and Ruth's accuracy improved, even when up to ten items appeared on the template. So now with ten photographs, there were four lights within each target area. I also learned that it didn't matter if I added more cognitive demands to the task. Whether I asked them to find a specific picture of a cup, to locate something they could drink from, or to actually use the Expressor in class to designate that they were thirsty, they could do so accurately with up to ten targets per template.

With this revelation, I implemented three useful strategies for success:

First, Ed and I created several templates of ten that reflected activities related to school, the wards, or personal matters.

Second, for lessons or questions that required more than ten segments per template, we would resort to the original selection strategy, where I would watch them and stop the light at their bidding. This way, the picture selected would be of their choosing rather than mine because they were signaling me to stop the light's movement.

Third, we would continue to practice motor control, with a goal to increase the number of possible target areas that could be accurately and easily selected on a single template.

Education is about change and progress, but I knew that if large academic leaps became the standard by which I measured the success of my instruction, I was in the wrong business. The past eight months of teaching had taught me a great deal, but perhaps most importantly, I had come to understand that modest progress was a realistic benchmark. For most students with learning difficulties, or for those who had difficulty with motor control, noticeable improvement was often slow in coming, and the extent of progress could be minute. Whether minuscule or massive, the operative word had to be *improvement*.

That Ron and Ruth could now independently and spontaneously choose items from a field of twelve photos might have seemed like a small improvement, but in my view, it was momentous. To transition from having no symbolic expression to independently answering questions and providing information—it may not have been a miracle, exactly, but it was a dazzling achievement to behold.

CHAPTER 28

I loved the month of May in the Northeast. For me, it was the true beginning of springtime—the real deal, not the teasing variety that April typically offered. In May, taking in a Red Sox game at Fenway Park no longer required a winter coat and gloves, real flowers began to bloom, and everything seemed to come alive. The dance had turned out to be a success, the Expressor had arrived, and Ron and Ruth were making wonderful progress.

But the customary joy of May in 1970 was about to change.

I found the letter sitting in the middle of my desk when I arrived at my classroom, and I put it aside for a moment as I rearranged some papers. Really, I was delaying what I knew was going to be unpleasant news. I shuffled everything around again, trying to recall the original position of all my stuff. Then finally, reluctantly, I picked up the envelope.

I checked the corridor for potential intruders and returned to my desk, wondering why I had even bothered to look. Then, I tore open the sealed envelope. As I unfolded the paper, I checked for the author of the brief letter first. I was not surprised to see "Dorothy Sharp" at the bottom of the page.

The message was succinct and direct:

This letter is to inform you that your contract to teach at Belchertown State School will not be renewed for the 1970–71 school year. Thank you for your service during this academic year.

I read the letter a few times, then crumpled it and tossed it over the edge of the desk, blindly shooting at the brown metal trashcan. After the failed throw, I retrieved the letter from the floor and unfurled it to get another glimpse of the words.

I rested my elbows on the desk, placed my forehead into the palms of both hands, and stared at the letter before me, wrinkled but legible. I read it again.

I stood, rather dazed, and walked out of the room and up the stairway to the second-floor landing. As I started to unlock the door to the corridor, I saw too much activity through the glass, so I turned around and retreated to the first floor. Here I found my key ring, rubbed my thumb over the number 836 on the brass plate, and let myself into the corridor. I walked down the center aisle and entered the small room set aside as a combination dental office and barbershop, then re-locked the door behind me.

An archaic chair occupied the center of the room, a dental chair from another era perched on a heavy iron base. I climbed onto its worn leather seat and pumped a metal handle on the side of the chair several times, raising the seat about a foot, then leaned back against the headrest. Looking out the dirty window onto the lush green grounds, I reflected on what Mrs. Sharp's note really meant. I thought of all the words to describe being fired. "Terminated." "Canned." "Dismissed." It was obvious what the note meant for me, but the sickening feeling in my stomach wasn't for myself—it was for Ron, and Ruth, and Jack, and Dennis, and Carla, and Teddy, and Barbara, and Paula, and Danny, and Wendy.

I imagined having to tell Wendy that I wouldn't be seeing her anymore.

Mrs. Sharp's note broke my heart, but at the same time, it stiffened my resolve. Whatever I called it, or however I said it or tried to explain it, I had lost this job, and for my students' sake, I needed to see what I could do to get it back.

The noise of the elevator clanking across the hall reminded me that I had to get back to my classroom. Before returning to the basement, I made my way to the main office, looking for Bernie. She wasn't there, but I ducked in anyway and used her phone to call Mrs. Sharp.

"Dorothy Sharp here," she answered.

"Mrs. Sharp, it's Howard Shane."

"Yes, Mr. Shane, what can I do for you?"

"I'd like to meet with you after school today."

"And what will we be discussing?"

"Please, Mrs. Sharp. I would like just a few minutes after school."

"Suit yourself," she said. "Come by after your students leave for the day."

I hung up without another word. I felt better already, knowing I would at least have the opportunity to confront the enemy by day's end.

Before heading back to my classroom, I took a detour to Ward 1. I scanned the ward, looking for Wendy, hoping her sweet voice might cheer me up. I found her lying in her cart, wearing a lovely white dress with light pink piping along the skirt line. As always, she was delighted to see me.

"Wendy, can you tell me a joke?" I asked.

"Okay, I can," she said. She thought for a second, but her initial enthusiasm vanished and tears welled in her eyes.

"What's wrong, honey?" I asked.

She looked up into my eyes. "I can't find the joke in my head."

"Wendy, you told me about the cat yesterday. Do you remember?"

She smiled. "What is a cat's favorite color?

"Is it yellow?" I responded.

"No, silly Mr. Shane. It's purr-ple."

"I knew you would cheer me up with a great joke," I said. "Thanks, Wendy. I'm going to head down to class now, and I'll see you when you get there."

She seemed content again, and I left.

As I returned to my classroom, I decided that my news should be kept under wraps. It was unfair to burden my students until I had a better sense of what it meant for their future, as well as how best to break the news. Besides, I was holding on to the hope that I could talk Mrs. Sharp into reconsidering my dismissal.

Teddy was the last to leave that day because he was writing a letter to his parents and asked me for some guidance. It must have been obvious that I was distracted, because he asked if he should come back tomorrow. Before we settled the matter, an attendant from Teddy's ward arrived, announcing that Teddy had to go upstairs to see Dr. Ivanok.

When he heard where he was going, Teddy glanced at me with a grin and asked, "Do you have a Russian dictionary?"

"Get upstairs and behave yourself," I said. "He's a very good doctor even though he is sometimes hard to understand."

"It's easier to understand people who can't talk than to understand what he's saying. Last week I bumped my head, and when he got finished, I was toothless and my appendix was missing."

"Then why don't you have Norman or one of the other guys serve as your interpreter? Besides, now you don't need to worry about cavities or appendicitis. Now go upstairs, and I'll see you tomorrow."

"*Do svidaniya!*" he yelled, as he was pushed through the classroom door.

"Right, *do svidaniya* to you, too," I responded.

My classroom now empty, I left the infirmary and headed toward the parking lot. I noticed Henry's red four-door sedan and wondered why he was there on a Monday. Since I had time before my meeting with Mrs. Sharp, I went back to the infirmary and found Henry there, talking with two of the attendants in Ward 1. He smiled and gestured for me to wait.

"What's up?" he asked, when he walked over to me. "Why do you look so forlorn?"

"Do you have a minute? I need to talk to you about something."

He put his arm around my shoulder and led me out the door. "I always have time for a struggling academic. Where do you want to go?"

"How about outside the building?"

"Works for me."

We walked in silence to the same bench where I'd had my very first discussion with Ron's grandmother. It seemed so long ago that I had promised to help improve his life. I knew now that I had been incapable of fully appreciating the implications of that promise. It was a pledge driven by naïveté and a desire to bring comfort to his caring grandmother. But with these months behind me, buttressed by interminable reality checks, I could now appreciate that the path to an equitable life would be a lengthy struggle. I just didn't want the undeniable progress to be cut short. "I have a big-time problem, Henry, and I'm not exactly sure what to do about it."

I removed the dismissal letter from my front pocket. It was now folded neatly, but it still bore the scars of its violent morning. Henry took an unusually long time to read it. Finally, he said, "Yeah, so what?"

"So... I'm history around here," I said.

"What did you expect? Are you telling me you were actually surprised to receive this note?"

"Of course I'm surprised! Maybe I've pushed the envelope around here a bit, but I was a good teacher, wasn't I? Or have I gotten that part all wrong, too?"

"Sure, you were a good teacher," he said. "You were—are—a great teacher, but this has nothing to do with teaching. This has everything to do with attitude and conformity, and conformity is one of the hallmarks of American education. Not only do we expect the student body to conform, but we also insist that the faculty get in line as well. You were out of line all year, and they decided to do something about it."

"But don't you think my little transgressions deserved a reprimand, not a dismissal?" I was fishing for any ounce of hope.

"What I think doesn't matter on an issue like this." Shaking the letter in his hand, he said, "This letter is much more than a simple firing. This letter is a pronouncement that this institution is going back to business as usual."

"Do you really think Belchertown can ever return to business as usual," I asked, "given all the publicity it's received and the attention from politicians just itching for an issue that might get them re-elected? I know not much has changed yet, but the winds of change are certainly blowing."

"Personally, I agree with you, but unfortunately, son, I see no way that those changes will affect this decision." He paused. "Even though you'll never admit your role in helping the *Springfield Union,* you have to admit you did, in effect, create your own demise. So suck it up and get ready for a little change yourself. Change is good."

"Maybe, but I don't think change is what my students need right now. They need some harmony and consistency in their lives."

Henry shifted his weight on the bench. "I agree with you that this is not a good outcome for them." Then, without elaborating, he changed the subject. "I know this just happened, but do you have any ideas yet about what you're going to do?"

"Right now, I'm off to see my boss to review the details of my dismissal. After that meeting is over, I'm free. In fact, I have nothing booked for the rest of my life." I realized I was being hyperbolic, but my future suddenly seemed like a black hole, and the uncertainty of it all had my mind racing in a million different directions.

"What do you expect to gain from a conversation with Mrs. Sharp?"

"I don't know. Satisfaction, maybe."

"Let me give you some advice," he said. "Don't burn your bridges. Don't rush in there without thinking it all through and do or say something you'll regret later."

"Henry, I was fired, not given a warning. I'm out of here in less than six weeks. What difference does it make what I say to her now? And I have thought it through. I'm just going to talk with her, not behead her."

He nodded. "Listen, in a few days, after you have a chance to cool down, why don't you and I get together and talk about some other options you might have?"

"Like what, selling encyclopedias?"

"I have some better ideas than that, but you need to get your concerns and questions sorted out here first."

"Will do, Henry. I'll call you in a few days." I sighed. "Just one other question, though."

"What's that?"

"You didn't order my dismissal, did you?"

"I tried to months ago, but they insisted we wait until you really got hooked on the kids and actually thought you were making a difference." He elbowed me playfully. When I didn't laugh, he patted my back, too, realizing I needed comfort in addition to the humor.

"Well, at least you didn't do it on my birthday," I said.

"We tried to, but Mrs. Sharp didn't have time to dictate a termination letter."

"Thanks, Henry," I said, allowing myself a grin. "I feel a lot better now."

I marched up the stairs of the school building, carrying my briefcase in one hand and a tape recorder in the other. Mrs. Sharp's door was closed, so I knocked. She barked, "I'll be with you shortly!" The building was quiet, and it appeared we were the only occupants this late in the day.

I stared at her office door, feeling quite exposed. I slowly backed up and leaned against the wall opposite the door. If having me wait was a calculated move to gain a psychological advantage, it was working. As I stood there alone in the wide corridor, a range of emotions swept over me, but anger, frustration, and hopelessness were the predominant ones. The lack of a bench or seat to rest on while I waited only added to the indignity of the moment.

When Mrs. Sharp opened the door several minutes later, she found me sitting cross-legged on the floor, talking into my tape recorder. "Mr. Shane, you can come in now."

I fumbled to turn off the recorder but apparently took too long. Mrs. Sharp stepped closer to me and shouted, "You can come in now!"

"What?" I said it softly and slowly as I looked up at her, consciously making every effort to appear as calm and under control as possible. She turned abruptly and marched back into her office. I got up and followed.

I took a seat in the metal folding chair a few feet away from the center of her polished desk. For some strange reason, I really was feeling better.

"Do you mind if I record our meeting?" I asked, placing the tape recorder on her desk while striking the record button. I still held my briefcase on my lap.

"To what purpose?" she asked.

"For the record," I answered.

"Mr. Shane, I'm not amused by you at all. You can't record in here. It's against the rules of this institution to record a conversation without my—without permission. And you do not have written permission now, do you?" She leaned over and hit the off button with excessive force.

"Apparently not," I said, trying to regain my composure. "Very well."

"Let us move on then."

She conspicuously checked her watch. I countered by removing my pocket watch and examining it in the most obvious manner.

She gave a little sigh. "So, you're here to discuss an exit strategy, I presume?"

"No, I'm here to discuss why I'm being exited at all," I said.

"Surely you aren't serious. You can't think for one minute that I could continue to tolerate a teacher like you? Someone so impertinent, so thoroughly dismissive of our rules?" She scowled.

"Mrs. Sharp," I said, "I think you've misinterpreted my behavior. Furthermore, I think you've allowed your anger about my conduct, and perhaps your opinion of me, to cloud your judgment about my teaching performance."

"Oh, and how else should I characterize your insolent behavior during this entire school year?"

"Look," I said, trying to humble myself. "I'm not going to sit here and tell you I wasn't aware that my behavior was causing you some distress. However, I really thought that you would see beyond that and recognize my motives were always to benefit the residents. I also thought you would notice the value I brought to the students and the school program in the infirmary. That program was failing, but over the past year..." I leaned forward, my voice rising with emotion. "I've worked my *tail* off to bring life back to that program and to teach and boost the lives and self-esteem of those kids. And I offer the achievement of each and every one of those students in defense of my conduct and as justification for my methodologies. Yes, I was oppositional at times. But never *once* did I neglect the intellectual or educational interests of any student."

"Really?" She lifted an eyebrow. "I seem to remember that you refused to use the film strip series on nature and earth that we purchased just this year. Teachers like you complain about a lack of curriculum materials, and then when they're available, they're not capitalized upon."

"To remind you, Mrs. Sharp," I said calmly, "I did not ask for those materials, and I also never said that I wouldn't use them. What I did say was that I might use them at some point in the future. Nature touches most of us routinely, even in our humdrum daily lives, but that is not true for the students in the infirmary building. So for the past few months, my approach to the natural sciences with my students has been to encourage observation of the real thing—not pictures. And that's why I asked to take them outdoors and let them feel the breeze, touch the grass, run their fingers in the dirt, smell some flowers. One day the filmstrip material might be a supplement to these other experiences. But they will never grasp the meaning of these filmstrips if they can't experience any of it in the real world first. It's that simple."

Mrs. Sharp acted as if she hadn't even heard me. "So, you didn't use those materials, did you?"

"I did not."

"How about we talk about the spring dance, then? Let's discuss bringing a whole unexpected group of residents to the dance, practically a brigade."

"No, let's not discuss that," I said, "because you and I both know that the appearance of my kids at that dance was the best thing that happened to you this year, not to mention the students. Or would you like to revisit this issue with Dr. Bowser?"

Her jaw clenched. I got the feeling she was still furious about the whole dance episode and how, remarkably, the superintendent took my side on that one. "See, it's just that attitude that makes it impossible to work with you," she said. "Maybe if I'd had more time and supervised you more closely, things might have worked out differently."

I saw a glimmer of hope and sacrificed my pride. "Now, that's a really good idea," I offered. "Why don't you serve as my direct supervisor next year and work with me on a closer level? Wouldn't that be better than firing me?"

"Mr. Shane," she said quickly, "let me be perfectly clear. You are not fired—you are just not re-hired, and you never will be hired to work here again. *Never.*"

"So, let me get this straight," I said. "I'm not fired, just not re-hired, and I will never be hired here ever again despite all my good work and my agreeing that perhaps having assistance from you as a supervisor might help with my attitude and skill development."

"Correct, that is what I just said, and that's what I said in the letter I sent you, and that's precisely what I mean." The corners of her mouth turned upward. She seemed to be enjoying this part of the conversation.

I stood up and said, "I see." Then, I headed for the door.

"Oh, Mr. Shane," she said. "Aren't you forgetting your tape recorder?"

I turned back to her, now clutching my briefcase like a newborn against my chest. "No, no, that's okay, Mrs. Sharp. That tape recorder belongs to the school department—so you keep it. Besides, I have my own running in here." I tapped my palm against the leather case, turned away, and strolled out the door, leaving Mrs. Sharp to pick her jaw up off the floor.

CHAPTER 29

"I heard," Bob said solemnly.

I found him in Ward 3 the day after my encounter with Mrs. Sharp. He was working with an elderly resident, Margaret, before my school day began. He gently bent her leg, holding it just beneath the knee.

"How are you doing?" he asked me.

"Oh, I've had better days. And Henry was real comforting. His exact words to me were 'What did you expect?'" I sighed. "I was a little annoyed with him at first, but he was right."

"Right or wrong," Bob said, helping Margaret unbend her leg, "it still stinks. Look, I have to finish up here, but I want to continue this discussion."

"Sure, sure. My calendar is wide open."

"I'll find you later. Maybe we can get a drink or something."

"Okay, but we'd better do it quickly. When the news of my dismissal gets around, you may have to consider the risks associated with being seen with me."

"Not a problem," he shot back. "I've avoided being seen with you for the past nine months. Nothing's changed in that regard."

"I appreciate the empathy." I checked my watch. "I'd love to hear more of your kind and compassionate sentiments, but I have to get to my students. Goodbye, Margaret," I said to the woman he was working with. "I'm sorry I took up some of your time with Bob. I'll see you again soon."

I rushed out of Ward 3 en route to my classroom and ran into my female students, who were crowded by the elevator to the basement. Everyone greeted me enthusiastically, and sadness hit me all over again. How would I tell them I wouldn't be with them again next year?

After a moment, I saw that the congestion on the corridor was due to an elevator car completely stuffed with sacks of clean laundry. This meant that school would be delayed for at least half an hour. I had planned to meet with Bernie to discuss my new status and decided that this lull was as good a time as any.

I knocked and opened her door before she invited me in. She glanced up at me, her eyes a little sad.

"Hey, Bernie," I said. "I've got a good one. So, a priest, a physical therapist, and a first-year teacher who just got canned walk into a bar..."

"I heard," she said, ignoring my usual nonsense. "I'm sorry. I really am. God knows you were a pain, but you were a good fit for these kids and for this building."

"Thanks, Bernie." I took a seat in her guest chair. "I sure thought so."

"So... what's next for you?"

"Having a drink with Bob Bergquist is as far as I've gotten."

"As good as that sounds, I think something even better will come along for you." She folded her hands on the desk. "By the way, do you recall that little talk we had a while back?"

"You mean the one where you thought I was a carpetbagger, or was it an interloper? That talk where you suggested I was working here because the pay was so good and the work was so glamorous?"

"Yes," she said, smiling. "That one."

"Sure, I remember."

"I want to add that I don't know what you're going to do after you leave Belchertown, but I hope you keep on being a teacher. You shouldn't stop working with students like our kids."

I stood and extended my hand. "Bernie, I can't tell you how much that means to me," I said. "Now comes the hard part—telling the students."

While I knew I needed to inform the class I was leaving, I had a more difficult time deciding exactly how and what to tell them. I knew that for some of the students, whose reasoning skills were still undeveloped, no explanation I could offer would clarify the concept of my departure. Life for them was concrete and absolute: either I was there or I wasn't, and my absence would not be easy to explain in words. Other students, like Teddy, Ron, Jack, Dennis, and Ruth, would undoubtedly experience my departure as a form of loss. I envisioned for them a loss of educational opportunity, the loss of an advocate, and—perhaps most importantly—the loss of an individual they had come to depend upon.

I spent less time thinking about how I would break the news of my unexpected career change to friends and family. If my dismissal had occurred earlier in the school year, they no doubt would have reminded me that this job was nothing more than a way station on the path to something else, much as Bernie had implied. But over the course of the academic year, as I became more entrenched in the school and the idea of education as a profession—*my* profession—I had begun to realize that there was no "something else." I now had to own up to my dismissal and acknowledge that this, on some level, had been a personal failing.

The institution had a unique system for spreading information and especially delivering gossip. I once joked that there were three ways to communicate in this place: telephone, telegraph, and tele-resident. I knew that once I spoke to my class, the word of my dismissal would spread faster than the recent outbreak of lice in A Building.

My plan to explain my exit was simple. I would relay my dismissal to the students as a group. I would tell them in as direct, calm, and impartial a manner as possible and save the interpretations for others. For those who were bruised by the meaning of the message and wanted a further explanation, they could seek counsel from me, if they chose, or take it up with any attendant, nurse, or visitor with whom they felt comfortable.

Since the students would remain after I departed, it would be cruel and of no benefit to further insult and belittle the institution or its administrators. I could easily trash them as insensitive, uncaring, unjust, and so on, but at the end of the day, the residents still had to rely on those bureaucrats for their comfort and wellbeing. This was going to be hard for everyone, and I wanted to keep as much negativity as possible out of my talk with the class.

Once everyone had made it to the classroom following the delay with the elevator, I gathered them by my desk and told them I wanted to speak to everyone at the same time.

"I know," Teddy said. "You want to tell us why you're quitting."

I was shocked for a second—but given the way gossip spread here, I knew I shouldn't be totally surprised. "Where'd you hear that?"

"One of the attendants said it last night."

"Where'd they hear it?"

"Well, are you going?" Teddy pressed me.

"Whoa, hold on, folks," I said. "Let's slow down. I'm still looking into what the next steps are, so let's not get ahead of ourselves."

I scanned the faces of every student, searching for telltale signs of their emotions. Everyone was silent. Dennis, looking glum and pale, lowered his head until his chin was resting on his chest and stared intently at the floor. Ed slowly drifted from his usual place in the corner of the room to a spot right among the group. Ron and Ruth always emoted through facial expressions, and the fact that they now appeared expressionless told me they were contemplating the meaning of this announcement. Barbara and Paula's silence was probably an indication that they were reading and responding to social cues from the rest of the class, a skill they'd both improved. Wendy rolled her head from side to side as she observed the other students. I wasn't sure what she was thinking, but she, too, was likely seeking out social cues; she often looked to others as a gauge for whether she should be happy or sad.

The group didn't stay quiet for long. Jack blurted out, "I can't believe this! You're really leaving?" Then, the whole class exploded in confused chatter. I tried to regain their attention, but no one could hear me over the hubbub. Teddy was talking directly to me. I couldn't make out what he was saying, but I tried to speak to him over the noise:

"I'm going, but it's not what you think," I shouted. "Where'd you hear that I quit?"

Teddy yelled back, "I said is it true or what?"

I placed my index fingers in my mouth and let out a sharp whistle, which immediately quieted the noise.

"I will not be here next year," I said calmly, "but I did *not* quit."

"Yes, you did!" Jack shot back. "They said so last night, and they said you quit because you don't care about us."

"Jack, you know better than that," I said. "I didn't quit, period. You all know that I've never lied to any of you." I was curious to know who had started the rumor that I had quit. I was also angry that someone had gotten to my students first and told them I didn't care about them. Of course, I couldn't help but wonder if it had originated from the very top of the school administration. My quitting would certainly deflect from the negative publicity that the firing of a teacher, even a controversial one, would produce.

"Well, I'm quitting school right now, I'll tell you that," Teddy said.

"Me, too!" Jack yelled.

"Me, too!" Carla shouted, anger evident on her face.

Danny muttered something, but in his extreme level of excitement, his words were not intelligible.

I was immensely frustrated by now, but a glance at Ron helped to calm me. He was in an extended body position, eyes gazing at the ceiling. It was his way of saying that he agreed that I was not a liar. I smiled at him.

"Why are you leaving, then?" Teddy demanded.

"Because I was fired. I'm not being asked back to teach next year. They don't want me back. I don't have any choice."

"But *why* are you fired?" Jack asked, propping himself upright as far as he could with one arm.

Before I could respond, Wendy broke the tension in the room. "You're not on fire, Mr. Shane," she said.

Everyone was quiet for a second. Then, Ruth began to laugh. She laughed with such force that she drew the attention of the entire class, and soon several of the students were laughing along with her. I couldn't help but chuckle a little myself.

"No, I am not *on* fire, Wendy. You're right," I said. "But I *am* fired. When a person is fired, that means they have to leave. That's why I can't work here anymore."

"So... is this the last day of school?" Teddy asked. Some of the anger in his tone had dissipated, and now he mostly sounded sad.

"No way," I said. "I still have almost three more weeks to torture all of you. In fact, I'll be here until this day." I walked over to the wall calendar, flipped the next page over, and pointed to June 19th.

"Mr. Shane," Jack said, "Ron wants to say something."

Ron's hard stare toward the communication device in the corner of the room told me what I needed to know.

"Ed, would you mind linking Ron to the Expressor?" I asked.

Ed brought Ron to the communication machine, attached the mercury switch to his right wrist, and fitted the circle with a template we had labeled *Emotions*. Months before, I had informed the class that although Ron and Ruth's messages took an extended time to compose and unfold, we had to be respectful and patient. The class, out of both habit and respect, now became silent.

The light slowly and steadily traversed the circumference of the circle, passing the icons that represented different feelings. Ron's face was a lesson in determination. He stared intently at a single icon as each bulb was illuminated by the moving light. When the light aligned with the symbol denoting *mad,* he rotated his shoulder and twisted his wrist. The light stopped.

"Mad," Teddy repeated. "He's saying he's mad."

Ron blinked, reiterating the sentiment.

"Me, too, Ron," I offered, not knowing what else to say. "I'm really mad, too."

We didn't discuss my firing any further, and the school day chugged along unremarkably, though Dennis's mood showed little improvement as the day went by. When class was over, Teddy didn't show any interest in leaving as the attendants came to return the students to their wards. As the other students left, he lingered behind.

"Teddy," I said, before he could say a word. "I didn't quit, I promise. If I was going to quit, I would have told the class before I told the school administration. You wouldn't have heard about it first from one of the attendants or whoever told that phony story. I didn't know my days were running out until just yesterday. When I got to school, there was a letter waiting for me that told me my job was over next month. If you still don't believe me, I'll show you the letter. Do you want to see it?"

Before he could answer, an attendant from the second floor came back to the classroom. "Time to get lively, Teddy," she said. "Everyone but you has gone upstairs."

"Would you mind if I brought him back up in a little while?" I asked. "We're still trying to work out a problem here."

"That's fine," she said. "I'll see him upstairs."

"*Adios,*" Teddy called after her.

We were quiet, listening to the click-clack of the attendant's heels as she walked back to the elevator.

Teddy spoke first: "You can write to the governor. He'll tell them to let you teach here."

"It won't do any good, Teddy."

"Okay, then *I'll* write to the governor," he stated. "I know how to write now, you know."

"Go ahead. It would be good practice for your penmanship—and you know, I do believe it's important to speak up and tell powerful people about the changes you want to see. But in this case, Teddy, it's not going to get me my job back. Mrs. Sharp has made that decision."

"Why don't you talk to Mrs. Sharp and make her take you back?" he asked.

"Already did. And she said bye-bye. I mean, she said *adios*."

Teddy chuckled. Then, we were silent again.

"Can I go back upstairs now?" he asked. He turned his chair and slowly propelled himself toward the classroom door.

"Yeah, let's go. It's getting late."

Just as we passed through the door, he stopped and asked, "Can I borrow your tape recorder? I'll bring it back tomorrow."

"Sure, but why do you need mine? Don't you have one upstairs?"

"It's broken, and I have to record something," he said.

"Why don't you keep moving, and I'll go back and get it. Do you need a fresh tape?"

"No, I have a lot of them in my trunk."

I retrieved my tape recorder from my briefcase. Realizing the battery might be nearly depleted, I grabbed the spare AAs I kept in my desk and slid in a new one for Teddy. Then, very carefully, I popped out the cassette tape from my meeting with Mrs. Sharp. The tape seemed to vibrate in my hand as I thought about the plan I had for it. I knew I needed to keep it safe, so I tucked it in my shirt pocket.

After escorting Teddy back to Ward 5, I scanned the room for Dennis. I was most concerned about him and sought him out first. Over the course of the school year, I had gained a good appreciation of his moods and how downcast he could become. When I didn't find him in Ward 5, I ventured into the adjoining day room. Other residents sat in a cluster talking with an attendant, but Dennis had isolated himself in the corner, where he leaned against his crutches and stared out the window.

He must have heard my approaching footsteps, because he wiped his eyes with the sleeve of his wrinkled plaid shirt. I slowed my pace to give him sufficient time to ready himself for a face-to-face encounter.

I stopped just behind him and asked, "What's up?"

"Nothing," he said in a neutral tone.

I came around to his side and joined him at the window. Together, we gazed through the bars, our eyes on the grass and trees in the distance.

"Dennis, I never thought I would have to leave," I said, "but they decided it would be the best thing for the school if they got another teacher."

He didn't move a muscle, nor did he speak.

"I'll bet the next teacher will be really great." I didn't know what else I could say.

"Stop lying to me, okay?" he said.

"I'm not lying to you. Now that everyone's shown they like to go to school so much, I really do think Mrs. Sharp will find a really good teacher to take my place."

"She's a shit ass," he said, and then added, "just like you." He looked straight at me and made no attempt to hide the tears pooling in his eyes. "Everybody just leaves. Nobody wants to be here."

A feeling of utter helplessness rushed through me. This was the moment my termination became real.

I'd been distracted by Henry's lecture and my argument with Mrs. Sharp, but the second I saw tears well up in Dennis's eyes, the fact of my leaving felt genuine and inevitable. I was losing control, and the clearest indication of this was the realization that there was nothing I could do or say to make this boy feel any better.

I had no comforting words. I could suggest that we stay in touch or tell him I would visit often, but the last thing he needed to hear were more half-truths and empty promises—as much as I wanted to come back and visit my students, I wasn't sure I'd be allowed on campus. I certainly didn't want to become yet another person who would tell him anything to provide temporary comfort. Like his father, I could say I'd return, but the reality was that my coming back was unlikely. Dennis didn't need a school bag under his bed just like his suitcase, symbolizing yet another person who had let him down.

"Look, it's not fair," I said. "I agree with you. But we still have a few more weeks of school. Let's make the most of it." I placed my hand on his arm, but he pulled it away.

"Do you think I'll ever see you again?" he asked.

"I don't know, Dennis," I said truthfully. I couldn't hide how much it disappointed me to say that. "I hope so, but it will depend on where I go. Now, there's a chance I'll stay local, and if I do, I promise I'll try to see you, if they'll let me."

He turned back to the window, focusing on the tree line in the distance. "Do you think Ron will be able to use his communicator when you're gone?"

My eyes filled with tears at this question, and I wasn't sure what to say. After a moment, I managed to gently tug on his arm and tilt my head to signal we should walk back toward the ward. As we moved along, he must have sensed that I was too emotional to talk, because he didn't press me for an answer. Once we got to the ward, he started to move ahead of me, maneuvering smoothly on his crutches.

Before he was out of earshot, I said, "Dennis?"

He turned to me slightly.

"I think the machine is just the beginning for Ron. This will go on whether I'm here or not." I blinked back tears. "I think it's just the beginning for all of you."

He glanced back at me, this smart and brave boy who had sprayed me with water on his very first day in my classroom. I thought about how much he'd learned, how far he'd come, how much potential he still had.

I raised a hand, and he nodded. Then, he turned around and kept moving on, until he was out of sight.

I took a moment to collect myself before moving on. It was my plan to talk to everyone individually, and Ron was next. I found him sitting with a small group that included Norman, Teddy, and a few attendants. When I approached, they became quiet, and I suspected they had been discussing my leaving.

"Mind if I steal Mr. Benoit for a few minutes?" I asked. The attendants nodded.

"Ron, is that okay with you?"

He blinked a yes.

I grabbed the handles of his wheelchair and moved him toward his bed space. When we were out of earshot from the group, I asked, "You okay?"

He blinked.

"Are you upset?"

He responded with a half blink and a half headshake that I interpreted to mean, "Somewhat."

Once again, I felt the helplessness I had experienced with Dennis, and I couldn't find the right words to comfort him. I knew this would be difficult for Ron, but I wasn't sure what I could do to help with this loss or prepare him for the future. Ron and I had established a special bond. We had connected in a unique way, and the importance of that connection would have been impossible for me to describe in words.

Without question, the depth of Ron's communication difficulties had shaped much of my educational itinerary for the year. While all of the lessons and the work of the classroom had been interesting and important, my time spent on the development of his and Ruth's communication had been the pinnacle. As vital as I knew I was to Ron, he was just as important to me.

"I wish I could do something or say something that makes this easier," I said. "But I can't. I want you to know as far as the Expressor goes, I will do everything I possibly can to be sure that work continues. I promise."

As I spoke, he blinked repeatedly. It was his way of saying, "I understand, and I believe you."

My mind wandered to *The Wizard of Oz*. At that moment, I felt like Dorothy during her big farewell scene—when she had already offered goodbyes to the Tin Man and the Lion, and she told the Scarecrow she thought she would miss him most of all.

CHAPTER 30

Two weeks after the termination announcement, my students had become more uneasy and excitable. Holding their attention became a challenge, and I knew my upcoming departure had everything to do with this behavior. Although I tried to act normal after the announcement, no doubt the reality of the situation was on most of the students' minds.

One day, a knock at the classroom door caused a mild uproar, and everyone got in on the act.

"Ed, there's someone knocking on the door," Wendy announced.

"Come in!" Paula yelled.

"Go away," Teddy added.

"Who is it? We don't want any," Dennis said.

The students who couldn't talk were moving and writhing in their chairs.

I raised my voice to get everyone's attention. "Guys, guys, quiet down!"

A young resident messenger came in carrying a sealed manila envelope with the insignia of the institution printed in the left corner. "Here," she said, handing me the envelope. Taped to the front was a note from Bernie saying that the envelope had just arrived and she thought it might be important.

I tore it open and found a handwritten letter inside. I also felt an object in the envelope. I tipped the mailer, and a cassette tape fell on my desk.

"Hey, that's my tape," Teddy said.

"What do you mean, Teddy?" I asked, picking it up.

"It's the tape I made last week for Mrs. Sharp," he replied.

I thought back to the other day, when he'd asked to borrow my tape recorder. "But how do you know that this one is your tape?" I asked, as gently as I could.

"Because I signed it."

I turned the tape over and sure enough, there on a strip of white medical tape was his telltale signature—the very one we had been working so hard to produce all year. Now I was really curious, so I read the typewritten note I was holding in my other hand.

Dear Mr. Shane,

It is unfortunate indeed that you would stoop to using one of your students in an attempt to keep your job. This was extremely insensitive, immature, and inappropriate to make Teddy do this.

Dorothy Sharp

"Can we talk out here?" I asked, already pushing Teddy's chair into the corridor. I closed the classroom door behind me and walked around to the front of his wheelchair to face him directly. "Teddy, what's on this tape?" I was trying to be kind, but I felt a rising anxiety in my gut.

"I sent it to Mrs. Sharp," he admitted. "I asked her not to fire you."

"I see."

"Are you mad at me?" As he asked, the upper part of his face wrinkled, his round eyes becoming tiny slits. His concern about my feelings was touching.

"Of course not. I think it was a very nice thing for you to do—but she just isn't going to change her mind. Can I listen to this after class?" I asked, waving the cassette in front of him.

Teddy nodded and pushed back a strand of brown hair that had fallen in his eyes.

"Thanks," I said. "Let's head back in."

I was anxious for the lunch hour so I could hear the tape that had caused Mrs. Sharp such obvious aggravation. When the last student had left for the break, I closed the door and popped the tape in the player. There was about a fifteen-second period of silence before Teddy's voice began.

Mrs. Sharp, I have a favor to ask of you. I wish that you would reconsider keeping Mr. Shane here next year. I just asked him if I could borrow his tape recorder to make this tape. This wasn't his idea. This was my own idea. Everybody else has got the wrong impression of him. He is not as bad as you think he is. He is teaching us the same things that we have been learning, like reading and writing and everything else. If you get rid of him, we're only gonna have to wait another year till you get somebody else. 'Cause if he leaves, I'm not coming back to school, even if they do get somebody else. And I'm gonna tell my parents, too. They have hippie teachers in the public schools, you know, that wear long hair.

He finally convinced me that I had to use a pencil and do arithmetic. I'd never do those things before—but I am doing them now. I don't see why you'd have any reason to throw him out. Even though you don't like him, you can try and get used to him. But I mean it seriously: he is not as bad as you think he is. I know this isn't going to do any good, but I hope it will at least get through to you, anyway.

Thank you.

Teddy must have forgotten to hit the stop button on the recorder, because the tape continued to play back the evening sounds of the infirmary after his narration was complete. I heard occasional screams and moans, the clang of metal on metal. Several requests for help with lifting a resident were audible, as were various reminders to do this or don't forget to do that. The nighttime noises of the infirmary created an eerie soundtrack to Teddy's appeal.

I was deeply moved by Teddy's effort on my behalf. And the more I thought about it, the more I realized that his pleading wasn't just about me: it was a statement about the irrational world that he and his fellow residents here were forced to endure.

I did see some hope and optimism in this narrative. Teddy had not yet lost his willingness to fight. Even though, as he had admitted, he did not hold out much hope that his request would be respected, he at least had been willing to try. I couldn't help but wonder how long this spunky teenager could sustain his fighting spirit and continue to seek change. How long might it be before he, too, lost the spark that enabled him to resist? I hoped he could hold onto it, even nurture it into a roaring flame.

Teddy's tape was one of the defining moments of my year of teaching. It was the most important, tangible item I could keep as a reminder that this was all worth it. I have held onto that cassette and listened to Teddy's sorrowful voice from time to time for over five decades as a reminder to keep moving forward on the hardest days.

But on that late-spring day in 1970, I took out a sheet of paper and scribbled a note back to Mrs. Sharp:

Dear Mrs. Sharp,

It's not important what he said. It's only important that he said it.

Respectfully,

Howard C. Shane

After school, I tried calling Henry at the university but ended up reaching him at his home office.

"Henry, it's your humble servant here," I said.

"And how is the Belchertown pariah holding up?"

"You said I should talk to you when I was ready to move on."

"And? Are you?"

I sighed, part of me still resisting my departure. "Well, my bags are nearly packed with the few possessions I own," I admitted, "so I guess that's a sign that I'm ready to make some decisions about the future."

"Who did you say this was?" he asked.

"Funny. So, what is it I'm supposed to do now that I have neither a job nor future prospects?"

"I will make this simple: graduate school."

"That's it?" I asked. "That's your recommendation?"

"What do you mean, 'that's it'? That's all it needs to be."

"But I want to work, not go back to school."

"Answer me this," he said. "Do you plan to change fields or continue working with children who have disabilities?"

"Continue working with kids. Which, for the record, I actually thought I was pretty good at."

"Despite being fired?" he asked.

"Despite being fired," I confirmed.

"Let me warn you, then, that you'll be on a long road of continuous disappointment if you stay in this field and continue butting heads with any administration, as you have at Belchertown. I suspect you'll need to grow accustomed to being fired."

"Let's say I believe you," I said. "How is graduate school going to fireproof me and keep me from being terminated on a regular basis? It seems to me that if I was going to get fired as much as you say, maybe I need a union, not a degree."

"You know, it reminds me of *The Wizard of Oz*," he said, surprising me with his reference to the movie that had crossed my mind just a few days earlier. "The scarecrow takes this long, dangerous journey just to get a brain. Then, he meets the Wizard, and he learns that he doesn't need a brain—he just needs a diploma. I have the same advice for you: you don't need a lesson in how to conduct yourself around children. You need a diploma. With a diploma, you'll be able to act as you do now, and instead of being ostracized, you'll be considered a maverick or maybe an eccentric. It's simple. Put yourself in a position of power. And the only way to do that in the education world is to get a diploma."

I let his words sink in. They were making more sense than I wanted them to.

"And then, of course," he continued, "there's one other little detail that you seem to have neglected... or maybe you're unwilling to face."

"And that is?"

"Your project—your communication device," he said. "Think about all the time and work you put into that device for Ron and Ruth. Are you just going to let that whole effort die? Remember, we've been talking to Professor Fitch about building the next version of the Expressor. That undertaking is, in my opinion, just as important as all the advocacy on behalf of these residents. Go back to school and continue that work. It shouldn't stop just because you've had a temporary setback. Hell," he chuckled, "for you, it wouldn't be any fun if there weren't any roadblocks."

"So—are you saying you think I could work on the communication project as part of a graduate program?"

"Yeah, I do. Improving Ron and Ruth's ability to use that device could be part of what you'll do in graduate school."

The line went quiet, and I knew he'd said all he intended to say. I felt overwhelmed by his advice. I wasn't sure I was ready or even capable of handling graduate school. But I knew his recommendation was sincere and carefully considered.

"Henry, I appreciate your advice," I said. "I really do. You've given me a lot to think about."

"I know you'll do the right thing," he said, and then hung up.

After I spoke with Henry, I walked slowly back to my car, his words running on a loop in my mind. He had more confidence in my judgment than I did. *Do the right thing.*

It sounded so simple.

My last day at Belchertown was a blur. I'd spoken with each of the students already and said my special goodbyes, but it didn't make that final classroom day any easier. Wendy and I exchanged one last joke (in which I learned what was "fast, loud, and crunchy"—a rocket chip). Barbara and Paula presented me with a card they had worked on together. Teddy handed me a folded piece of white lined paper printed with four legible words in royal blue ink: *Thank you Teddy McNeil.* I kept a smile on my face, shook their hands, and gave them words of encouragement. I wouldn't let myself think too hard about the significance of this day, or the fact that when I switched off that classroom light, I would never be switching it on again.

Before my emotions could sweep me away, Bob and Bernie called me into her office. Bob closed the door, and we all stood silent for a moment.

"Look, I don't have much time to talk now," I said, forcing a light-hearted tone. "I'm having the oil changed on my taxi, and my mechanic hates it when I'm late."

A small grin formed on Bernie's face, and dampness filled her eyes. The blank expression on Bob's face lingered; I guessed he hated goodbyes as much as I did.

"I know there's no point in me telling you what I could have or should have done differently and how that might have changed this outcome," I continued. "But one thing I want to make crystal clear is how much the two of you meant to me through all of the ups and downs." I broke into what I hoped they would interpret as a mischievous smile. "And make no mistake, there were many more ups than there were downs. Right?"

They both nodded their heads.

I extended my hand to Bernie and said, "Thank you." She brushed my hand aside, and we hugged instead.

I was teary-eyed following that heartfelt embrace, and I wasn't sure I could take another one. "Don't you get any ideas about hugging me," I said to Bob. "You can show your love by buying a few rounds of beer some night next week."

He grinned as if the muscles in his face had been reinnervated.

"You're on," he said.

———————————

It was unseasonably warm for mid-June, and since I hadn't cracked any windows, the interior of my car was blistering hot. I fidgeted against the leather and fumbled for the window. In its twenty-year life span, the Austin had acquired a host of odors that had been baking in the car all day. I breathed in the familiar funk of gym clothes, spilled soda, crushed potato chips, and who knew what else.

Since my termination notice, my ride home had become a daily countdown to the last day. As I edged out of the parking lot once more, I instinctively checked the speedometer, careful not to exceed the institution's speed limit of ten miles per hour. I thought about pushing down on the accelerator just once and gunning around campus. I could just hear the screeching of the Austin's wheels, could see the perturbed faces of Mrs. Sharp and the other administrators who would rush to the windows as I roared past, leaving a cloud of dust in my wake.

That was how it would've gone down in the movies. But for now, I was content to move on.

Maybe Henry was right about me, I thought, as I took my foot off the pedal to keep my speed down. Maybe I needed to take the lessons from Belchertown and apply them to my future.

Slowly, I eased past the school building's granite steps. My mind took me back to the night of the dance—my students in their finery, dancing in wheelchairs to the Kinks, making connections with each other. Enjoying a magical night off from their monotonous lives.

I passed the picnic table where I'd sat with Jack on our special outdoor adventures. Where he'd taught me the value of stillness, of simple joys, as he smiled at the touch of the spring breeze and sun.

Cruising by the administration building, I pictured Ron cracking a smile in spite of his discomfort in that ridiculously small chair as the two state workers carried him up the stairs and into the building for our meeting with the superintendent. I passed the bench where I'd made the promise to Ron's grandmother on that first day. I hoped I had lived up to my vow to help him—and would, one way or another, continue to do so.

Still traveling at Belchertown's speed limit, I came to the meadow with the merry-go-round at its far end. The smell of freshly cut grass overpowered any scent that might have lingered in the car. This carousel was a tangible reminder of my Belchertown orientation, an imprint so profound I relived it every morning and afternoon as I arrived and left campus. I slowed to watch some residents, likely older than me, eagerly clutching colorful wooden horses.

I recalled one day earlier in the spring when I'd taken a noontime stroll and ventured into the metal building that housed the carousel. I was blown away by the exquisite sculpting of each horse. I later learned that each mount was hand-carved by an artisan from Brooklyn, New York. A local benefactor had purchased the entire herd and then established this merry-go-round for the enjoyment of the residents of Belchertown State School.

The building had been deserted that day, so I threw a leg over one of the stallions. As I took in the splendor of the intricate hand-carved detail of the horse's mane, his vivid expression, his elegant muscles, it was hard not to contrast the beauty of the carousel with the ugliness and foulness that pervaded so much of this institution. Sitting atop that wooden steed, I also realized that this structure and its frozen inhabitants were emblematic of so much about Belchertown: how it infantilized its residents, how days and weeks could pass by here in a mechanical blur, how the same infuriating issues and roadblocks kept coming around again and again during my year here. I hoped we could get off this ride someday. I hoped the system would change. I hoped that I, in some small way, would be a meaningful part of that change.

I knew there would be a flood of Belchertown memories in the days to come—the battles, the small victories, the frustrations, the laughs and smiles with my students and allies—but for now I was moving on, ready to see what the rest of life had in store. I would take a little time to clear my head. I would think about how to be part of the solution. And I would ditch the idea of disclosing the secret tape recording of my last confrontation with Mrs. Sharp. I had once considered it an ace up my sleeve, but now I realized that going public with it wouldn't magically change things for my students, or for other people in institutions like Belchertown. Real and lasting change would happen slowly but steadily, as people like me found better ways to fight for it.

As I approached the main road, about to leave the grounds for the last time, I stopped the Austin for a second. I sometimes click my blinker on before turning, but today I didn't. I glanced in the rearview mirror and stared at my familiar brown eyes, which widened a bit as I felt the weight of Henry's assignment: *do the right thing.*

Although my next path was still unclear, I knew that for me, doing the right thing would mean using the rest of my life to make a difference for kids like my students. And I knew that whether I turned left or right, I'd be heading in the right direction.

EPILOGUE

After I wrapped up my final weeks in the basement classroom of the infirmary, I applied to become a master's student at the University of Massachusetts, Amherst, where Henry was a professor. With his support, I was accepted into the communication disorders program, where I was able to personalize a curriculum to accommodate my interest in people with cerebral palsy who were nonspeaking. At the time, the field of communication disorders was focused on strengthening spoken communication, with virtually no part of the profession dedicated to people who were minimally verbal. That, too, was somewhat understandable, because people with communicative disabilities like Ron and Ruth's had been locked away in places like Belchertown, and the world—including professionals interested in disability—knew very little about them.

As part of my master's program, I did return part time for the next two years as a consultant in the newly formed communication disorders program at Belchertown State School. This program, the direct result of numerous state-imposed mandates for change, was upbeat, innovative, and unafraid to take risks. Thankfully, work with the Expressor went on uninterrupted.

My return to Belchertown did stir up some controversy. Dr. Bowser claimed I was a troublemaker, but Henry indicated that if I wasn't offered the consultant position, Dr. Bowser would learn firsthand the true meaning of trouble. This new position gave me a welcome chance to reengage with my former students and provide more focused treatment to Ron and Ruth using a newer version of the Expressor. Henry also stayed in my life as an invaluable mentor—and, more importantly, a dear and trusted friend—for the next four decades.

Bob Bergquist, too, stayed in my life long after my time at Belchertown ended. He completed his physical therapy internship, established a highly successful private PT practice in Western Massachusetts, and was a very respected professor of physical therapy at Springfield College for forty years. We remained in contact until his death in 2013.

As for me, I graduated and immediately began doctoral studies at Syracuse University under the mentorship of Dr. Ruth Lencione, a professor who studied and specialized in the communication disorders associated with cerebral palsy. I then completed a doctoral fellowship at the Mayo Clinic with a concentration in neuromotor speech disorders. During this time, I learned that other inventive people across the country were creating innovative tools and processes for those unable to speak. For many years, I have served as the Director of the Center for Communication Enhancement at Boston Children's Hospital and an Associate Professor at the Harvard Medical School, where I have worked for over four decades. As of this writing, I've made a plan to step back from my role in June of 2021, but I plan to keep working with patients and families for as long as life will allow.

For the forty-plus years I've been at Boston Children's Hospital, I've kept photos of Ron Benoit and Henry Peirce above my desk to remind me that they both were instrumental in bringing me to this point in my career. I estimate that I've now seen and worked with more than ten thousand children with significant communication impairments. I have been witness to, and have helped to shape, a discipline that hadn't even been conceived of during my tenure at Belchertown. It has truly been a privilege to be a part of the creation, adaption, and implementation of transformative technology and devices that give access to people who previously had no voice. How could I have predicted that I, this son of a truck driver from a mill town in Massachusetts, would one day have his work featured in a Smithsonian exhibition on technology—or have the honor of contributing to the development of a computer voice for Professor Stephen Hawking?

All this began with that basement classroom and those remarkable young people who had been cast aside by society. In the 1970s, because of the growing activism and outrage surrounding institutional living, many residents were transferred out of these institutions into smaller group homes or other facilities in the community. Belchertown itself was wracked by scandals and waves of failed reforms until it was finally shut down in 1992 as part of the state's deinstitutionalization plan. At an event to mark the school's official closing, Ruth—using her communication device and computer-generated voice—addressed the crowd with these words: "Today is a day of celebration for me. I am so very happy and grateful that I was able to leave Belchertown State School and begin to enjoy my life. Now everyone who was living here will have the same opportunity to have a good life. We should celebrate their opportunity."

What happened with my students from the infirmary class of 1969–1970? Well, over the years, I heard from Teddy McNeil from time to time. Not surprisingly, he continued to make frequent wisecracks, but his feisty personality manifested in another way, too: he became a passionate advocate for the rights of people with disabilities. He conducted this work through a local advocacy group and lived in a community apartment in Western Massachusetts.

Ruth married Norman Mercer from Ward 6 shortly after leaving the institution in 1978. Ruth and Norman enjoyed a happy marriage filled with love, which was wonderful to see after the suffering both of them had endured for so long at Belchertown. Ruth wrote a popular book based on her life called *I Raise My Eyes to Say Yes*, and she became an inspiration to people with disabilities around the world. Regrettably, Ruth died suddenly at the age of forty-eight, following several months of declining health. On a cool and sunny fall day in 1998, I—along with well over a hundred people—gathered to celebrate the life of Ruth Sienkiewicz-Mercer, and I was gratified to see all the people whose lives had been touched by my former student.

As promised, I visited Dennis regularly in the years after I left the institution. I suppose it was maturity that enabled him to accept that he'd likely not reconnect with his family. I drew that conclusion during one visit when I noticed the missing suitcase. When he saw me eyeing the empty space under his bed, he just said, "Let's not talk about it." And we never did.

By the early 1990s, all residents of Belchertown State School had dispersed into the community, and I lost track of many of them. They influenced my life immeasurably, and it is my utmost hope that they made that transition with ease and enjoyed a happier life in the community. I maintained the closest relationship with Ron after he left Belchertown. He and I worked together for another two years at the school, primarily on the next version of the Expressor. While I was off doing my graduate work, Ron moved to a community residence, and I often received updates from him highlighting his easy integration into community life. He was dearly loved by the staff at his group residence, which often facilitated fun excursions: rock concerts, rowdy evenings at local bars to watch Boston sports, trips to the Foxwoods Casino in Connecticut. On Labor Day 1982, Ron asked me to be the best man at his wedding. Three years later, his son, Andy, was born, and in 2017 he became a grandfather to Sylvana Ron Benoit.

In the decades following our time at Belchertown, Ron regularly came to my center at Boston Children's Hospital, where he was re-evaluated and learned to use the most current communication technologies. Ron and I also kept in touch through regular email exchanges once that technology became available. Our email communication was usually about daily happenings and holiday greetings, but one exchange in particular stands out in my mind. I don't know the reason for his historical reflection, but from out of the blue Ron wrote about that homemade wheelchair we had built decades before:

MARY! CHRISTMAS TO HOWARD SHANE, YOU MAKE ME A WHEEL-CHAIR FROM A CAR AND tricycle, AND BRING ME IN TO YOUR HOME, AND THE WHO COULD FORGET THE OLD WOMAN
December 11, 2007

When I asked him about this note, he just laughed. Mrs. Dorothy Sharp, he confirmed, was "the old woman." Who could forget her, indeed.

In 2014, forty-four years after the invention of the Expressor, Ron successfully operated an iPad using a special interface he could control with a switch positioned next to his head. He used the iPad for Skype and a number of other apps made possible by this transformative technology. In addition to our get-togethers around new technologies, Ron and I met up socially a few times every year because of our deep bond and lasting friendship. One of our favorite annual events was taking in a Red Sox game at Fenway Park.

In December of 2017, I received a call from Ron's friend and personal aide to let me know he was in hospice care at his residence. I immediately drove to Western Massachusetts to say goodbye and express my gratitude: not only for the significant effect he'd had on my professional career, but also for his friendship and the countless ways he'd influenced my growth as a human being. I wanted him to know that because of his strength, and because of the experiences he had endured and shared with me at Belchertown years before, he had by association affected the lives of thousands of individuals who now used assistive technology to speak. He had started it all, and I wanted him to know that.

When I arrived to visit him, I was escorted back to Ron's room, where he lay asleep, propped up in bed. He awoke after a moment, as if he'd sensed me standing by his bedside. Just an inch or so from his left temple was a small red disc which served as the switch interface to a modern communication device that allowed him to compose messages and speak with a computer-generated voice.

He stared at me for a moment, still processing that I was there. Before I could say a word, he moved his head slightly to the left. His device activated, and a cursor he controlled began to move uninterrupted over a display filled with words and letters.

"Thank you," he said, by way of the synthetic voice.

"You don't need to thank me for coming," I said.

"No. Everything," he responded.

That was the point where I lost it. I had to pause for a moment and wipe away a few tears before I could say what had been on my mind during the entire two-hour car ride.

"Ron," I started, "you really don't get it, do you? All the thanks here should be *me* thanking *you*." Ron stared into my eyes. I pressed on: "You're the one who kick-started my entire professional life. If it wasn't for you, I wouldn't have had the wonderful life I've had. I wouldn't have helped all those people. So, no... this is all about me thanking you." I smiled, blinking away new tears that had collected in my eyes. "Is that clear, Ron—crystal clear?"

He gave me a slow, strong blink. His "yes" was as unmistakable to me then as it had been the first time I'd seen him answer in the affirmative some forty-eight years before.

Ron's mother sent me the text message I had been expecting the day after my final visit with him. It read, "Good morning, Dr. Howard. Ron passed away this morning at three thirty. Thank you so very much for being there for us through this journey."

I read the text message several times and then retreated to my backyard for a private moment of silence. Images and memories of Ron's life flashed through my mind. I thought of Ron's mother, of the other families who had surrendered their children to Belchertown. I understood now that they were also victims—victims of the limited options society offered them at the time. When Ron was an infant, his mother had gone without the community supports that now provide help to families with children with disabilities. I liked to think that Ron had led a good life after all—but I couldn't help wondering how things might have been different if he had been born now.

I could be angry as I reflect on Dorothy Sharp and Lawrence Bowser and the way we treated one another over four decades ago, but my feelings are more complicated than that. On one hand, I've come to realize that they, too, were products of a different era, caught in the crossroads of a historic shift in policy and attitudes. Although advocates such as Burton Blatt, Dean of Education at Syracuse University, had begun to write passionately about the benefits of community care over institution life, this ideology had not yet found a foothold with administrators such as Mrs. Sharp and Dr. Bowser. They had not been charged with educating people and getting them ready to live productive lives outside Belchertown; their task was to prepare the residents to live out their days within the institution. Even if they both had been more enlightened, they likely would have struggled to find the budget or resources to make the lives of the residents more humane and enjoyable. Mrs. Sharp's stances, especially, seem indefensible to modern sensibilities—but she wasn't evil for the sake of being evil, as I had once accused her of being.

While it's clear to me now that Mrs. Sharp and Dr. Bowser were doing their jobs in a manner consistent with the times, it still disappoints me that their thinking never evolved. Even the newly appointed state officials who oversaw the running of Belchertown in the '70s began to adopt a more progressive attitude, but Dr. Bowser and Mrs. Sharp were not part of that. In fact, Dr. Bowser was forced to resign as superintendent in March of 1971 following an unprecedented uprising by the staff. Seventy-one school employees submitted a petition to the joint investigative committee seeking his dismissal, citing his "deplorable lack of concern" for the wellbeing of people with disabilities. Mrs. Sharp remained at Belchertown during my continued involvement as a consultant, but she never softened toward me, and we had no contact.

Today, the buildings of Belchertown are in ruins, and the grounds no longer boast the manicured lawns of my time there. As you drive past the few remaining buildings or make your way through the brush and overgrowth, you won't hear the echoing cries of frightened babies who scream for mothers who never came to comfort them. You won't hear the howls of unprotected and unsuspecting men, women, and children whose teeth were drilled or removed without the application of modern anesthesia. There is no trace left of the noiseless abuses, either: the man who was never shown how to eat without assistance, the woman whose bones calcified and broke after years of disuse, the people who missed out on any form of education. Lives were wasted there, and people suffered in immeasurable ways—but thankfully those doors are closed now, never to be opened again.

Bernie's employment prophecy didn't come true for me. I didn't go into business or law. My lifetime of work with children who can't speak—greatly influenced by the advent of modern technology—has allowed me to invent communication solutions used worldwide for more than four decades. My friends and family, who once wondered why I did this work, have changed the discussion from questioning my career choices to making fond statements such as, "You're still doing the same thing you did at Belchertown." It's true, on some level. My year at Belchertown State School, spent in the basement of the infirmary building with my wonderful students, was the seminal event that evolved into an unexpected, surprising, and incredibly satisfying career and existence.

Now it's time to leave the past, for it is just that. My concern now turns to the future. Although I marvel at how far we've come in the past four decades, I still worry about the next generation of babies who come into this world with physical or intellectual disabilities. I am uneasy that what happened at Belchertown could repeat itself in some way. While the old institution system has been dismantled, prejudice, bias, ignorance, and fear have not yet been eradicated. Humans have a short memory, and I fear that without a watchful eye, an invisible pendulum could someday swing back. As George Santayana once wrote, "Those who cannot remember the past are condemned to repeat it."

The next generation of professionals, parents, and self-advocates will need to work hard to maintain and expand on our current ideological position, which supports the right of all people with disabilities to live, work, and socialize in typical ways within society. We need to put our collective shoulders against that invisible pendulum so that it can't ever swing back, can't reverse the arc of freedom and dignity we've been working so hard to achieve.

We've come so far, and we still have far to go. I have hope that together, we can achieve true equity and inclusion for all. And I am confident that our continued march of progress will be led by people much like my smart, creative, and determined students at Belchertown State School. Unsilenced and empowered now, they will use their voices—whether biological or computer-generated—to speak loud and clear for themselves.

DISCUSSION QUESTIONS

1. In this memoir, Howard Shane describes the institution system of the late 1960s and 70s. He points out that these places existed because societal norms of that era were based on separation and segregation of people with disabilities. Compare and contrast how the philosophy of that era relates to our treatment of individuals with disabilities today. What has changed, and what still needs to change?

2. Dr. Burton Blatt, the former Dean of the School of Education at Syracuse University and author of the poetic anthology *Christmas in Purgatory*, once wrote, "There's nothing that's done in an institution that can't be done better in the community." Do you agree with this position? Why or why not?

3. Before starting his teaching job at Belchertown, Howard says he believes that "everyone learns and excels when doing something of strong personal interest." Giving specific examples, describe how he put this educational philosophy into action during his year with the infirmary students. Does his philosophy resonate with you? Can you think of a time when you used someone's personal interests to help them learn a new skill?

4. At Belchertown, Mrs. Sharp and Dr. Bowser are both rule-bound antagonists who show little compassion and refuse to embrace change, while nurses like Bernie and Pauline consistently show genuine care and concern for the residents. Since all of these staff members are products of the same era, how would you account for the differences in their attitudes, behaviors, and practices?

5. In Chapter 18, Bernie and Howard disagree about the prospect of organizing a strike to protest the conditions at Belchertown. Howard is eager to stand up for the residents, while Bernie points out that the institution's workers depend on their jobs (and the residents, in turn, depend on them). Which point of view did you empathize with more? Is it the responsibility of a workforce to speak up against injustice and become whistleblowers, or do they have a right to prioritize their livelihood?

6. At several points in this narrative, Howard indicates that his goal is to bring about change—for both his students and for Belchertown as a whole. Do you believe he was a catalyst for lasting change at Belchertown? What did he change the most: the curriculum, his students, the institution, or himself?

7. Describe a situation from your own professional experience that changed you forever. What happened? What was the outcome? In what ways did that situation help you grow as a person and a professional?

8. Howard was a young and passionate educator who frequently bent or broke the rules if he believed that doing so would benefit his students. Do you believe that Belchertown's rules were "made to be broken," and did you find yourself disagreeing with any of the choices Howard made? Was there any situation you would have chosen to handle differently, and why?

9. If you were given the opportunity to have dinner with someone from the book, who would it be? What are the top three questions you would ask your dinner companion?

10. Imagine that the moment Howard drives off the Belchertown grounds for the last time, you are given the responsibility of determining the fate of the institution. What actions would you take to ensure a better life for the residents?

11. In the epilogue, Howard reflects on the profound impact his student Ron had on his life. How was Ron instrumental in fostering the author's personal and professional growth, and how did Howard help change the course of Ron's life in return?

12. For several decades, Ron remained connected with Howard as a friend and a consumer of assistive technology that grew increasingly sophisticated. Discuss how advances in technology have changed the lives of Ron and other people with communication disorders. In what areas of life do they now enjoy control and choice, thanks to technology such as tablets, smartphones, and apps?

13. As research has shown the benefits of including students with disabilities in general education classrooms, more and more schools have been

working toward that goal. In your opinion, what are the most significant benefits of inclusive classrooms? Do you believe today's teachers are equipped to support students with a range of disabilities? What supports would they need to fully realize the benefits of inclusion?

14. Memoirs can be written for many different purposes, such as clearing up a misconceived notion, enhancing a person's professional profile, or promoting a philosophy or an idea. What do you think was the author's primary motivation for writing this book?

15. What is the most important lesson you took away from this book? How do you think you might apply it to your own life in the future?